Best wishes and Happy Landing
C. Windsor Miller, March 7, 1945
Bridge at Remagen,

A TANKER'S VIEW OF WORLD WAR II

The Military Experience of C. Windsor Miller

by C. Windsor Miller

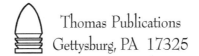

Thomas Publications
Gettysburg, PA 17325

Copyright © 2004 C. Windsor Miller

Printed and bound in the United States of America

Published by THOMAS PUBLICATIONS
                 P.O. Box 3031
                 Gettysburg, Pa. 17325

All rights reserved. No part of this book may be used or reproduced without written permission of the author and the publisher, except in the case of brief quotations embodied in critical essays and reviews.

ISBN-1-57747-110-5 (hardcover)
ISBN-1-57747-111-3 (softcover)

Cover illustration "Taking the Remagen Bridge" by Larry Selman.

THOMAS PUBLICATIONS publishes books about the American Colonial era, the Revolutionary War, the Civil War, and other important topics. For a complete list of titles, please visit our website at:

        www.thomaspublications.com

Or write to:
        THOMAS PUBLICATIONS
          P.O. Box 3031
          Gettysburg, Pa. 17325

Dedicated to the memory of my late wife,
Grace Joyce Miller,
and to our daughter,
Marilyn Louise Borrell,
who was the inspiration and motivation for this book.

Editor's note:

C. Windsor Miller, World War II combat veteran, has an extraordinary story to tell. As the editor of this work, I felt compelled to let him tell it in his own words. To submit to any editorial urge to condense or alter Mr. Miller's writing, other than with punctuation, would undermine its value as a first-person account. This, then, is his story as he wrote it.

CONTENTS

Preface 6
Foreword 8
Chapter 1   Into the Military 9
Chapter 2   Conversion from Civilian to Soldier 12
Chapter 3   An Officer and a Gentleman – by Act of Congress 20
Chapter 4   Assignment to the Ninth Armored Division 31
Chapter 5   Farewell Ft. Riley – Hello Camp Ibis 42
Chapter 6   Next Stop, Camp Polk, Louisiana 49
Chapter 7   All Aboard-and Bon Voyage! 57
Chapter 8   Closer and Closer 63
Chapter 9   Battle of the Bulge — Part One 68
Chapter 10   Battle of the Bulge — Part Two 75
Chapter 11   Recovery and Replacement 81
Chapter 12   The Drive to the Rhine 85
Chapter 13   Capture and Crossing of the Bridge at Remagen 92
Chapter 14   Expanding the Bridgehead — the War Goes on 99
Chapter 15   Some R & R, and None Too Soon 104
Chapter 16   Rendezvous with Russky at the Elbe River 109
Chapter 17   Are We There Yet?—No, but Soon 114
Chapter 18   Post-war Duty in Burgkunstadt, Germany 117
Chapter 19   One More Stop, Then Homeward Bound 125
Chapter 20   That's All Folks 130
Appendix A Roster of Company "A" 14th Tank Battalion 134
Appendix B Firing Tables 136

PREFACE

For ten years after I returned home from the battlefields of Europe following World War II, I said very little about the horrors of combat that I faced on a daily basis. It was not because I did not want to talk about it, but I knew there were twelve million others who had stories to tell and people probably had heard enough. Then on March 7, 1955, to celebrate the tenth anniversary of the capture and crossing of the only bridge remaining over the Rhine River at Remagen, Germany, President Eisenhower invited some of us to the White House. It was at that time the President created what he called "The Society of the Remagen Bridge" and presented each of us a personalized certificate of membership in that Society. In so doing, he made these remarks:

> Gentlemen, I have asked you to come here this morning because you know old soldiers' minds are bound to turn back once in a while to dramatic events of war – particularly of the kind that took place at the Remagen bridgehead. Now, of course that was not the biggest battle that was, but for me it always typified one thing: the dash, the ingenuity, the readiness at the first opportunity that characterizes the American Soldier.
>
> You men are only a typical group of the great forces that were in Europe, but it did seem to me that here, on the tenth anniversary of the day you went across the Rhine, you might not mind coming in and saying hello to the man who was responsible for directing this whole over-all strategy. I also brought with me General Spaatz. He typified the unity between the ground-air team on the battlefield that was responsible for victory.
>
> Now I must confess to you that I have done something on my own responsibility. I have organized here The Society of the Remagen Bridgehead. I have prepared for each of you a little certificate, which I hope you will keep and retain as of some sentimental value. It is nothing except to say in my little way to you and through you to all of the Ninth Armored Division and all of the whole Army, Navy and Air Force behind you that was responsible for this thing, my own personal thanks.
>
> Incidentally, one of these certificates is made out to all the officers and men of the Ninth Armored Division, and General Leonard says he is going to send it down to Fort Knox as a memento.

The publicity that accompanied this event resulted in immediate phone calls from friends who asked why I never told them about the action, and my response was, "You never asked me." That was the beginning of a constant demand to give talks on the subject, which continues to the present time.

After almost every one of my talks, I would be asked if I had written a book or someone made a suggestion that I should. I accepted these remarks as a way to compliment me for the talk and I certainly never took them seriously. In recent years pressure started to build in an effort to persuade me to do a book, but I was never convinced that there was sufficient interest. My daughter Marilyn Borrell from time to time had casually mentioned that it was her opinion it should be done, and when she began hearing how insistent people were becoming, started to really come down pretty hard on the need for me to put my words on paper.

There were a number of people who had heard several of my talks and had expressed a very strong interest in having my military history made a matter of public record. Some of these people got together with Marilyn and other members of my family and bombarded me with their demands, leaving me with no alternative but to give some serious thought to the idea of writing a book. Now that it has become a reality, I feel it is imperative that recognition be given to those who have played such an important role in this endeavor.

First of all must be my daughter Marilyn, who was so persuasive in her urging that I do this, and appealing to my paternal affection, told me she would consider it my greatest gift to her. Her encouraging remarks and complimentary opinion of my work in progress provided the ongoing motivation to continue. Next is my son-in-law Fred Borrell who was always there when needed, taking pictures, transferring the manuscript to compact disks, running countless errands and tolerating the many requests I made of him without complaint, which must have tried his patience to its limit. There were many whose encouragement was a great inspiration to carry on, among whom were Steve and Barbara Shultz, owners of Aces High Military Art Gallery in Gettysburg, Pennsylvania, where I had been invited to give several of my talks; Curt Vickery, president of the

Military History Roundtable of Baltimore; the Andersons, the Smiths, granddaughter Rebecca Voltz and many others. Finally, Dick Golden of Aces High. How can I thank a man who suffered through my horrible handwriting to provide the beautifully typed pages that he emailed to Fred and Marilyn who assembled five copies of the manuscript for presentation to the publishers? Dick also provided me with a terrific morale boost with his very favorable comments about my work as he struggled to interpret my hen scratching. Whenever I apologized to Dick for the condition of the writing, his only reply was that he was honored to be a part of the project. I will just say to him and all the others "THANK YOU," because their support contributed so much to whatever success this book might enjoy.

I gave a lot of thought about whom I would ask to write the foreword, and among those were a couple of authors, several generals, a number of history teachers, and so on. From the very beginning I have tried to write in a style that would appeal to the younger generation and it seemed most appropriate that I should ask Stephen Voglezon, a young high school student who for a long time has shown a deep and abiding interest in me and my military history. The wisdom of my decision is obvious from the excellence of his remarks, which are inscribed herein.

ENJOY!

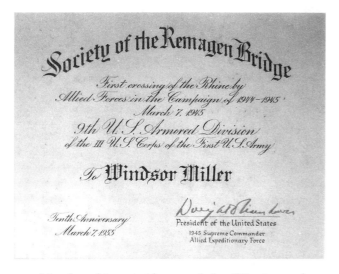

Membership certificate of the "Society of the Remagen Bridge" presented by President Eisenhower on the tenth anniversary of the capture and crossing of that bridge, March 7, 1955.

A photo with the president to celebrate the tenth anniversary of the bridge crossing. The author is seated at the president's right.

FOREWORD

C. Windsor Miller is a compassionate ninety-year old man who once achieved spectacular feats as an American Soldier in WWII, which includes leading a tank platoon across the crumbling Ludendorf Bridge while blinded by smoke, dust, and the dark of night, and winning the Distinguished Service Cross. With the ability to capture his audience through his unique charisma and charm, he tells the story of tragedy and triumph that made him an American hero. Thanks to Mr. Miller, my eyes have truly been opened to the harsh reality of combat and army life in the World War II era. Mr. Miller had done what no history book or teacher can do: he has brought the war to each and every member of his audience.

I first met C. Windsor Miller as a seventh grade student at St. Mary Star of the Sea School, located in Indian Head, Maryland, when he was invited to share his war experiences with the middle school students. I must admit, when I first heard that a World War II Veteran was coming to preach us a homily on his war accounts, I assumed that it would be just another boring talk with no thrills, and that I'd have to force myself to stay awake out of politeness. Boy was I mistaken! I have never seen a middle school history class so energized and full of awe.

Since meeting Mr. Miller for the first time in 1999, we have become dearest of friends and steady pen pals. In November 2000, I had the privilege of performing Taps for this American hero in a Veteran's Day celebration, and in July 2003, my family and I had the honor of attending Mr. Miller's ninetieth birthday bash. Mr. Miller and I have appeared in various newspapers and websites together. Even though I have since graduated from St. Mary Star of the Sea School and now attend Gonzaga College High School, I never miss his talks at St. Mary Star of the Sea whenever he is in town. Mr. Miller has truly touched my life in an inexplicable fashion. By writing *A Tanker's View of World War II*, C. Windsor Miller will touch the lives of his readers in a unique and unforgettable way.

R. Stephen Voglezon
Third Year Student
Gonzaga College High School
Washington, DC

Windsor Miller, left, with R. Stephen Voglezon at the author's nintieth birthday party at the Aces High Art Gallery in Gettysburg, PA.

Chapter 1

INTO THE MILITARY

Let's go back to the year 1940, when I was working for a real estate office and things were heating up in Europe, thanks to one Adolph Hitler. That was the year of the Selective Service Act and my number was not the first to be drawn. Not being of very sound mind and eager to get into the fray, I decided to try to enlist. Since I was married and 27, I was classified as 3A and the recruiting officer told me they were only accepting men classified 1A. There being no improvement to my mental condition, I was determined to make some contribution to the war effort.

Our government was providing the British with war material and equipment under a recently enacted "Lend-Lease" program and offices had been set up in Washington to implement the program. I applied for a position with the British Army Staff, Ord 3, whose function was the purchase and shipment of tanks and other armored vehicles and their spare parts to the Middle East where the British were already engaged with the Axis military forces. The British Army Staff consisted mainly of United Kingdom military personnel with one other American male civilian and several American female civilians. I soon realized that a language barrier existed and I would have to learn to speak English rather than American, which I was taught in school. For instance: your home is your "digs"; "bloody" is an expletive; the British line officers don't wear bars, they wear "pips", one for second lieutenant (pronounced leftenant) two for first lieutenant and three for captain. This very important work for the moment satisfied my need to be involved in the allied military build-up, especially on the occasions when I would receive a call in the middle of the night to report to the office. Although it wasn't mentioned, I knew it meant one of our shipments had been sunk by enemy submarines and a replacement of the materials lost must be provided immediately. It was always a bit amusing to me but certainly enjoyable when at mid-afternoon, business came to a halt and I was served a cup of hot tea and cookies. At that point the war became of secondary importance, but their sincerity of purpose and dogged determination to get the job done taught me a new respect for the people who we often made the brunt of many jokes. The demands on all of us to keep the vital supply lines open resulted in a kind of bonding between those of us who shared this great responsibility. Many lunches at our desks and hurried dinners at a nearby restaurant brought us closer together, enabling us to indulge in some good-natured teasing about each other's customs and language.

I was getting pretty well settled in with this fine group of people when, on December 7, 1941, the Japanese attacked Pearl Harbor and rekindled that insane notion that this war couldn't be won without me. So it wasn't long before I again confronted the Recruiting Officer with my request to sign up. One of the first questions he asked me was what was I presently doing and after I explained in some detail, he said he wouldn't think of permitting me to leave what he described as "essential war work," and that I was doing more for the cause than I could possibly do in the service. After reprimanding me for wanting to leave that work, he complimented me for my noble contribution to saving the world from enslavement and said I should be very proud of what I was doing. Well, he almost convinced me that maybe I could win the war from that office on "K" street in Washington, D.C., so back I went with renewed vigor and confidence that mine was the most important job in the world. He was a better salesman than I was.

I really liked what I was doing and the people I was working with, but something was missing. I was wearing this good-looking suit, the latest

English draped shoulders and tapered waist and I thought I looked pretty sharp, but something was missing. Enemy subs were taking a heavy toll, London was being firebombed, Rommel's tanks were shoving the British back in North Africa and the Japanese were causing heavy American casualties in the Islands of the Pacific, but something was missing. I wasn't in uniform. All around me were these fine men in their uniforms and I was wearing this handsome, stylish, civilian suit. That was what was missing — my uniform.

Now it is early June 1942, and I hied myself back down to the Recruiting Office where we are on a first name basis. Well maybe not, since I probably didn't see the same man each time, so I repeat my usual request that I would like to enlist and he asked for my Draft Card. He said he would check my file and be right back. What would be the excuse this time? Sure enough, when he came back he had an excuse and you won't believe it. This is what he said. "Sorry, you cannot enlist because in about two weeks you are going to be drafted." How about that. Having waited this long, I figured another two weeks couldn't hurt and he was right because in just about two weeks I received my "Greetings." So finally I was going into the Army, but my problems were not over and I would have another opportunity to prove my low intellectual level. The next morning, I went down to the office to report to Major Macloud, who was the officer in charge of Ord 3 of the British Army Staff. I said, "Major, I will be leaving you because I just received this draft notice," which I handed him. His response was, "Oh, no! This is considered essential war work and I will get you a deferment." Now here it comes. I said to him, "Major, I am standing before you in a civilian suit, while you are wearing the uniform of your country. Would you deny me the privilege of wearing the uniform of my country?" Then he said, "Well, since you put it that way I guess I have to let you go and I will give you a letter of recommendation," which he did, along with a leather-bound travel clock engraved with my initials and containing the signatures of all the people in Ord 3. I still have the clock although it shows signs of severe aging after 60 years. Following a brief farewell ceremony during which we were served tea and cookies, I said my farewells to my friends and returned home to prepare for my departure.

I have not mentioned my wife Gracie's reaction to all of this because it was typical. She naturally did not want me to leave, but understood my eagerness to serve and I believe she was proud of that. You will hear more about Gracie in the days to come.

The clock presented to C. Windsor Miller by the British Army staff when he resigned to enter the United States Army.

My draft notice instructed me to report to Ft. Myers, Virginia, on a certain day and time for formal induction into the U.S. Army. After the swearing-in ceremony, we were all given two weeks to take care of personal business. It was difficult to say farewell to family and friends, who promised prayers and letters. Gracie was a pillar of strength, which was a big help to me since I felt a little guilty that I wanted this so much. I later heard that she really took it very hard.

It was then time to report back to Ft. Myers for transportation to Camp Lee, Virginia, for processing. This consisted of a physical exam, several shots, issuing of uniforms and accessories, and a mental or psychiatric exam during which I was asked if I liked girls. I had to admit that I did, hoping Gracie would never find out. The final phase was an interview to determine where I might fit into the overall scheme of things. I could have told him and saved him a lot of trouble, but some guy by the name of Eisenhower already had the job. It was at this time I handed over the letter of recommendation from Major Macloud, having not a clue of what it contained. We were then assigned a barracks and given a package in which we were to mail home our civilian clothes. We were also given a list of several assignments, from which we could select one to keep us busy during our stay there. They were: 1) Kitchen Police, 2) Fire Police, 3) Grounds Police. The word "Police" suggested some authority and we raw recruits thought Kitchen Police would see that things were going smoothly in the kitchen, nobody lifting any goodies or wasting food and so on. Fire Police probably made sure people were using the butt cans in the barracks and not creating any fire hazards, and the Grounds Police would check the barracks for any disorderly conduct or loud talk and the like. I selected Fire Police and soon found out that I was to keep the coal-fired furnaces going to heat the water for several barracks, and I was kept busy shoveling coal during our tour there. Of course now, everyone knows that Kitchen Police involves washing dishes and peeling potatoes, and Grounds Police had to pick up butts and trash all around the outside of the barracks, so we learned an early lesson to exercise caution when electing to do certain duties in the Army and NEVER VOLUNTEER.

We were issued a Soldiers Training Manual and told how to salute, fall in, dress right, face left, column right, and halt, all of which are necessary to move large groups from place to place in an orderly fashion. Soon we were separated into sections according to which training center we were to be assigned, and loaded onto trains headed for these locations. Our contingent finally arrived at the AFTC, Armored Force Training Center, Ft. Knox, Kentucky, and immediately marched to the area where we would spend the next thirteen weeks of basic training.

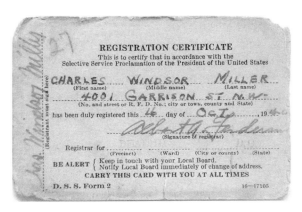

My Draft registration card.

Chapter 2

CONVERSION FROM CIVILIAN TO SOLDIER

So here I am at Ft. Knox, Kentucky, the Armored Force Training Center, wondering how come Armor, when it dawned on me that Major Macloud's letter of recommendation quite understandably related the function of Ord 3, which was buying and shipping tanks to the British Battle Zone. The Army in its great wisdom determined that since I worked in Ord 3 I must know all about tanks. In truth, I had never seen a tank, and didn't even know what they looked like except for the pictures and drawings in the catalogues we used for reference. However, it wouldn't be until we finished basic training that they would make a final decision what our permanent job assignment would be.

Upon reaching our company area, we were told to remain in formation for an official greeting, not by a brass band, not by a shower of flowers, not by a glowing speech of praise and encouragement by a high-ranking officer — no, none of this — but an address by a tough regular Army sergeant who informed us that "your heart may belong to Mamma, but Uncle Sam owns your buttocks now." He used a more graphic term for that part of the anatomy that "Uncle Sam owns now." I suddenly became aware that I would have to learn a third language used by the military where every third and sometimes second word must be profanity, an obscenity, or one of your own origination. This might present a communication problem for me because, while I knew these words, I never used them except when hitting my thumb with a hammer or when some character cut me off in traffic.

Our company consisted of four platoons, each having about eighty men with a sergeant in charge of each platoon. The first sergeant was regular Army and did not hold these raw recruits in very high regard. His name was Sergeant Cross. Sergeant Ward was my platoon sergeant for whom I had great respect. Ward was a rather mild-mannered man who really knew his business and could disassemble and assemble a machine gun blindfolded. Following our somewhat-less-than-cordial welcoming address, we were herded into our barracks, some hurriedly built two-story wooden buildings which would be "home" for the next three months. We filed into the building in a column of twos and went to the far end of the room, where we halted and were told that the bed we stopped beside was the one to which we were assigned. These were single beds and not the double bunk beds that the earlier recruits had, which was a break. We then received a demonstration on the Army method of making a bed with the traditional bouncing of a quarter.

The next stop would be the supply room to obtain sheets, towels, and other accessories that were not issued to us at the Processing Center. Among many instructions was to always check the bulletin board in the barracks for the next day's schedule, including first call, roll call, breakfast, and duty. Now I really felt like I was in the Army and the excitement and enthusiasm I experienced was overwhelming. I just couldn't wait for tomorrow to come when I would start learning how to be a soldier, so that I could go take care of those guys overseas who were causing so much trouble.

The next morning, right on schedule at 6:00 a.m. was first call and I jumped up, ran to the latrine, showered, shaved, and other things that you do in the latrine, dashed back and jumped into my clothes in 25 minutes and was ready for roll call by 6:30. Following roll call, I went back to the barracks to get ready to report to the Mess Hall for breakfast at 7:00. Going through the line, I picked up a glass, poured some grapefruit juice and drank it. The cook's helper put some powdered eggs on my tray, some potatoes which I can't describe, and unceremoniously introduced me to the Army's version of cream chipped beef on toast, more popularly referred to as S.O.S. – a loose interpretation would be "Stuff on a Shingle," but any old Army man would well know that I am lying. Placed on the table were large pitchers of coffee, and if you got to these soon enough you might have hot coffee. When we finished breakfast, we scraped any remaining scraps from the tray into a large garbage can and placed the tray on the counter to be attended to a little later by some people specially selected from the ranks.

Returning to the barracks, we had a few minutes to make beds, straighten clothing racks – left sleeve out – and organize footlockers. At 0800 hours, that's military time for 8 a.m., we lined up outside in formation to receive orders for our next activity, and were divided into work details: one group for latrine duty, another to police the area, the third to mop the barracks, and the fourth was the specially selected people I referred to above for kitchen duty. My group was to police the area, which meant picking up little scraps such as burnt matches, cigarette butts, chewing gum wrappers, etc., which I had a hard time relating to learning to fight an enemy. Some time later, I found out that this comes under the heading of discipline and taking orders, with which I had considerable experience as a married man. Following a ten-minute break, we formed up for a period of calisthenics and close-order drill at 0900. I found I was in much better shape than most of the others when it came to push-ups and pull-ups, since I did those kinds of exercises on a regular basis prior to entering the service. I also did well with the close-order drill, inasmuch as I knew my left foot from my right, and those who didn't were required to carry a rock in their left hand because when marching you lead with your left foot. The way it was explained was "right was wrong, and left was right," which only complicated the matter for most.

At 1000 hours, that's 10 o'clock, we were assembled for two periods of lectures on military discipline, rules and regulations on proper conduct, and proper dress. One interesting fact was that the Armored Forces wore their hats tilted to the left, as opposed to the rest of the Army that tilted to the right. We were also advised of the consequences of breaking the rules, some of which were a bit unpleasant to say the least.

Next we broke for lunch, which generally consisted of those things that people made derogatory remarks about but which I enjoyed, strange person that I was. After lunch, at 1300 hours – one o'clock if you still don't get it – we were marched down to the motor park where all these different military vehicles were, and we were halted beside this huge iron monster with a big old cannon sticking out of it. It finally dawned on me that this was a tank, the kind of thing that Ord 3 of the British Army Staff bought and shipped by the thousands. Since my work with Ord 3 made me a tank expert, I tried to hide how shocked I was at the immensity of this gigantic hunk of metal. Well, our catalogues gave us pictures and specifications with size and weight and so forth, but it sure makes a difference when you stand beside one of these suckers. I could hardly contain myself from the excitement of realizing that some day soon I would be driving one of these babies and firing all of its guns. The afternoon was spent learning about the tank, its guns, its capabilities, and its limitations, but not until combat did we learn about its weaknesses. This was all so fascinating to me that I was disappointed when we got the order to "fall in" and were marched back to the company area and dismissed at about 1630, in time to wash up for supper (I call it dinner) at 1700.

Dinner or supper consisted of ham, green beans, boiled potatoes, bread, coffee, and a piece of cake, and as usual I thought it was great. The rest of the evening was free time to visit the PX to buy goodies and necessities, or go to the rec hall for pool, table tennis, writing letters, or just hanging out. "Lights out" in the barracks was at 2200, and "Taps" was sounded at 2300, so I hit the sack shortly before "lights out." As I lay there contemplating the events of my first full day of basic training, I realized that this was the Army and I was a member of that great and powerful organization, and I could feel an overwhelming sense of pride swelling up within me. As the last notes of "Taps" faded into the night, I too faded into a deep sleep from total exhaustion from a day the likes of which for thirteen weeks would convert me from civilian to soldier.

I have described in considerable detail the events of the first day, which provided the format of the days to come but with constant change of the activities of those days. Each day brought new knowledge, new information, and new discoveries necessary for the creation of a fighting machine from a normal human being.

Miller as a private during basic training at Fort Knox, Kentucky.

Early on, we started instructions on the use of the various weapons we would be using in combat. One day we would hike to a wooded area where we would spread out a blanket and disassemble then assemble a rifle; the next day, a pistol; then a sub-machine gun; and finally a ground-mount .30-caliber machine gun, which we were to learn was basically the same as the .30-caliber machine guns mounted on a tank.

In the event of inclement weather, we would watch training films or listen to lectures on many and varied subjects. With each new thing I learned, I felt "now I am ready, let me at them," only to find out I had a long way to go before being combat-ready. This was all so new to me and totally fascinating, and I was enjoying it so much I was afraid someone would notice it and recommend I be discharged on a "Section 8," which is mental incompetence.

Well, somebody did notice, because after about the fifth week, the entire company was marched to the parade ground where a number of officers were assembled. A couple of them gave short speeches complimenting us on the progress we were making, and suggested that we showed promise of some day becoming soldiers, which I thought was encouraging. Then another officer stepped forward and called out, "Private Charles W. Miller, front and center." Hey, wait a minute, that's my name. Is this good or bad? Well, I will soon find out. I broke ranks, marched straight ahead, did a "column left," and halted in front of the officer, did a "right face," gave him a snappy salute and said, "Private Miller reporting, sir." He then proceeded to read an order which in effect said: "Due to Private Miller's attitude, aptitude, and determination reflecting the true spirit of the Armored Forces, he is herewith appointed a Lance Corporal, with the responsibilities and privileges commensurate with that rank." He then slipped an armband with corporal's striping over my sleeve, shook my hand and said, "Congratulations, Lance Corporal Miller." I snapped another salute, did an "about face" and marched toward my position in the ranks, and I became aware that the whole company was cheering and applauding. Man, I felt like I was just elected Pope. What a surprise. It must have been Sergeant Ward who recommended me. He told me later that usually a man from each of the four platoons was recommended, but I was the only one ready for that move.

Being named a lance corporal is quite an honor, especially since I was the only one out of over 300 men, but it carried with it very limited authority, some additional responsibilities, no pay increase, but excused me from all the housekeeping duties mentioned previously. Within the next few days, there were two situations that offered me an opportunity to prove if I was worthy of this recent recognition.

One of my early assignments was to run a squad of men through a period of close-order drill, which is supposed to be performed with snap and coordination in a military manner. It didn't take but a few moments for me to realize that I had a problem here. The men were out of step, talking, laughing, and generally goofing off, so I promptly called them to a halt, gave them a "left face," and stood there for a moment, staring at them and gathering my thoughts. I then said, "Gentlemen, we are in this Army for the duration, which could be years. I intend to make the most of the time I spend in the military by learning all I can about soldiering and taking seriously every second of our training. Certainly, the more we know about this business, the longer we will live in combat. Now, you can go along with me and start working toward a successful military career, or you can continue to clown around like you have been this morning, which makes us all look bad, and I will have to admit to Sergeant Ward that this drill didn't go well. He will then give you extra duty and make a note in my file about inability to maintain order. You can make us all look bad or all look good. The choice is yours, and if you are as smart as I think you are, I know what your choice will be."

Again I took a moment to observe any reaction to my talk, and as they stood at attention, I was aware that there was not a single smile among them, and on many I could see their jaw muscles flexing as they gritted their teeth while making a decision that would affect their lives for the foreseeable future. I immediately gave them a sharp "Left face, forward harp," and they stepped off like they had been doing it for years. I counted "Hut-twop-threep-fourp," then the order, "Count Cadence – Count," and in perfect unison and loud enough they could be heard in Washington, D.C., they counted. We did "By the left flank – Harp; by the right flank – Harp; to the rear – Harp; to the rear – Harp." You say "Harp" rather than "March" because "Harp" is sharper and clipped, and the whole drill went off like clockwork. After about 20 minutes, we marched back to the Company area, right up to where Sergeant Ward was standing, and I brought them to a halt, snapped a "Left face" and said, "Thank you, Gentlemen," turned to Sergeant Ward and said, "Sergeant, you have a fine group of soldiers here," and walked over and took my place at their side. Ward said, "Take a ten-minute break. Dismissed." As the men broke ranks, they brushed beside me, and one said, "Nice going, Miller," another, "Good job, Miller," some, a pat on the shoulder, a punch on the arm, or a whack on the bottom, and I knew then I was on my way.

The second incident that I referred to earlier happened one night in the barracks, where we were getting ready to turn in. Some of the men were reading for the fourth or fifth time the mail they received that day, some were shining shoes, and others were engaged in idle chatter, joking with one another using language I promised myself not to write in these pages. However, there were two big men, both Texans, whose remarks to each other became increasingly loud and unfriendly, and I sensed they were becoming rather belligerent. I put down the boots I was polishing just as they stood up and started swinging at each other. Although both were considerably larger than I and against my better judgment, I immediately jumped in and grabbed the man nearest me and swung him around away from his opponent, placing me in between these two big hunks. Then I said, "If you two want to beat each other up, that's fine with me, but you will go outside to do it. I'll not have you guys busting up my barracks, which are my responsibility." That seemed to calm things down, and as one of them turned away, the other one whom I grabbed said to me, "If you ever do that to me again, I will run a knife through your belly," and I said, "Well, you can try, but you better not miss because you will never get a second chance." I am not sure what I meant, but it seemed to take the sting out of the situation, and I am happy to say nothing more ever came of it. Since all of this was rather new to me, I was unsure if I was handling these incidents properly, but my actions seemed to remedy the problem so I must have done something right.

Each day for the next couple of weeks brought new discoveries and experiences, including trips to the firing range where we would fire the various weapons we had been learning about. One day, the rifle, another day, the pistol, then the submachine gun, and finally the ground-mounted .30 caliber machine gun, which required the "buddy system" to feed the cartridge belt into the chamber of the gun. There were long marches with full pack, and tent-pitching exercises mixed in with numerous trips to the motor park; then finally we were permitted to "fire up" a tank. That is army for "starting the motor," and what a thrill that was to hear the frightening roar of that powerful engine. All of this activity only added fuel to the tremendous enthusiasm I had for this totally new lifestyle.

At about the eighth week, the schedule called for our khaki uniform, and the company was marched to the parade ground and I suspected they were finally going to name lance corporals for the other platoons. Sure enough, one man from each platoon was called to stand before the formation of officers. I was surprised when they called one of the men in my platoon, but I thought that was great because I would have some help. The order was read naming each of the four men a lance corporal, and they all received their armbands. They then returned to their places, and one of the officers stepped forward and commanded, "Lance Corporal Charles W. Miller, front and center." I marched up and halted in front of the officer, who proceeded to read the order making me a lance sergeant. I just couldn't believe it, and once again I was the only one in the company to receive a lance sergeant's armband. As I marched back to my platoon, I think I busted a couple of buttons off of my shirt from an over-expanded chest. Later that day, during a "ten-minute break," Sergeant Ward called to me and quietly congratulated me on receiving my lance sergeant rating, and complimented me on my progress since coming to the center. I didn't think these things happened to a raw recruit, but as I said before, Sergeant Ward was somebody special.

On the following Monday, we were to reach another milestone on this amazing journey where this man had never walked before. We were loaded into trucks and transported out to the driving range where the tanks were awaiting our arrival. It didn't take a brain surgeon to figure out what was about to happen. We were going to drive

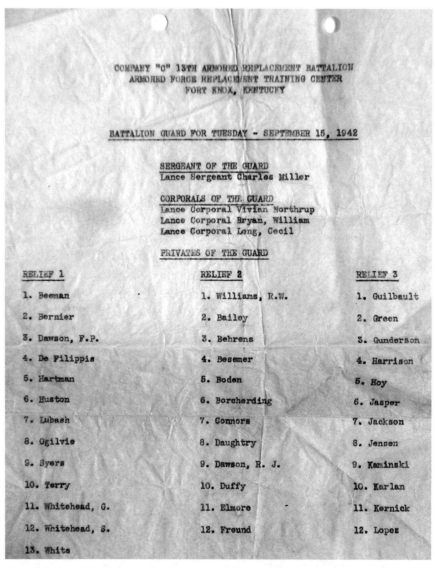

Guard roster listing Miller as "Sergeant of the Guard" at Fort Knox, Kentucky.

these gorgeous hunks of steel – the moment I had been looking forward to since I first arrived at Ft. Knox. During those weeks of preliminary instructions, I realized that this could be a real challenge for me. You see, many of the men had driven large trucks or heavy construction vehicles or heavy farm equipment, some of which were even track-driven, all of which gave them an advantage over a guy who had never driven anything larger than a Mercury two-door sedan. I had never heard of "double-clutching," "gearing up" and "gearing down," "increasing power" and "decreasing power" depending on the r.p.m.s (that's revolutions per minute). All I had ever been concerned with was m.p.h.s (that's miles per hour) and whether the gas gauge showed "full" or "empty." We had been told all about these things, and now we were going to put them to use.

The adrenaline was rising fast as I slipped through the hatch into the driver's seat with a tech sergeant seated next to me, who said, "Ok, let's fire it up." Now back then, all cars had stick shifts, so I was familiar with engaging the clutch before putting in gear, but my car had three forward speeds. This thing had five. Also, my car had a steering wheel, while a tank has two steering levers, one to turn right, the other to turn left, and to stop, you pulled both levers back. Here's the problem: you need two hands to steer and a third to shift gears, and since I was a normal human with only two hands I felt somewhat at a disadvantage, but we had already been shown how to cope with that situation. It would take a lot of time to describe to you the thrill of moving down the tank trail in second gear for just a short distance at first, and gradually each day increasing speeds and performing various maneuvers, becoming more comfortable as I soon began to realize that I could really handle this machine as easily as my Mercury – well, almost.

Another big event was driving out to the firing range and firing the tank guns. This gave us some idea what it would sound like in combat, although no one was shooting back at us. That would come later. All of this activity was intermingled with the many other instructions described earlier.

The tenth Sunday of our basic training period had been designated visitors' day for those having friends or relatives within driving distance of Ft. Knox. I had mentioned this to Gracie, and while she agreed it was too far to drive, she wanted to hop a train to be with me on visitors' day. Well, if you knew Gracie, you would know that what Gracie wants, Gracie gets. So I told her about a little hotel in nearby Elizabethtown, better known as "E-town," and looked forward to seeing her that Sunday.

It so happened that the Friday before visitors' day, our company was to stand Retreat, which meant wearing the khaki uniform and marching to the retreat area. As lance sergeant, I was in charge of our platoon and marched beside the men and gave the necessary commands to move them to our designated position, which was along side of the road. I took my place in front of the platoon, facing the road. While we were waiting for them to sound Retreat, a post shuttle bus came up that road. Since it was summer and no air-conditioning, the windows of the bus were open, and just as the bus passed in front of my platoon and me standing at attention, a young lady leaned out of the window, and so the whole world could hear, yelled, "Hi, Snookie!" Who else could it be but my Gracie, subjecting me to one of the most humiliating experiences of my life, which I had to live with for the rest of my basic training. We were able to have dinner together that evening, and when I told her how embarrassed I was, she couldn't stop laughing. If the truth were known, I actually thought it was kind of cute, and my guys had a lot of fun with it.

It was just a few days later that I was called to the Orderly Room where I was told to get dressed and report to the Officers' Review Board at the Administration Building, that I was to be interviewed as a possible candidate for Officer Candidate School. Only then did I realize that because of my total involvement in the learning process, I had completely forgotten my original intention to apply for OCS. Obviously somebody, thinking I might be officer material, had submitted my name for consideration and I have to believe it had to be Sgt. Ward. I hurried to my barracks, showered, and dressed in my recently laundered and pressed uniform, hoping to make a good impression. In spite of being so excited, I was amazed how calm, cool, and confident I felt as I walked toward the Administration Building to keep the appointment that could, and did have a tremendous influence on the rest of my life. Although I arrived a few minutes early, I was immediately ushered to the Officers' Conference Room, where sat the Review Board consisting of a major and two captains. I moved forward and came to a halt in front of the major, saluted and said, "Lance Sergeant Charles W. Miller reporting as ordered, Sir." The major returned my salute, and proceeded to read some of the regulations relating to the formality of determining a soldier's qualifications and eligibility for appointment to the Officer Candidate School. After asking if I understood, he started to ask a series of simple questions, which I assumed was to break the ice and either loosen me up or tighten me up, depending on my disposition. "Where are you from?" "What is your favorite sport?" Then out of the blue: "How does Mrs. Miller feel about you being in the Army?" I replied, "Concerned but proud, Sir." Now the questions got a little more serious. "What is your opinion of your basic training?" I answered, "Very informative and sometimes even inspiring, Sir." He asked me to explain, and I told him, "I realized that all of the instructions and knowledge I recently received was to convert me from a civilian to a soldier in the United States Army. I found that to be very inspiring, Sir." Next, "Do you want to be an officer?" "Yes, Sir, I do." Then, "Why?" Oh, boy, but I immediately replied, "Sir, I feel that as an officer, I can be of greater service to the Army and my Country." Did I detect a look of approval in his eyes, or was it my imagination? Anyway, I felt good about it. The major then turned to the officer on his right and asked, "Captain, do you have any questions you would like to ask?" The captain turned to me and said, "Miller, can you give me four ways to write "for?" I quickly rattled off, "For, fore, four, and the numeral 4, and a fifth way could be the Roman numeral IV." At that moment I could have bitten my tongue, because I was afraid I sounded like a smart aleck adding something he didn't ask for, but I was relieved to see a slight smile on his face, and he said, "Very good, Miller," with emphasis on "very." The major also seemed somewhat amused as he turned to the other officer and asked the captain if he had anything he wanted to add. The captain said, "No, Major. I thought it was an excellent interview, and I am impressed. I have nothing further." He was probably complimenting the major, but it sounded good to me. The major said, "Very well, then. This interview is over, and Lance Sergeant Miller, you may be excused." With that I said, "Thank you, Sir," snapped a salute, did a sharp "about face" and marched toward the door, which seemed a mile away.

As I emerged from the building into the late afternoon sunlight, I slowly began to realize what had just taken place, and was amazed at my own performance during this vital session – how I was able to maintain my composure, how quickly I responded to each of the questions, how smoothly the words seemed to flow and without any hesitation. Please forgive me if I say I was extremely pleased with myself, and I know that a little Guardian Angel was sitting on my shoulder, guiding me through the entire interview.

The word of my whereabouts that afternoon reached some of the guys in my outfit, and when I returned they were anxious to know how it went. With considerable effort, I was able to muster up a degree of false modesty and said we would just have to wait and see.

Since there were still more than two weeks left of our basic training, our daily routine consisted of repeating over and over what we had learned in the early stages of our training. It was less than a week later that I was called to the Orderly Room, and the first sergeant held out his hand and said, "Congratulations, Miller, you have been accepted to the OCS," and handed me a letter informing me that a company of officer candidates was being formed and should be activated within the next 30 to 60 days, and I should remain at my present location until I received orders giving me the exact date to report. When I left that Orderly Room, I could no longer hide my pride, my feet wouldn't touch the ground, and I was walking on cloud nine.

I returned to the motor park where my group was getting instructions on repairing a tank track, and Sgt. Ward walked up and congratulated me. Obviously, he had already heard when he told me to report to the first sergeant, but said nothing because it was information to be given by the first sergeant on behalf of the company commander. I joined my group, some of whom looked at me with rather inquisitive expressions on their faces, but kept their attention on the business at hand. They were able to keep their curiosity under control until we returned to the company area and were dismissed for the day, when the floodgates of questions were opened. "What's going on with you?" they asked almost with one voice, and it was with subdued pride that I told them what had happened, and they were all genuinely happy for me. Although we continued to work right up to the last day of basic training, from that hour on, it seemed to be a breeze for me. For one thing, I noticed all the "non-comms" in the company were much more sociable, which of necessity was limited during the training period.

When the final day arrived, it was good-bye to these men with whom I had spent thirteen fascinating weeks that seemed to have gone so quickly. I was the only one left at the Training Center where I would await my orders to report to OCS. My lance sergeant armband was turned in, and the "non-comms" told me to just hang loose and there would be lots for me to do when the next batch of recruits arrived. They gave me the room of one of the "non-comms" who lived off the post with his wife, which was a real luxury. I was now able to leave the post, and got a pass from noon Saturday until roll call Monday to visit my grandmother in Cincinnati, Ohio. The only problem was that the pass limited travel to within fifty miles of Ft. Knox. What do I do about that? Well, it was suggested that I not get drunk, not get in any fights, or cause any kind of public disturbances necessitating my producing the pass to an inquiring MP (Military Police). I did visit my grandmother who was living with one of my aunts, had a great spaghetti dinner, went to church on Sunday morning, another nice dinner, then back on the bus to Ft. Knox where I arrived before lights out, to learn the new batch of recruits had arrived that afternoon. When I walked into the barracks, I realized what a terrific difference thirteen weeks of training made.

It was hard to believe that those well-disciplined, confident soldiers who just shipped out a couple of days ago were once like these confused, unsure, RAW recruits I saw before me. As I walked through the barracks, I paused briefly to introduce myself and explain my present situation and assure them that I was just a private, just like them.

For the few remaining days until I was to report to OCS, the "non-comms" used me to demonstrate various movements such as right, left, and about face, the hand salute and stand at attention, and I was a "gopher" for whatever they needed for the instructions they were giving.

Finally the day came for me to leave AFTC and report to the office at OCS. While I was packing my "A" and "B" barracks bags, Sergeant Ward came in and said, "As soon as you are packed, come on out. I have a Peep waiting to take you over." I certainly didn't expect that, but I was really glad because I had added a few items to what I had been issued, and those two barracks bags had gotten pretty heavy. I dragged them down to the Peep, threw them into the back seat, jumped in and off we went. Note: A Peep is what the Armor people called a Jeep and to this day, I don't know why. It was just about a five minute ride, during which I told Ward how much I appreciated everything he had taught me and the recognition I received during my training. His response was, "Just doing my job." He pulled up to the building where I was to report, and I reached over, grabbed my barracks bags, extended my hand and said, "Thanks for the lift, Sergeant." He shook my hand and said, "Good luck, Miller," and hurriedly drove off, leaving me standing there between my two barracks bags and thinking, "I will never forget that man," and I never have.

Chapter 3

AN OFFICER AND A GENTLEMAN — BY ACT OF CONGRESS

Picking up my bags I entered the building and was greeted by a sign near the door of an office that said, "New Candidates Report Here." I walked into the office where a staff sergeant was seated at a desk and said, "Hi Sergeant, I am a new candidate." He said "Good afternoon, your name and serial number." I responded, "Charles W. Miller, 33191617." He leafed through some manila envelopes and pulled out one with my name on it and handed it to me. "These are the rules and regulations and a directive advising you of your company, platoon, the building and floor where you will live," and he added, "it's the second floor of Building B. Find yourself a bed that is not taken and be prepared to be in formation at 1600." I thanked him and headed toward Building B, which fortunately was only two buildings away, climbed the stairs, and spotted a bed which I dumped my things on. There was a fellow unloading his stuff on the bed next to mine and we introduced ourselves. His name was John Egan and I immediately felt that he and I might become friends because he suggested that I read the contents of my envelope as soon as possible, which I did, and learned that not knowing the rules was no excuse for messing up. It listed the dozens of things for which you could receive demerits, which were called "gigs," and after ten gigs your record would be reviewed to determine if you are officer material or should be dropped from the rolls. Some of the misdeeds that will get you a gig are: soiled uniform, improper uniform, unpolished shoes, unpolished brass, late for formation, failure to salute, bed not made properly, clothing not hung properly, foot locker not arranged according to diagram, maintains proper posture when seated in the mess hall, just to name a few. True to form, I thought all of this was just great, but I wondered if I could remember it all. I was glad to learn of these restrictions before the 1600 formation, just so I wouldn't get a bad start on my first day. However, the officer who greeted us at that formation advised us that penalties would be imposed starting the next day. While his words were not threatening, he explained honestly and frankly that at least thirty five percent of our company would not obtain commissions. Many would drop out of their own accord, others due to failing grades, and some because of excessive gigs. He mentioned that we had been selected because it was believed that we had a good chance of becoming officers, able to lead men and willing to take responsibility for the lives of those under our command. He warned that the days ahead would be difficult, with heavy demands on mind and body sometimes pushing us to the very limits of our abilities. We were told that there was so much we had to learn and so little time to learn it, and how we used the knowledge we gained here could determine whether or not we and our men would survive in combat. This was pretty much the nature of his talk, which lasted nearly an hour and which was very thought provoking, impressing upon us the seriousness of the job ahead.

This talk was so different from the one we received when we first arrived at the Training Center where the sergeant spoke to us like we were a bunch of dummies, which most of us were, militarily speaking. This talk tore into your brain, ripped at your nerves, and touched your heart with the intention of reaching out to a group of men who at least had completed basic training, but there were many who had considerable military experience and even some who had been first sergeants with the units they left to find out if the grass was greener as an officer. Although I was already totally committed to the proposition of becoming an officer, I found renewed inspiration from the remarks of this officer. He closed by wishing us good luck and success in our endeavors here and throughout our military careers. After being dismissed we proceeded to the mess hall to partake of our dinner and to practice our new rules of table etiquette according to OCS.

Following dinner, Egan and I decided to take our coats to the PX to have the OCS patches sewn on which were worn several inches above the left cuff, as opposed to the military unit patches which are on the left sleeve just below the shoulder. Some of the men were going to do it themselves but we wanted to make sure it was done exactly right. We were glad we did because later some of the men were gigged for not having the patches on correctly. We also bought some Simonize, an auto wax, for our shoes and some clear nail polish for our brass. These were a couple of tricks I learned from the non-comms after basic training. It was hard work rubbing that Simonize to a shiny gloss, but from then on just a quick buffing made your shoes sparkle. After polishing your brass, a light coating of fingernail polish preserved the shine for a long time. Egan and I split the cost because one can and one bottle was enough for both of us.

It did not take long after the start of the next day for us to realize that the remarks of the officer the day before were right on target – it was tough. First call was at 0600, but I continued my practice of getting up at least 15 minutes before so I could get to the latrine, shave, and be in the shower before most of the others got there. Roll call at 0645 and breakfast 0700. Now I must remember at mess to sit with my back at least three inches from the back of the chair, the hand not in use at my side, and keep talk soft and to a minimum. Food was placed on the table in bowls sufficient for four people and you could take only your share. When finished, you scraped your plate into a garbage can and placed it, your cup, and silverware into a cart. The sleeping quarters being upstairs, you returned to make your bed, straighten the clothing in your locker and arrange your footlocker properly, then line up in formation outside at 0800. The next 50 minutes were spent in a mixture of close-order drill and light calisthenics, after which we had a ten-minute break to freshen up or perform bathroom duty. Then at 0900 we lined up to proceed to our first classroom assignment which was in a building several blocks away. As we moved out, we immediately got the order "Double-Time-Harp" which is an easy jog but in cadence, and from that time on, movements from one class to another were in "double-time."

We soon reached our destination and as we filed into the building we were handed a Training Manual on Military Courtesy – Military Law. During the next two hours, with a ten-minute break, we watched a training film, heard a lecture, and had an open discussion and received a stern warning on the consequences of violating any of those regulations. Most were just common sense or those regulations normally applied to civilians, but some were related to the conduct of military officers, such as never carry an umbrella or walk a dog, and meet all financial obligations promptly and maintain a flawless credit record. As usual I approved of all of these rules, but there were some who referred to them as "chicken stuff," which I again have altered to keep these pages clean as I am determined to do. We were dismissed at 1100 hours, then double-timed back to the barracks where we were reminded to check the bulletin board for the afternoon instructions. When checking the bulletin board we learned that the subject for the afternoon would be Wheeled Vehicles and figured we would be driving some peeps and light trucks. We dashed upstairs to wash up for chow and back down to the mess hall at 1200 when we were served our noon meal. One thing about OCS – we didn't have any kitchen duties other than what I mentioned earlier, but we would later receive full instructions on Mess Management. At 1300 we were in formation to proceed in the usual

OCS patch.

manner to the area designated for Wheeled Vehicles. To our surprise, it was another classroom where we received training manuals on the subject, listened to a talk on the concept of internal combustion engines, the firing sequence of four and six cylinder motors, the function of the carburetor and the spark plugs, and much more detail that I knew so little about. I was sure that I was in a heap of trouble but it certainly was interesting. Another two-hour session with a ten minute break, and at 1530 we returned to the barracks for 30 minutes of close-order drill.

At this point one of our company officers had us stand at ease while he reviewed our first full day at OCS. "This was probably the easiest day you will have while you are here," he stated, at which time you could hear a lot of sighs and deep breaths because we were pretty beat at the end of the day. The officer continued, "Now you are looking forward to an evening of relaxation at a movie or the rec hall, but I would suggest that you sit down with the manuals you received today and review everything you learned because at the end of the week there will be exams, which you don't want to fail." With that warning he dismissed us, and we slowly went upstairs and flopped down on our beds with one of the manuals and studied until chow time at 1730. Some of the whispered remarks around the tables at chow revealed a little uncertainty about their ability to successfully complete this course, some made jokingly, others with a degree of seriousness. Those who really seemed concerned received words of encouragement to "stick with it, you're going to make it" from the guys whose confidence remained unshaken. As far as myself, there was no doubt in my mind that I would survive no matter how rough they made it.

The next three days were pretty much carbon copies of the first, except each day we received new information about each of the subjects we were studying. However, on the fourth day we went to the Motor Park and drove some of the wheeled vehicles over a short test track. It was fun, except when shifting gears on the two and a half ton six wheeler I ground the gears a little, but nobody said anything so I guess I did all right. Just as we had been told, we had exams on Friday and I was a little nervous about Wheeled Vehicles because as a civilian about all I knew was how to drive. I did pick up a good bit of knowledge in basic training and I really studied that manual all week so I felt I was ready. Although both of the exams were long and tough, I did feel that I did well enough to pass. That evening at chow there seemed to be a deadly quiet, which seemed strange because there was so much to talk about, but I suppose we all waited until the meal was over when we could speak freely in the barracks. Boy, did they speak freely. When they realized they had given a wrong answer, there were a lot of words that I won't repeat. Since we had to turn in our manuals the day of the exam we had to compare our answers with each other, which resulted in a lot of conversation and included a lot of good old army cussin'. Egan and I discussed a number of questions we were in doubt about and to my surprise we were pretty much in agreement – but were we right? Results of the exams were supposed to be posted on the bulletin board Sunday night so we would find out soon enough.

Now it was time to prepare for Saturday inspection, so I took a mop and swabbed around and under my bed, moved my footlocker to mop there and under the clothing locker. Then I mopped the aisle at the end of my bed and across to the bed on the other side. We were only expected to go half way but we all mopped all the way so the aisle was really clean. Next, shine shoes and brass, check clothing for any spots and see that they were hung properly, and make sure the contents of the footlocker were in order. When it was time for "Lights Out," none of us had to be told to go to bed. We were one tired bunch of soldiers and welcomed the opportunity to get some sleep.

Saturday morning we followed our usual routine until after breakfast, when we went back to the dorm to make final preparation for the inspection, which was scheduled for 0800. The procedure, which was described in the material we received earlier, was for an officer and a non-comm to enter the dorm and the non-comm would call "Attention"– actually he says "Attent-hut." The officer would immediately give the command "At Ease" and we would move in front of our opened footlockers and stand at ease, but when they approached, you would snap to attention. He would then start down the line of men from their right, asking each man's name and serial number, and the non-comm would start checking items on the sheet on his clipboard. They inspected the man front and back, glanced down at his foot locker, moved along beside the bed, the non-comm looked under the bed, went around the head of the bed to the clothing locker and checked it, and finally returned to face the man and said, "At Ease." Since we were on the opposite side of the aisle from the men being inspected, we were able to observe them moving from one to the next stopping occasionally for a brief comment, then the sergeant would make a check mark or write a word on his check sheet. We figured that was not a good sign. When they reached the end of that side they started back on our side, and since Egan and I were at the far end of the room we would be the first, with Egan and then me. I was close enough that I could hear them ask him his name and serial number, and then I remember hoping I could remember my name. There were no delays at Egan's position, and they soon reached me and I did remember my name, and serial number too. Like Egan's, mine seemed to go smoothly also and I was relieved when the officer gave me "At Ease." They followed this procedure until the last man and when they finished with him, the officer gave the command, "As you were," and left the room. It was almost time to form up for more close-order drill, which was scheduled for 1030 hours. Up to this point, either an officer or a drill sergeant conducted the drill and today was the sergeant who brought us to a halt after about 15 or 20 minutes and turned us over to an officer who had us "stand at ease." The officer told us that the inspection went pretty well but there were some gigs, which would be posted along with our exam grades Sunday evening. He also said that starting Monday morning, our close-order drill would be conducted by the candidates who would be called out of the ranks to take over for about a ten-minute period. Furthermore, drill would be held in the street and we would be required to move the unit in all four directions, front, back, left and right, and at all times keeping within the two curbs. If the unit were standing in the exact center of the street, one curb was about three paces in front, the other about three paces to the rear. For most of the men who had not conducted any drill before, this would be a real challenge but for those who had some time in the service, not too bad. Two things were in my favor: my experience as a lance corporal and sergeant, and the fact that I really enjoyed drilling, and so for me I felt it was my cup of tea and couldn't wait for my turn.

When the officer finished, he called us to attention and dismissed us for the day. It was almost time for lunch and after we ate, Egan and I went to the PX where we bought some more writing paper and a couple of candy bars. Egan said he was going back to the barracks and rest a little, but I decided to go to the rec hall to see if anything was going on and write a letter to Gracie. Saturday night chow usually left something to be desired with either cold cuts, stew, sometimes spaghetti, all of which were ok with me because I was in OCS, which was what mattered the most to me. I turned in early that night because I wanted to get up and attend Mass in the morning. After breakfast, nearly a dozen of us walked to the post chapel to hear Mass celebrated by one of the chaplains stationed at Ft. Knox. The chapel was used by various denominations so there was only one Mass to make room for other services. The midday meal on Sunday was pretty good as usual, and now began the nervous wait for our grades and gigs to be posted for all to see. To pass the time we read the Stars and Stripes or Yank, which were publications for the military services. It seemed like most everybody was hanging around but we were saddened by several beds that had been stripped down which indicated some had already left. It turned out that a couple of them were old timers who apparently felt that the job they were doing as first sergeant was as important as any job they would get as an officer. It was hard to argue that point.

Finally, someone called out from downstairs that the exam grades had been posted and my heart skipped a beat. Not that I was worried about passing, but I was anxious to know by how much and was I in for a huge surprise. Wheeled Vehicles was the one subject I knew the least about and so I didn't expect to do real great, but would you believe it, I scored 98 on that exam which as time would tell was the best mark I received for the entire course. Did I ever feel good and I did fine on Military Courtesy-Military Law, but I only remember my highest and my lowest exam grades. Egan did real well too and kidded me about my 98, saying that I had been bluffing all along about my limited knowledge of all things mechanical. I did listen intently to the instructions we received and really studied the manual, so I guess it paid off. There were also a number of gigs, a few failing grades and several with the word "Withdrew" beside their name. Both Egan and I lucked out in the gig department and we felt that our first week was a huge success. Now with only 12 more weeks to go we checked the bulletin board to find out what was in store for the next week, which was Map Reading and the Colt 45 Pistol.

Week number two saw the beginning of the rotation of the candidates to lead close-order drill, and I was hoping for an early call but soon realized we would be called in alphabetical order. That was too bad because the first man called was rather nervous and obviously had never done this before. He dragged out the commands instead of snapping them, gave them on the wrong foot and wasn't quick enough to keep us off the curbs. The men tried to help by adjusting but there was some disorder in the ranks which was expected for the first time. A couple of others had problems but we managed to get through the period without a major disaster. Another thing different about week two was we had instructions each day in the field. In the morning after drill we marched out to a field training area, double timing part way then "route order" going through the field. We were issued a map, an aerial photograph, a compass, and a manual. In the afternoon at a different location we received a Colt 45 pistol and a manual. The morning and evening drills went pretty much as described above but when a former first sergeant took over, naturally it went well. I thought it would have been better if the experienced men went first as it would have made it a little easier for the inexperienced, but the Army hadn't asked for my opinion. Egan did all right but his commands could have been a little sharper, which again was a lack of experience.

On Thursday of that week, when we reached the training area we were divided into groups, and each group was given a list of compass directions to various reference points to reach a certain destination. It was like a game and we had no difficulty in accomplishing our mission. I thought it was fun. In the afternoon we boarded trucks and were taken to the firing range to fire the pistol. I had fired the .45 in basic training and didn't like it very much because of the heavy recoil. Back then we were taught to stand with our side to the target and raise the pistol with our arm extended, and get the target in the sight and fire. Now you stand with your body facing the target with your feet firmly planted and hold the pistol with both hands, which makes more sense because you can control the recoil better that way. But I did fine, although I still didn't like that gun. By the time we got back from the range we were running late, but we lined up for close-order drill and a couple of the men were called to take over. They had some of the usual problems in spite of our efforts to help, but that was to be expected.

Finally I got my chance, which I had long been waiting for. I moved them out in column formation and immediately gave them a "Right Oblique," which moves the unit at an angle, then a "Forward Harp" to straighten them out again near the one curb, which left the rest of the street for flanking movements without reaching the curb. No one had done it that way before, not even the sergeants who could give the commands quick enough to keep the unit within the limits, and the men executed it perfectly. Then after about five minutes more, the cannon was fired signaling "Retreat." We often finished before "Retreat," but a couple of times the officer took over shortly before "Retreat" and had us stand at attention while he saluted during the bugle sounding "Retreat." But here I was in command so I quickly had them do a flanking movement, brought them to a halt facing the direction of the flag and gave the order, "By the numbers, Hand Salute" which is the command when you want the whole detail to salute. After "Retreat" had been sounded, I gave the order "Two" which brings the hand back down to the side. At that point the officer came up and said "I'll take over, candidate." I saluted and got back in formation and he dismissed us. Some of the guys complimented me, but Egan called me a "show-off" again and I admitted I was. I really felt it went well, and apparently too well because I was never called on again. Neither were the Sergeants and we concluded that drill time was assigned to those who needed it most. Egan got called two more times and that was it for him. He did very well and that finished his drill duty.

Friday, exams again, and the weekend was pretty much the same as the previous one, except inspection was held outside in formation which made it go much quicker. Sunday evening the grades were posted, with similar results. Egan and I did well, as did most of the others, but there were a couple more "Withdrew" and for the first time one marked "Dismissed." There never was much discussion about those that left. For one thing, you barely knew the men beyond those on either side of your bed so their leaving had little personal effect on you. There was Egan on one side of me, and a fellow by the name of Larson on the other, and while Egan and I seemed to pair up, Larson kind of teamed up with the man on the other side of him. So that was the way it was and you were just too busy to extend your social contacts beyond the bed next to you. Also, the bulletin board indicated the next week we would have "Supply and Logistics" in the morning and the "Sub-Machine gun" in the afternoon. Since we pretty much followed the same routine each day I won't go into further detail, but I should mention that in the event of rain we sometimes watched a film in the theater on various subjects. Also, as time went on most of the guys improved on their close-order drill and we could usually adjust to any miscues that they made.

Thursday we fired the sub-machine gun and Friday, exams. Saturday inspection was again in formation and Egan and I survived without incident, but more of the others were not so fortunate. Such things as a scratched belt buckle, a crooked insignia, a sloppy tie, unshined shoes, need of a haircut, all resulted in numerous gigs, which served notice that they were getting tougher and we could expect that none would escape unscathed. Sunday, the exam grades and gigs were posted and I don't recall that we lost anyone that week, although we may have. Both Egan and I did well, and the subjects for the coming week were Military Strategy and the .30 Caliber Machine Gun. Military Strategy was a lot of fun because we worked with a sand table, which was all set up with hills, streams, woods, roads, houses, and toy tanks and soldiers. It was like playing in a sand box but this was serious business. We were shown several situations and then given some problems to show how we would maneuver the tanks and men under various conditions. We also discussed the Table of Organization of an Armored Division – neat stuff. Thursday we fired the machine gun and as usual, Friday exams. The rest of the weekend was similar to the others, at least for Egan and me: no gigs and good grades. The fourth week was a little different, with the subjects being Engineers-Construction and Demolition and the .30 Caliber Rifle M1. In the mornings we would learn about the use of fuses, primacord, detonator caps, TNT, plastic, booby traps, satchel charges, laying mine fields, and going through a simulated mine field detecting and removing anti-personnel and anti-tank mines. We even detonated a low-grade explosive. Also there was a discussion about bridge building, the various types of bridges, and how to determine weight limits. In the afternoon, we drew the M1 rifle and the next three days we would disassemble and assemble the weapon, study how it operated, do close-order drill with it, learn the Manual of Arms including how to stack the rifle, and at the end of the day Wednesday, turn them in. Thursday, of course, meant out to the range to fire the rifle and as usual, exams on Friday.

Saturday was another barracks inspection which as I mentioned before was tough, and guess what? Egan got a gig. Our extra pair of shoes was to be shined and placed at the foot of the bed with the toe of the right shoe against the leg of the bed. As he told me later, while Egan was waiting for inspection he was sitting on his bed reading and when it was getting close to the time, he stood up and smoothed down his bed and unknowingly kicked one of the shoes under the bed, and he was gigged for a shoe out of place. Sunday night we were both pleased with our exam grades and sure enough there was that big old one gig beside Egan's name. I told him I didn't know if I wanted to associate with him any more since he got a gig and we both enjoyed a hearty laugh over the incident. Next week would be Mess Management and TANKS. Wow, at last we were going to start on tanks and I was raring to go. Also, Christmas was this week and Gracie had insisted on spending Christmas with me even though I only had the one day off.

That week started off pretty much like all the others and many of us, including me, felt that Mess Management should not be much of a problem, so back to the classroom to find out how wrong we were. There is a tremendous amount of detail involved in managing a company mess including keeping records of amount of equipment, kitchen supplies, number of rations served and to be ordered each day. Of great importance is the care and storage of the various types of rations including the perishables, and the need to keep waste to the barest minimum. Cleanliness and sanitation of equipment and personnel was absolutely essential. The preparation of meals ensuring proper balance and sufficient nutrition was high on the list of priorities of efficient mess management. I could list dozens of other details that needed daily attention, but suffice it to say mess management is not an easy task. The trips to the motor park each afternoon were full of excitement for me. We were reintroduced to these monsters of death and destruction, and made to realize that it was absolutely imperative that we become fully acclimated and acquainted with every feature of this vehicle which would become home to many of us for the duration.

I made reservations at the post guest house for Gracie and me for Christmas Eve, and got a twelve-hour pass to be off the post from 0800 to 2000 hours Christmas day so I could take Gracie up to Louisville for a nice Christmas dinner. The afternoon period the day before Christmas was cut short and we were dismissed at 1500 hours, so I hurried to take my second shower of the day, got dressed and walked (ran) over to the guest house to meet Gracie. I had told Egan that I would ask him to join us but I really didn't want him. He laughed, gave me a shove and said he would see me when I got back Christmas night. Gracie was waiting when I got there and we were so glad to see each other that we almost forgot to get dinner. We went to a little restaurant near the guest house right there on the post and had a nice meal and a lot of talking. Later back in our room we exchanged Christmas presents. Gracie bought me a wonderful military watch, non-magnetic, waterproof, shockproof, self-winding, with a sweep second hand and an o.d. (olive drab color) watch band. I wore it all through the war and long after. I am afraid I don't remember what I gave Gracie, but I know it was a little trinket. I bought it at the PX. Christmas morning we went to Mass on the post, and I introduced Gracie to some of the fellows from my unit, then told them to get lost. Gracie said I was "awfully rude" and told the guys to hang around but they got the message, laughed and took off.

After a while we checked out of the guest house and hopped a shuttle bus to Louisville to have our Christmas dinner. We had a rather unpleasant experience I think I should mention because it reflects a policy employed by many of the better facilities throughout the country. We walked into the dining room of a nice hotel and were seated at a table when after a few minutes, a gentleman walked up and said, "I am sorry but it is the policy of the hotel not to serve enlisted men in our dining room." I was dumbfounded and said, "Would you mind repeating that?" He said, "We don't serve enlisted men here." I told him I had never been so insulted in my life and that he should be ashamed of such treatment. I also said, "You may not recognize this patch on my sleeve but it indicates I am attending Officers Candidate School at Ft. Knox. In a short time I will be an officer. Then you would serve me, even though I will be exactly the same person that you refuse to serve today. This is my wife, who traveled all the way from Washington, D.C. just to spend this day with me and you want to make Christmas a disaster for us." He then repeated that it was the policy but he would make an exception in our case. I told him that I thought such a policy was a disgrace and that the hotel should reconsider it. I would have left but Gracie had to catch a bus and I didn't want to take the time to find another place. Unfortunately, too often the men would come to town, get drunk and make a nuisance of themselves, and the MPs would have to be called to take them away. I know it to be true because later on I had to be in charge of a detail to collect these guys for our battalion.

After I cooled down, the rest of the afternoon was terrific and we really enjoyed a great meal. There were two couples sitting at a table near us and one of the men said, "We couldn't help but hear that discussion and we all commend you for the stand you took." All four of them walked over and shook my hand and wished Gracie a Merry Christmas, so "all's well that ends well." Later I walked Gracie back to the bus station and saw her off, heading back home. I returned to Ft. Knox and told them about the incident and many said they had the same experience back in their hometowns. They had questions about our other activities and again I "rudely" advised them it was none of their business so they made up their own stories. The posting of grades and gigs gave Egan the opportunity to get back at me for kidding him about his gig because I came up with an 81 for Mess Management and he did a lot better. I can't imagine what I got wrong because we seemed to agree on most of the answers that we could remember. That was the lowest grade I would get for the whole curriculum. Egan jokingly blamed it on Gracie's visit.

Some of the subjects ahead of us were Personal Hygiene, First Aid, Censorship, Intelligence, Security, Customs of Other Countries, Aircraft and Vehicle Identification and Prisoners of War Treatment, Them and Us. Also from here on out, we would be concentrating on every detail about the tank and tank warfare. The next few weeks were fairly routine, with an occasional training film or a talk on one of the various subjects that we thought we were through with. Sometimes we were brought up to date on current events and the status of the war and to what degree we were building our military strength, the theory being that a well-informed army is a more efficient army. That concept, along with a number of others, went out the window in combat. Most important was the increase in time and attention devoted to the tank and its considerable impact on the various strategies employed to insure a successful conclusion of this gigantic war effort. More and more we began to realize that we were being put into a position where we could make a very important contribution to this endeavor. This tank was the instrument that would enable us to accomplish big things, but we would have to get into its brain, its heart, its very soul so we could function as a complete union of man and machine.

For the next few weeks everything went along pretty much on cue so to go into details would be rather repetitious, but then disaster struck. One Monday we were scheduled to fire the 75 mm tank gun and would ride out to the range in the tanks with sergeants driving them. We were aware that these sergeants liked to give the future officers a rough time, so on the way back from the range, I was riding in the turret in the tank commander's position and we were going across the field to get to the tank trail which would take us back to the motor park. I was aware that we were going a little fast for cross-country when I noticed we were approaching a ditch and the driver wasn't slowing down. We had learned if you were in a standing position to flex your knees when you hit a bump to reduce the jarring effect of the jolt, so I was prepared to do that. We hit that ditch pretty hard and when I bent my knees I felt my right knee suddenly come in contact with the sharp corner of an ammunition rack inside the turret. I was afraid I might have done some real damage because by the time we reached the motor park, my knee had swelled up like a balloon and the pain was excruciating, but I was determined not to let the sergeant know he had hurt me. It was a real struggle to get out of that turret and down off the tank but I made it, and then I had to get in formation and double-time back to the barracks.

I was really hurting and as soon as I got back, I told the officer in charge that I had injured my knee and I thought I should report to the orderly room. He took one look at my knee and immediately excused me, and the orderly room ordered a peep to take me to the hospital. After the doctor in the emergency room did a preliminary examination of my knee, he said to me, "Soldier, your military career is over." I said to him, "It can't be. Everything has been going so well." They then took some x-rays of the knee and after they had time to read them, the doctor came back and said, "Well, it isn't quite as bad as we thought, but there is a lot of fluid there and you will be laid up for a couple of weeks at least, so you will have to drop out of OCS" He might just as well have stabbed me with a knife, and I said, "Doctor, I have come all this way with these guys and I would like so much to be commissioned with them." The next few minutes were spent with me pleading with him to let me continue and him telling me how bad the injury was. Finally, he said, "If your company commander will excuse you from drill, I will release you." They strapped my leg from the calf to the thigh to completely immobilize the knee, and had a peep take me back to the orderly room.

The company commander was still there and I made my urgent plea to let me continue in this class. I think he must have heard from the doctor because he seemed to be prepared and mentioned that my record was good and he would like to see me stay in OCS. He said he would give it a try and see how it worked out, and I would be excused from drill but nothing else. I thanked him, gave him a salute, did a very shaky about face and hobbled out to the mess hall. I guess news travels fast because some of the kitchen crew was still there and even though chow was over several hours ago, they heated up some dinner for me which I ate standing at the counter. Who says the Army has no heart?

The next challenge was to negotiate those stairs up to the dorm, which was very difficult and I knew I had some very serious problems facing me. I've mentioned the way these men showed their mutual support for each other when they tried to compensate for the mistakes made by the one giving the commands for our close-order drill. Well, I was about to be the recipient of that support in a manner I could hardly believe. Each morning, Egan put on the sock and shoe of my right foot; at chow, someone always picked up my plates and silverware and cleaned them off for me. "Need any help Miller?" was a constant inquiry and I thought that with that kind of spirit and cooperation we were certain to win this war. There was not a man in our dorm who didn't offer to do something for me during the period I was incapacitated. Some adjustments in my morning routine had to be made, including getting up an hour early instead of 15 minutes and getting a head start to our classes. I would be present but not participate in the calisthenics and close-order drill, and at break time I would be on my way. We usually arrived at about the same time, or if I were a minute late they would wait for me before filing in. I remember how lucky I was that we only went to the motor park two days that week and everything was review – check water, gas, oil, tracks, etc. I wasn't able to get in the tank but the others got in and started it up to check the various gauges, oil pressure, rpms, battery, etc. A few guys were able to take a short spin and I was naturally upset that I couldn't, but I had already driven more than most, because I enjoyed it so much I never wanted to bring it back. Several of the days it rained and we followed the inclement weather schedule which took us indoors.

I must tell you about an incident that happened the end of the week when I was walking to the morning class. I saw the fellows coming up behind me, double-timing as usual, so I tried to pick it up a little which made my limp more pronounced. Just as they approached me they got the command "Quick Time-March" which is the normal marching time but it was further away from our area than when they usually did that. Then the order was given, "LIMP TIME-MARCH" and they all started limping in cadence as they passed me and I just couldn't believe what I was seeing. They had to have practiced that to do it so perfectly and I wondered when they did it. It seems that during the week, after the break following drill and exercise, somebody got this bright idea and they practiced on the way to the training area and out of my sight. These were the nutty characters who were going to win this war. What a bunch.

When I had been following this routine for a week I returned to the hospital for an examination of my knee, and the doctor seemed very pleased with the healing progress and said he was going to leave the tape off, but I still could not drill and I should favor that knee as much as possible. Boy was I relieved. Now I could take a decent shower without trying to keep one leg dry and could even get into a tank with a little help. They let me drive a little, which was not a problem because pressure was required of the left foot to engage the clutch while shifting gears, but the injured right leg only had the accelerator to operate which took very little pressure. Things were looking a bit brighter and I was feeling very encouraged, but then the schedule called for a forced night march across country on foot. Another break, which I am sure was designed, was when I was assigned to be in charge of the orderly room that night. Each night, one man had to spend the night in the orderly room to handle any emergencies that may occur during the night. There was a cot there that you could sleep on but with your clothes on. However, I stayed up so I could greet the guys when they returned, which was around 0130, and the men were really beat. Trying to bolster their morale I would say "Nice job fellows" or "Good going guys" and things like that, and most of the response was "Yeah, easy for you to say" or "How did you get so lucky" or "Yeah, thanks Goldbrick" which we called someone trying to weasel out of a job, but it was all good natured hassling. They knew that I would rather have been with them and I would have done well because I was in great physical condition, better than most. By the end of that week I again went to the hospital and was given permission to resume drill, which felt like the world was lifted from my shoulders. Everything seemed back to normal, grades were good, no gigs – whoa, wait a minute. Egan got another gig, this one for needing a haircut, which was really ridiculous. He didn't need a haircut any more than I did but time was running out and according to rumor, no one gets through Armor OCS without some gigs. Was I going to be the exception? Stay tuned.

The closing weeks were primarily drill, exercise, tank work, and lots of talks, lectures, and speeches about honor, duty, and country, new responsibilities, and one talk I will never forget. An officer who had returned from combat with the British in North Africa told us of some of the vicious fighting he had experienced, and displayed some of the wounds he had received to prove his point. One remark he made that remains with me today was, "You men might just as well make up your mind right now that you are going to get killed." He didn't say "Some of you" or "You might get killed"; no, he said, "You will get killed." Believe me, a comment like that from a man who had been there burns like a hot poker into your memory and was the subject of a lot of discussion among all of us for the next few days.

The next exciting event was when they took us to Louisville to be fitted for our new uniforms. I just cannot describe the sensation I felt when I tried on the blouse – that is what they call the officer's coat – and the tailor started marking it for alterations. My goose bumps were like mountains as I thought, "It is really going to happen. I am going to get my commission." About ten days later we were taken back to try on our uniforms, and if no more alterations were needed we could take them with us. We also received the insignia to go on the blouse but the gold bars for second lieutenant had to wait until we were sworn in.

Two weeks before we were to graduate, we were in formation for what was to be our final inspection, although we didn't know it at the time. As the officer stood in front of me he looked me over from head to toe, then kind of leaned to one side, looked down and said, "Spot on shoe – one gig." I just couldn't believe it. Then he proceeded down the line and came back behind us and stopped in back of me. "Spot on shoe – one gig" he said, and hurried on. Can you believe that? Two gigs for the same spot. After we were dismissed I looked at my shoe and saw a tiny spot on the side near the back of the shoe which I must have picked up walking through the grass to get in formation. I remembered the rumor that you never get through OCS without a gig. While this would never have been called early on, since this would be the last inspection they had to find something, like Egan's haircut. We all enjoyed a good laugh over the fact that I finally got a gig.

There was another tradition coming up: a talent show put on by the candidates on the last night before graduation. Any one who could play an instrument, sing, do comedy, or had any kind of talent was asked to sign up. I didn't think I qualified in any of those categories but I did have kind of a knack for poetry, so I wrote some words to the tune of *Among My Souvenirs*. Keep in mind that we were at war with the Japanese, the Germans, and the Italians, and our feelings toward them were of a very belligerent nature and any references to them were something less than flattering. With this in mind these are the words I wrote to be sung to the tune of *Among My Souvenirs*:

> At Last I've got my bars, for which I thank my stars,
> And now off to the wars, to get my souvenirs.
> The tank, the quarter ton, we'll use them, everyone,
> To sink the rising sun and get my souvenirs.
> Old Tojo we will stop, and then that greasy wop,
> Then Hitler's guns he'll drop, and we will free the nations.
> We'll shed some blood and tears, then victory and cheers,
> I'll have some dead Jap's ears, among my souvenirs.

At the time, I thought that was pretty good and still do, but thinking they would probably expect me to sing it, I never turned it in so this is the first time my masterpiece has been exposed for public consumption.

I made reservations for Gracie to stay at the guest house and was pretty well set for the big day. Our final gig report was posted and Egan was unmerciful in his efforts to get even for the bad time I had given him. Finally the notice we were all anxious to see was posted listing the names of those to receive their commission and where assigned. There was my name, and my assignment was 14th Tank Regiment, 9th Armored Division, Ft. Riley, Kansas. It was amazing that something I felt so sure about still was a great relief to have it made official. Egan was going to a tank destroyer battalion at Camp Hood, Texas, and Larson was sent to Army Headquarters, Washington, D.C.

Just a few days before graduation day we received our travel orders and our commissions, and my new serial number, 01016389. I was glad to find out that I could bring my wife and my car, and would be given a housing allowance to live off the post. Our final day was free time so I went over to the guest house about mid-afternoon when Gracie was expected to arrive, and sure enough, there she was waiting. There just seemed to be so much excitement, it is really difficult to put it into words. We went to the rec hall to get a soft drink, chatted a while, and then to dinner. We walked back to the guest house so Gracie could freshen up before going to the talent show. When we arrived there some of the men who had met Gracie came up to say hello and we went inside to watch the show. It was not mandatory that we attend the show and Egan had told me he thought he would skip it but I thought Gracie might enjoy it. It was really a lot of fun, although the talent would probably not win any awards and the comics poked fun at the officers and some of the remarks were a little colorful, but you had to give them an "A" for effort. After it was over, I walked Gracie to the guest house and said "Good night" because there were a lot of last minute details to take care of back at the barracks. Make sure shoes and all brass was polished, non-essentials in the two barracks bags, and uniforms and toilet articles in the new Val-a-Pack I had bought, shake hands with the guys and take a few moments with Egan to thank him and tell him how much I enjoyed meeting him and hoped we would meet again some day. Our orders did not give specific addresses so we did not know how we could correspond, but we both agreed that we had developed a great relationship in the thirteen weeks at OCS. Then, it was time to turn in because we had a big day ahead of us.

The morning routine was pretty normal except no roll call until later. Shower, shave, etc, get dressed, go to breakfast, straighten area, put on blouse, and go to the latrine to see how I looked. Man, I sure looked great – well, the uniform looked great – and pretty soon it was time to fall in for roll call and march to the auditorium. Gracie was already there and waved, but no "Hi Snookie" this time, thank goodness. The ceremony was very nice and shorter than expected. We were addressed by the post commander, who also administered the oath of office and requested that those who were to pin our bars on to please come forward and do it now. Gracie came running up to do the honors and added a big hug and kiss. We were told to be seated for a few last minute instructions and then we were dismissed. I was joined by Gracie as we filed out, and at the doorway I received my first salute by none other than Sergeant Ward. Tradition dictates that a newly commissioned officer gives a dollar to the first man who salutes him. I was never so glad to give away a dollar as I was to give it to Ward, who had come over to see me get my commission and give me my first salute. I shook his hand and thanked him for helping to make all this happen, and then he had to get back. We picked up my Val-a-Pak outside the Orderly Room and headed for the bus station to catch the bus for home. My orders provided for ten days' travel time, so we could spend a few days at home before we made our way to Ft. Riley and the 9th Armored Division.

Chapter 4

ASSIGNMENT TO THE NINTH ARMORED DIVISION

Upon our return home we visited friends and relatives and I stopped by the real estate office where I worked prior to going to the British Army Staff. The people I really wanted to see were the folks at the British Army Staff but they had moved and I wasn't able to locate them. In a few days we packed up and headed for Dayton, Ohio, my home town where I intended to see some of the relatives there, but upon our arrival at the hotel I was told that it had been taken over by Air Force personnel as had most of the hotels in town. Disappointed, I decided to move on and cover as much ground as I could before it got too late. Shortly after crossing the Indiana state line, I heard that nauseating hissing sound from one of my tires indicating that I had a puncture. I got out and looked at it, which was all I could do since I had no spare due to the tire rationing.

Getting back in the car I started to drive very slowly, hoping to reach a garage or service station before I did too much damage to the tire. Finally I came to a garage, which fortunately was still open as it was then after dark. I had driven too long and the tire was completely pulverized and I was lucky I didn't damage the rim. The garage man said he had tires but could not sell them without a certificate from the Office of Price Administration (OPA), and being Saturday night it was closed. I explained that this was an emergency because I was on my way to report to my Post at Ft. Riley, Kansas. He said he knew personally the man in charge of the local OPA and gave me his name and phone number and told me to call him after I checked in at the nearby hotel. He also said he would call and if the OPA man would give me a certificate we could all meet in the morning and work it out. We walked to the hotel and after checking in I gave the gentleman a call and believe me he was a gentleman. I told him my story and he said that the man at the garage had already called and agreed to open the garage Sunday morning so we could all meet and he would bring a certificate authorizing the sale of a tire to me. What a relief as I was getting desperate and now it looked like everything was going to work out. We had dinner and turned in right away because we were to meet at the garage at 7:00 a.m. Everyone was there, I met the OPA man, filled out some forms, he gave me a certificate for two tires which I gave to the garage man who had already put the tire on and the spare in the trunk, gave him my check, vigorously shook hands and we were on our way.

Gracie and I both said a little prayer thanking the Lord for our good fortune and started looking for a church along the way so we could attend Mass that Sunday morning. It wasn't long before we saw a sign directing us to a church after which we had breakfast and headed toward Kansas. As soon as we reached Manhattan we checked into the hotel and had some dinner, then I bought a local paper – Saturday's, no local edition Sunday, to look for an apartment. There were nothing but rooms, most of which had to share a bathroom and no kitchen facilities. I still had three days of my travel time left so we drove around the area looking for "For Rent" signs but they were just more of the same.

It came time to report in so I rode out to Camp Funston, a part of Ft. Riley that had been a horse cavalry post, and reported to the adjutant of the 14th Armored Regiment. I handed him my orders and he checked his list, then told me I was to report to Captain Chandler of "B" Company. He gave me directions to the "B" Company orderly room whereupon I immediately drove over to report as ordered. The first sergeant was sitting at the desk and I told him that the adjutant sent me over to report to Captain Chandler. He buzzed the captain and I was told to go in which I did repeating my introduction for the third time. Captain Chandler was very friendly and asked me to have a seat while he made a telephone call. I sensed we had a problem here and wondered what might have gone wrong. He obviously was calling the adjutant, telling him that while he was expecting a couple of new officers my name wasn't one of them. There was a little lull after which the Captain said over the telephone, "Very well Sir, I will take care of it," and hung up. "There has been a slight mix-up, you were supposed to report to "A" Company, Captain Zillick" he informed me and told me "A" Company was just a few buildings down the line. I was beginning to wonder how many times I would have to go through this reporting routine as I was greeted by First Sergeant Cerveny, an old cavalry man not happy about losing his horses. He told me to have a seat, that Captain Zillick was out but should be in soon. Shortly, Captain Zillick returned and I learned that he too was an old cavalryman, not too happy about losing his horses and apparently not too happy to see me. "I have been expecting you," he said. Then I explained to him about the mix-up. I thought at first that I had gotten off to a bad start but found out later that nearly everybody got off to a bad start with Captain Zillick.

He eventually offered me a seat and made a few inquiries about my situation and I mentioned I was staying at the hotel while looking for suitable accommodations. He told me he could help me because there was a lieutenant living in one of the apartments where he lived who was leaving that weekend. It was a house converted into three apartments occupied by the captain, the lieutenant, and the owner, and the captain said to come by after dinner and he would introduce me to the owner.

As we left the captain's office we met three lieutenants who had just come into the orderly room and Zillick introduced me to 1st Lieutenant James and 2nd Lieutenants Hall and Moskowitz. Since it was then lunchtime we all walked over to the Officer's Mess to grab a bite to eat. Zillick sat with some of his old cavalry cronies and we four lieutenants sat together giving me a chance to find out what was happening in Company A. They said things were kind of at loose ends with them just overseeing the activities while the platoon sergeants pretty much ran the show. The company wasn't long out of basic training and was just getting organized. At the moment James was acting motor officer, Hall first platoon leader and Moskowitz the second platoon, which sounded like Miller might get the third platoon. I just had time to give Gracie a call to tell her about the apartment.

Returning to the company area we found the men preparing to march back to the motor park and Zillick told us to fall in behind the column and go with them.. Here I was in shirt, tie, blouse and pinks, that's what they called officer's slacks back then and looking very much out of place since all the others were in fatigues. At the motor park the men moved to their respective tanks and I decided to go over to where the third platoon was working. I had not been introduced to anyone so the men didn't know who I was, but the platoon sergeant walked over and asked if he could help me. He told me he was Sergeant Weaver and at least for the time being was the acting platoon sergeant of the third platoon. I introduced myself and asked just what his men were doing. One crew was breaking a track to replace a damaged section, another was removing the radio to take it to the communications sergeant for repair, a third crew was disassembling the cannons' breach just for practice, and the other two were going through various before and after operation checks. I was impressed that everyone seemed to have a job and Weaver seemed to be in touch with what was going on. He excused himself saying he might have to help the crew repairing the tank track and I decided to visit each tank to see if all the men were busy.

When men are working they are not usually required to come to attention if an officer approaches but a couple of the tank commanders did call "Attention" and I quickly said "As you were" so as not to interrupt them and told the tank commanders to "Carry On." I was pleased to find that they all were doing pretty much as Weaver said they were and I noticed him leaning over the group working on the track. It was time for their ten minute break and I observed the smokers moved at least ten feet away from the tanks according to regulations, but there was one man leaning against a tank with a cigarette in his hand. I walked toward him and he came to attention and I told him "At Ease" and said "You aren't going to light that cigarette are you soldier?" He replied "No Sir, I don't smoke." I said "Good, neither do I," as I walked away.

Later that afternoon back at the company area Zillick called us into his office and told us that he might be getting one or two more officers but he wanted to start to get organized so he was having an officers' meeting tomorrow at 0900 hours. He also told Moskowitz to take me to the supply room to get my two barracks bags, which had been sent ahead, and get some Ninth Armored patches plus some cloth insignia. He dismissed us, and Moskowitz introduced me to the supply sergeant and proceeded to get the items for me. I was aware that he knew his way around the supply room because he knew where everything was, then he told the sergeant what he had gotten for me so the sergeant could record it in his books. He picked up my barracks bags and said he would walk me to my car, and on the way told me if I ever needed anything from the supply room let him know and he would take care of it. He tossed the bags into my car, I thanked him for his help and took off for the hotel where Gracie was waiting to go to dinner.

During dinner I related the events of the day including the arrangements for renting the apartment. We went by and saw the apartment, signed up and we were told we could move in that weekend. It was a small apartment on the second floor, but it had a bedroom, kitchen, bath and combination living/dining area. We felt fortunate and thanked the Captain and the owner. On the way back to the hotel we decided to park the car and walk around a little while. Gracie said she would like an ice cream cone and I told her I would have to eat in the store, so she got her cone and I had a dish of ice cream. It wasn't proper for an officer to walk down the street eating an ice cream cone. After a while we returned to our room, having picked up my barracks bags from the car, and I showed Gracie the patches and insignia which she could take to the tailor the next day. I had to put the metal insignia on one of my coveralls which I would wear to camp.

That morning we reported to the Captain for his meeting at 0900 and he immediately assigned duties to his officers. James was named Maintenance Officer, responsible for the care and maintenance of all company vehicles; the other three would be tank platoon leaders, Hall the first, Moskowitz the second, and Miller the third platoon. Then the Captain said, "When I say platoon leaders, I mean just that. You will lead your platoons in drill, calisthenics, marches and any tank road and field exercises. The platoon sergeants have already been notified that these orders will be in effect as of Monday morning. In addition, James will be Communications Officer; Hall, Weapons Officer; Moskowitz, Supply Officer; and Miller, Mess Officer." You gotta be kidding. Mess management was my worst subject and I am to be Mess Officer. Naturally, I didn't say anything but I couldn't believe the irony of this situation, although I was quite satisfied with the assignment. The other officers all knew the sergeants they would be working with: Phillips, Motor Sergeant; Best, Communications Sergeant; Key, First Platoon Sergeant; Doering, Armorer; Humphrey, Second Platoon Sergeant; Reed, Supply Sergeant; Weaver, Third Platoon Sergeant; and Woodward, Mess Sergeant, but being new I didn't know Woodward, so Moskowitz took me to the kitchen to meet him. Woodward was another old cavalryman who wasn't happy about losing his horses and obviously not too pleased to have this green lieutenant as his mess officer. I thanked Moskowitz and told him I would like to hang around to get acquainted with the kitchen setup and observe the mess hall procedure.

Furthermore, the Mess Officer is required to have one meal a day with the troops so I figured I might as well stay for lunch. Woodward definitely knew his job; he had attended Cooks and Bakers School and had already spent considerable time as a mess sergeant. He showed me around the kitchen, where the staples were stored and how perishables were kept refrigerated, and then the layout and procedures in the mess hall. I told him that I would be leaning very heavily on his experience, and that my training in mess management was rather limited and I would be learning by doing. We talked for a while over a cup of coffee and I told him I would stay for lunch, where upon he walked over to where his cooks and helpers were working and apparently told them to set a place for the lieutenant. I thanked Woodward and said to carry on that I would be just roaming around until lunch. I made myself quite visible to the men as they entered the mess hall so they wouldn't get the impression I was sneaking around. They were quite orderly but I was very much aware that the atmosphere here was a far cry, understandably, from that to which I had become accustomed at OCS. The place was buzzing with conversation with an occasional glance in my direction and an obvious comment about the new "Shave-tail" in their midst. I moved to where they had set a place for me and one of the kitchen help came over with a filled plate and a cup of coffee. I thanked him and told him that wasn't necessary that hereafter I would go through the line. I wanted to be sure I was eating the same food the men were so they would know that I wasn't getting something that was especially prepared for me.

After lunch I wanted to observe the cleanup procedures but thought I should get back to the company to join in the afternoon work detail, which again was at the motor park. In accordance with Zillick's orders, I took over the platoon and marched them down to the motor park thinking Weaver had done a good job since they responded to the commands with snap and precision. I did notice one man who, out of curiosity I guess, looked over at me and I immediately gave him an "Eyes Front, Soldier," which seemed to correct the situation. When we arrived I told Weaver to take over, and he ordered the men to move to their tanks and continue the work they were doing in the morning. As I stood there, Hall and Moskowitz came up and asked how I was doing and did I need anything. They must have noticed that I marched the men so I explained that I didn't see any reason for waiting until Monday and I felt that the sooner the better. I told them I realized they had been here a while longer than I and were better acquainted with their men and this would help me get to know them quicker. They said they thought it was a good idea and if I needed anything let them know, and went back to their men.

It was then I noticed that the men who were repairing the tank track were struggling to pull the track over the support rollers and Weaver was helping them along with a couple of men from another tank. The ideal way to do this would be to fasten a cable to the track and have a vehicle pull the track but they apparently wanted to use the manpower for training. I couldn't resist the urge to help so I just stepped in, grabbed hold and said "Heave" and the thing really picked up the pace and was soon in place. I then stood back while they worked to fasten the connectors to the two ends and I moved on to the next tank. The rest of the afternoon was spent jumping on the other tanks to look into the turrets and other hatches to see if everything was in order. I did see some candy wrappers in one turret and told the tank commander to have them picked up and disposed of. Someone obviously was snacking while working and I wanted to find out if this was acceptable or were they expected to wait for their break. It would be my judgement that they should wait because removing the wrappers and holding a candy bar would be a distraction and a deterrent to what the man was supposed to be doing, but was this my OCS training showing again? At the end of the day I discussed this matter with the other platoon leaders, both of whom felt that Zillick would be displeased and would probably have us conducting frequent checks to see if any of the guys were goofing off in that manner. It was their thinking that it would be better just to handle such situations as I did that afternoon and I realized that at times I might have to back off from my concept that strict discipline is an essential ingredient of an effective combat soldier. At dinner that evening I was all set to relate to Gracie all that happened that day, but she beat me to it by telling me about the many shops she visited just to get acquainted and tell some of the folks she would need their help in keeping within the rationing restrictions. I suspected she was planning to use her charm to obtain more of certain items than she was limited to. I cautioned her not to do anything that might be illegal and, of course, she assured me it was not her intention.

The uniform for the next day was to be O.D.s with field jackets, and the schedule called for a training film which was often the case for Saturday mornings since most of the men went into town Saturday nights. The subjects generally had to do with conduct, proper dress, excessive drinking, personal hygiene, etc., things we had heard about before and many more times in the future. Back at the company area the officers made a brief inspection of the men, then announced they could report to the orderly room after 1400 if they wanted passes to go into town. We had lunch and I hung around for a while before driving back to the hotel. James and Hall were not married, Moskowitz's wife wasn't with him so Zillick and I were the only ones living off post. Gracie and I discussed plans for our move the next day and decided there wasn't anything we had to get except food since the apartment was completely furnished. Gracie had brought bedding and a few mementoes so all we had to do was pack our clothes and check out of

(Above) The Hotel Wareham in Manhattan, Kansas, where my wife Gracie and I stayed while looking for housing during the time I was stationed at Fort. Riley. (Below) The house we found. These photos were taken in 2003 by Fred Borrell during a Company "A" reunion.

the hotel. Following Mass we had breakfast, loaded the car, paid the hotel bill, and drove to our new "home."

The owner was out front as we drove up and greeted us with a cheerful "Welcome." He said that he and his wife had done a little straightening and cleaning and all was ready for us to move in and handed me the keys. Since I had added my two barracks bags to our luggage and Gracie had a couple of boxes she had packed, it took several trips up the stairs to get the car unloaded. We put our clothes in closets and dresser drawers and Gracie put out some knick-knacks she had brought from home, which gave the little apartment a homey touch. Pretty soon it was time for some lunch and we decided that while we were out we could buy a few groceries on Sunday. Gracie said she had seen a deli on her tour Friday so she guided me to a nearby small but neat Mom and Pop store and proceeded to give her order for milk, bread, eggs, sausage, cereal, coffee, and quite a few other items. When she was through, I walked up to the counter to pay the man and asked Gracie for the ration coupon book. With that the gentlemen said, "Oh it won't be necessary. We had a few extras we can let you have and since you are just setting up housekeeping, we can waive that." I was very surprised and wondered how he knew we were just setting up housekeeping when it suddenly struck me this had to be one of the places Gracie visited and had cultivated their friendship in anticipation of our market trip. I certainly didn't argue with the gentlemen because I was sure he knew the regulations better than I did so I thanked him, paid for our purchases, and started to leave. When the man and his wife said "Thank you Gracie, come back and see us anytime," I gave Gracie a knowing glance and she couldn't help busting out laughing. That was my Gracie.

At the apartment we put the groceries away then sat down to snack on some of the munchies that Gracie had picked up and I started a list of fruits and vegetables and other things that the little deli didn't carry. Opening a couple of cans and a little imagination was all that it took to provide us a very nice dinner for our first meal in our new home.

The next day at camp following drill and calisthenics we were in formation ready to march to the motor park when the first sergeant came out to announce that the tanks were to be ready for an all day series of tank field exercises tomorrow. He told the men to bring mess kits and to fill their canteens first thing in the morning because we would be eating in the field. At the motor park I asked Weaver if the men had done this before and he said a little but not all day. I told him I would like to talk to the men but I would wait until after lunch and for him to assemble the men at my tank at 1400. The rest of the morning I was pleased to see the crews gassing up, checking oil and water and a couple with grease guns. I could hear radio operators testing 1-2-3, and I walked over to ask the tank commander about the tank with the repaired track, if it was ok and he assured me it was.

Weaver assembled the men right on schedule at 1400, and I proceeded to advise the men to take these field exercises seriously, that we are not playing games but being prepared to act efficiently under fire. I told them that I had been informed that when you are being shot at, the brain doesn't function too well and your actions have to be automatic in order to do what you learn in training to stay alive. I also said that I thought they were the best platoon in the company but our goal was to be the best tank platoon in the Division. I then instructed them to return to their tanks, each man to be in his assigned position and do a dry run of his duties for fifteen minutes as the driver starts the engine and lets it idle for that period. Weaver was to accompany me as we visited each tank to make sure it was ready to go. All went well and there didn't seem to be any problems, so after 15 minutes, engines were cut and the men dismounted for a 10-minute break. At that time the First Sergeant drove up and informed us that the Captain wanted to assemble the men at the Company Area at 1600 for further instructions on the next day's activities. The Captain said that the morning would be spent attempting to move our tanks without revealing our position and in the afternoon we would practice various attack formations. He also reminded the men to bring mess kits and filled canteens and when crossing the highway each platoon would be responsible for putting out crossing guards to flag down civilian traffic while their platoon crossed the road.

The next morning at the Motor Park, while we prepared to move out, I told my assistant driver and the assistant driver of my number two tank that they would be the crossing guards for our platoon. Shortly, the Captain gave the order to mount up and we moved out of the Motor Park in column formation with the Captain in the lead followed by the first, second and third platoons in that order. We soon came to the highway and one man from each of the two tanks in the Headquarters Section dismounted and halted traffic from each direction, then as the first platoon arrived its two guards ran up to relieve the other two and so on, in order to keep any delay in the tanks crossing to a minimum. No cars were permitted through until all seventeen tanks had cleared the road, but there was very little traffic due to the gas and tire rationing. We continued along some tank trails until we came to a tank training area where we closed up and the men dismounted for their break. The Captain called all Tank Commanders together to brief them on the exercise we were about to perform. Off in the distance there was a hill about a quarter mile wide, and running along the front of it was a draw which would give cover to the tanks moving laterally along it. The Captain would lead us along the draw and we were to make sure our tanks could not be observed beyond that hill. After we reached the end of the draw, the Captain would move to some high ground about a half a mile away and take a position where he could determine if we kept out of sight as we backtracked down the draw. We were to turn our tanks around with the platoons remaining in their present positions, which put the third platoon in the lead, and at a specified time, move back down the draw. One thing that concerned me was our antennae that rose about six feet above the tank turret, which I thought the Captain might be able to see through his binoculars. So after we got turned around, I called my Tank Commanders together and told them that when we moved out, to bend their antennae down so they wouldn't extend above the crest of the hill that we would be driving behind. At the designated time I ordered my driver to move out, and reached over to bend my antenna toward me and looked back to see all of my guys doing the same thing. We moved carefully and slowly down the draw so as not to raise a lot of dust. In about 25 minutes we reached the end of the draw where we stopped to wait for the Captain to come back to tell us how we did. He brought his tank up to the center of the column and had the Company meet there, and proceeded to say that he thought we did pretty well but only one platoon kept their antennae out of sight. He said if in combat the enemy were looking for us through their powerful binoculars, they would have detected those antennae, which would have given away our position. He also pointed out that this was the reason for these exercises so we could determine what we were doing wrong and correct our mistakes. We would do them over and over to make sure we would do it automatically in combat. Then he said, "By the way, which platoon lowered its antennae?" and I raised my hand and I could just hear old Egan saying, "Show-off." I did wonder why the others hadn't done that when they saw my platoon, which was in front of them. I give you these details so you can realize all the preparation necessary to bring us up to "combat readiness." The next exercise involved moving our tanks up this hill in line formation by platoons to a point where we could observe and fire on a distant target, exposing as little of the tanks as possible. This was kind of a delicate operation because it required coordination between Tank Commander, gunner and driver. It was essential that we move up to a position for the gunner to see the target through his gun sight and for the driver to halt at that very point so as not to make too much of the tank visible to an enemy weapon. When the gunner gave the signal to stop, I felt that standing up there in the turret I could be seen by the whole world, which was a rather uncomfortable position to be in. We repeated these exercises a couple of times during the morning, then stopped for chow which had been prepared using the field kitchen equipment. I had brought my mess kit, but the Captain had a table set up for the officers with some folding chairs and I thought that this probably wasn't the way it would be in combat. I did take note that our plates were filled from the same food containers from which the men were served. During lunch Zillick described the exercises for the afternoon, which would be executing the various battle formations, including 'in line by platoon'. This meant each platoon would place its tanks side by side and move forward one platoon behind the other. Next would be the platoon wedge formation, with each platoon forming a wedge with the first platoon in front, the second platoon off to its left rear and the third platoon to the right and rear of the first platoon. Also right and left echelon, forming a diagonal line to the right or left of the platoon leaders tank; and finally a Company wedge with the first platoon in wedge formation, the second platoon, echelon left and the third platoon, echelon right. The terrain and enemy location would determine which of the various formations would be used. I really enjoyed maneuvering my platoon into the different positions. These are the types of things that we did on a daily basis, intermingled with talks, training films, days at the firing range, and tank maintenance.

A terrible tragedy occurred over one weekend when Lieutenant Hall got a hotel room and killed himself. I was told that he was having problems with his girlfriend but there was no indication of trouble that any of us had observed. His family came to claim the body and I met them because Captain Zillick had told me I was to escort the body and attend the funeral in Lieutenant Hall's hometown, which was not too far away. It was such a sad situation where this young, good-looking officer, took his own life over a stupid lover's quarrel. Such things are hard to understand.

One morning during close-order drill, Sergeant Swayne said something that made a couple of the men laugh. I halted the platoon and called Swayne aside and told him there would not be any talking in the ranks during drill, which he knew as well as I did. Again he said something, so this time I yelled. "Swayne, I told you to stop the chatter. Now cut it out." Since I didn't correct him publicly the first time, I was mad when he continued to talk so I thought I was justified in chewing him out. During the break he was talking to the guys loud enough for me to hear and said, "These people think they are tough just because they have those gold bars on their shoulders." I walked over to the group and said "Swayne, I am sure you wanted me to hear what you just said so I will tell you what I will do. At the end of the day today, you go over to the athletic department and check out a set of boxing gloves. Tonight, after chow at 1900, I will come over to the barracks without my bars and we will put on the gloves to see just who is tough." He said "OK." He was over six feet tall and I was a little less than six feet but I had done a lot of boxing in the gym, so I felt my knowledge would overcome his weight advantage. I called Gracie to tell her I would be a little late for dinner, took my bars off and walked over to the barracks at 1900. Some of the men were standing around but no Swayne. I said, "Have any of you seen Swayne?" One of them said, "Yes Sir, but he told us he didn't want to fight you." Then I said, "When you see him, be sure you tell him that Miller was here without his bars." That may not have been the proper way to handle the situation but I was mad. Too often people think because you don't use a lot of foul language you are a wimp. Then you have to take matters into your own hands. I didn't say anything more about it to Swayne and the incident was soon forgotten.

Now it was time for one of many trips to the firing range because that is what war is all about. The schedule indicated that the next day we would fire the .30 caliber ground mount machine gun, and tradition required that the first round be fired at sun up. So first call would be 0430, breakfast at 0500, and assemble to be transported to the range at 0530. Guess who the order said would be Range Officer? Yeah, you got it. None other than Lieutenant Miller. My first thought was, I have never been a range officer before, what do I know? Of course, I had been to the range many times during basic and OCS and knew pretty much what to do and the rest I would just wing it. At dinner I told Gracie I would be getting up very early the next morning and would grab a quick breakfast at the mess hall. I set the alarm at quarter to four and when it went off I tried not to disturb Gracie, but it was dark and I had to turn on a light. I went into the bathroom, shaved and showered and came back to find Gracie was up and in her tiny kitchen frying up some bacon and eggs with toast, juice and coffee. How about that girl. By the time I was dressed, breakfast was on the table and I was soon out the door and on my way. I arrived at our Orderly Room at 0530 and a peep was already there to take me to the range. At the range, men were busy setting up the weapons and a man was up in the tower testing the sound equipment, so I went up there to see how to operate it. Pretty soon the trucks bringing the men arrived and they immediately dismounted and lined up by platoon. The first platoon was temporarily taken over by James since Hall was gone. Moskowitz was with his second platoon and Sergeant Weaver was in charge of my third platoon, which was no problem. The first platoon took their places at the gun positions while the others busied themselves checking ammo cases and setting up some more guns that they would be disassembling and assembling later in the morning. It seemed to be getting a little lighter and I could see off on the eastern horizon that the sky was starting to brighten. I turned on the mike and said "Gunners load your weapons." After about two minutes it became light enough to see the targets so I said "Ready on the right" and I could see all the men on my right raise their hands, then "Ready on the left" and again the hands were raised and I said "Ready on the firing line — commence firing" as the sun peeked over the horizon. It was a great feeling to look through my binoculars and see that all guns were working, the gunners firing in short bursts, and his buddy at his side feeding the ammo to the weapon. Soon the firing gradually came to a halt and I gave the order "Cease firing," then "Clear your weapon", and finally "All clear on the right", and again the raised hands, followed by "All clear on the left," then "All clear on the firing line — move away from your weapons." This procedure was repeated over and over until all had fired, with a break for lunch which consisted of sandwiches and beverages. At the end of the day I ordered that all gun positions be thoroughly policed, all targets replaced and that the range be left in better condition than when we arrived. That is pretty much a standard order when a unit leaves any area where it has been training. As the men mounted the trucks to return to the company area, the range detail moved in to collect the weapons and the Communication Sergeant came back up to the tower to pick up the P.A. System. "Nice job, Lieutenant" he said, and I replied "Thank you, Sergeant" and I really felt it went well. I got a surprise the following week when I received a directive that "B" Company was to use the firing range and Lieutenant Miller of "A" Company would be the Range Officer. I asked Zillick how did this happen, and he told me it came from Battalion, that someone there had heard that I did a good job so they would have me do it for "B" Company. I guess I should have been flattered but I told Zillick that I hoped this wouldn't be a regular thing because I didn't like being away from my platoon. He said he didn't like it either and would see what he could do. He spoke to the Battalion Commander who told him he would not have me do it any more after "B" Company.

Something I had been doing since about the second week was to have the men "double-time" for part of the fitness period, starting with five minutes the first time and adding five minutes each week until finally we used the full thirty minutes double-timing in formation in perfect cadence. I thought there might be some griping, but I was pleased to hear some of the men bragging to the other platoons about what they had done. To me, this combined conditioning, discipline, and coordination, and these three elements should prove beneficial in combat.

Another toughness activity was a 24 hour tank field exercise, which was to start in the morning with a tank road march to a distant maneuver area where several situations were given to the Captain, who had to develop various tank movements designed to solve each strategy problem. These situations would occur during the rest of the afternoon and throughout the night, requiring maps to locate certain enemy positions and at the same time avoiding heavily defended areas. It was a warm mid-April day and so the uniform of the day was fatigues, the green twill coveralls that were pretty heavy and rather ill fitting. Since we were to simulate combat conditions as soon as we moved out, it was likely we would be using the "C" and "D" rations which were issued to us in the morning. When we reached the point of departure, the Captain called the officers for a briefing showing us our first objective on the map and he would give us our orders as we moved up depending on terrain and enemy resistance.

I thought things were going pretty well during the afternoon, but judging from his language and tone of voice, the Captain wasn't very pleased. I also noticed as we moved into the evening hours that the air had become considerably cooler and a brisk wind was blowing. We got a little break and managed to gulp down some cold corned beef hash and a cracker, then Zillick called the officers together to discuss the next phase. He also jumped some of us for using what he thought were incorrect formations for the specific situations. Although none of us said anything, I felt that he should have ordered the formation he wanted since this was a Company exercise. It was now getting dark and the temperature was dropping fast, signaling a very uncomfortable night before us. It seemed that we accomplished the next mission in total darkness which brought us to about 0200 hours and freezing, windy weather. We were about to start the final phase so the Captain called the officers again to explain the next move. He had a shelter half which we held over our heads while we stooped down, and Zillick spread the map on the ground and turned on his flashlight. I never will forget, it was so cold that the Captain's nose kept dripping as he leaned over the map, and we all were shivering from the biting wind. I went back to explain the problem to the men, who were about frozen and kept saying it's too cold and wanted to go back to camp. I told them this could happen in combat and at least now they weren't being shot at. I had always said that I never felt the cold, but that night, I WAS COLD! The coveralls we were wearing certainly were not sufficient to ward off that severe and unexpected drop in temperature, but we all seemed to survive without any permanent affects except for the beefing that continued for a long time afterward. We completed the exercise and were back at the Motor Park by midmorning, where we performed the usual servicing of the tanks before heading back to the Company for some much needed chow and hot coffee. We were dismissed for the rest of the day following a brief formation to instruct the men to rest and clean up because the next day we would be going to the firing range, which would require an early first call. I was able to get a little sleep during the afternoon and Gracie fixed a great dinner for us that night.

We received two more Lieutenants, Walkowitz and DelCampo who were just as green and considerably less enthusiastic than I was when I arrived. They seemed to be nice guys, but as usual Zillick was not impressed and made no secret of it. They were to take over the first platoon, and James, Moskowitz and I helped them get oriented so James could resume his duties as Maintenance Officer. I liked the two new officers but I sensed that they might have a difficult time due to an attitude problem. It seems that they took too seriously the old saying RHIP (Rank Has It's Privileges) and would take some liberties that made the Captain furious, resulting in some ongoing friction between them.

The weeks ahead were spent in non-stop intensive training in the effort to prepare us for the ultimate goal — combat. Along the way, several little incidents occurred that I feel are worth relating here, the first being when I was in the Mess Hall one day during lunch and I noticed a man who needed a haircut. He was eating as I walked up behind him, pulled the hair on the back of his neck and said "Soldier, you need a haircut." "Sir, I just got one this morning," he replied. I repeated "Soldier, you need a haircut." He leaned down and mumbled a few unintelligible words but I had a pretty good idea what he was saying. A few minutes later he got up from the table and started toward the door. "Hey Ward, where are you going?" asked Sergeant Humphrey, his platoon sergeant, and Ward answered, "Lieutenant Miller said I need a haircut." "You just got a haircut this morning" said Humphrey and Ward replied, "Lieutenant Miller said I need a haircut," and walked out the door. As Ward sat down in the barber's chair the barber said, "What are you doing back here, didn't I just cut your hair this morning?" To which Ward repeated "Yeah, but Lieutenant Miller said I need a haircut." To this day, Jack Ward loves to tell that story, especially when I am around. It was on a Saturday night that I took Gracie to the Officer's Club for dinner where one of my drivers, John Whitehead, was tending bar. We walked over and I introduced Gracie to Whitehead, and she engaged him in conversation when I stepped away to speak to another officer. During dinner Gracie showed me this tiny Tank Insignia that Whitehead had given her and she was thrilled to death. Although Gracie is gone, we still have that little tank she received from one of my men. While we were still in Manhattan, Kansas, Gracie asked me to go to a local studio and have my picture taken so she would have it when I went overseas. The significance of this incident will be explained in a later chapter. During the latter part of April 1943 rumors were circulating that President Roosevelt was coming to Ft. Riley, and on Easter Sunday we were marched up to the main road to form a solid line on both sides of the road. Two hours later, a convoy of black sedans came speeding down the road so fast we barely had time to render a salute as the President's car zoomed by, leaving us a bit disappointed.

During May we started getting hints that we would be moving out of Ft. Riley, probably to another Post because we spent some time receiving instructions on loading and unloading tanks onto and off of train flatbeds. Near the end of the month, the rumors were confirmed that the Division would be transferred to the Desert Training Center at Camp Ibis, California. We were also told that there would be very little available housing and living conditions would be unpleasant at best and it was suggested that wives not make that move. Funny thing, Gracie told me about the Division moving even before we heard the rumors at camp. It seems that the civilians knew more about our activities than we did so we had discussed this possibility for some time. She packed up our belongings and gradually shipped them home, keeping our bedding until the last. I didn't want her to be subjected to the discomforts of desert life and she agreed that it would be better for her to return home but she didn't want to take the car. This presented a problem because we were advised that the officers would be required to travel on the train with the troops but the enlisted men could drive their cars, so I asked Whitehead if he would be interested in driving my car to California. He said he would be happy to and I wondered if it was a good idea to have a tank driver drive my car, and it turned out that it wasn't. Just after the first of June Gracie bid me a tearful goodbye and went back home while I moved into the B.O.Q. at camp. We were kept busy making preparations for the move and attending numerous sessions relative to desert training. Heat, of course, was the primary problem requiring such things as water conservation, gradual exposure of the men to the sun, the use of lotions and salt tablets. The preservation of food was of great concern to me and the kitchen crew, but we would have refrigeration in camp, though none for meals served in the field. Maintenance of the vehicles would be more difficult because of intense heat and the sandy, dusty environment, which could foul up engines and any moving parts of the vehicles. Finally about the middle of June we were told we would be moving out the following week and to make sure everything was in readiness. All activities were stepped up a notch higher, moving the tanks to the staging areas, boxing up supplies and provisions, thorough policing of all areas and checking and double checking to make sure all orders were carried out to the letter. It was about 20 June when we marched to the trains to start the long journey to Camp Ibis, California — the Desert Training Center. I had given Whitehead the keys to the car and my gasoline ration book, and he had a pass for four days' travel time which should have been more than enough. Late afternoon, the trains departed Ft. Riley where I had experienced just about every emotion known to mankind, except maybe fear, but there was joy, sadness, anger, confusion, and on and on. Most of all however, I would have fond memories of our stay in Manhattan.

Chapter 5

FAREWELL FT. RILEY, HELLO CAMP IBIS

The train ride could best be described as uneventful to be polite, boring to be honest, with the men whiling away the time playing cards, reading, watching the landscape go by or catching some much needed shut eye. As dull as it was most were glad for this break after the very hectic weeks getting ready for the big move. Our meals were the rations that were handed out prior to boarding the train and the kitchen crew came through with small cartons of cold drinks. They had also baked some cakes while still in camp which would be our desert. I decided to walk back where the kitchen was located and saw the dining car was converted to storage but the kitchen portion was intact and the huge refrigerator was operative. All mess Sergeants love their coffee and despite the hot June day Woodward and the First Sergeant were drinking some when I walked in. Of course, Woodward poured a cup for me and I really enjoyed this pleasant surprise even though I was sweating profusely.

There were frequent stops when we were switched to a siding to let other trains come through and I thought it was strange that all other traffic had priority over troop trains. It really did make sense because the other trains were on a strict timetable and had to keep on schedule so they were given the right-of-way. Sometimes the other officers would come and sit for a few minutes and I too would visit with them while looking in on the men and inquiring how they were doing. After each meal the kitchen crew would come by with large trash bags for the men to deposit their trash, so I would check in on the men then because I wanted to make sure that they were keeping their areas well policed.

There is little more to report about the train ride, but as we neared our destination I kept thinking that spending the summer on the Mojave desert was never one of my secret ambitions and I wondered whose idea it was anyway. Of course, the usual explanation for unexplainable actions was, this is the Army and we are at war. It was late afternoon of the second day when we were advised that we would arrive at our destination in about thirty minutes and to get ready to detrain. In a short while we pulled onto a siding where there was a board walkway, a few buildings, and a line of two and a half ton trucks to transport us to our respective company areas. The heat was almost oven-like in intensity and I realized it would take a lot of getting use to in order to perform effectively. Peeps were provided for the Platoon Leaders and their Platoon Sergeants and the rest of the Platoon mounted the trucks for about a twenty-minute ride to our homes in the desert sands.

The men were lined up for a few instructions from the Captain and the First Sergeant who reminded them of the lectures we had received at Ft. Riley about desert life, heat, and water discipline. Since it was already past time for the evening meal they were told to use their rations and there would be breakfast in the morning at 0730 with first call at 0600 and roll call at 0900. That indicated we would be easing into the work schedule in order to avoid as much as possible any incidence of heat exhaustion. The First Sergeant pointed in the direction of the kitchen area where a Lyster bag was located and said that was the only source of drinking water and that canteens would be kept filled at all times with water from that Lyster bag. A Lyster bag is a large canvas-like bag with several spouts around the bottom to draw the chemically treated drinking water. Zillick then dismissed the Company and the men immediately went to fill their canteens after which they were directed to these huge tents each of which would accommodate a platoon less the non-comms. We officers also filled our canteens and Zillick led us over to a long line of smaller tents labeled "Officers' Row." He pointed out the tent for "A" Company's Junior Officers, which included James, Moskowitz, Walkowitz, DelCampo and myself. The Company Commanders were further down the line and the higher the rank the further their tent from the junior officers. I had taken notice before I left the men that Whitehead was not among them but he still had more travel time so I was not surprised.

The next morning I decided to practice a little water discipline so I poured some water into my helmet and brushed my teeth, then with the same water, I washed my face and shaved. I believe it must have been the first time I ever shaved with cold water but it would be far from the last as time and conditions would prove. It was a long-standing tradition in the Cavalry to grow a thick mustache when on maneuvers and quite a few of the old guys did just that and some of the new ones did also to reduce shaving as much as possible.

I arrived at the kitchen area well ahead of the men just to observe how things were going, and I again felt fortunate that we had an old hand like Sergeant Woodward as our Mess Sergeant because we had to switch from garrison to field rations with emphasis on desert conditions. Things were really humming in the kitchen area preparing a menu of scrambled powdered eggs made with powdered milk, creamed chipped beef on toast, you know SOS, individual boxes of cereal that had a slit down the middle in order to eat right out of the box, pitchers of powdered milk and coffee. The three large cans of boiling water for washing the men's mess gear, two soapy and one clear were all ready for use. Woodward filled my canteen cup with coffee, so I decided to go ahead and have my breakfast before the men arrived. As usual it tasted good to me and I was able to finish and wash my gear by the time chow was served.

Everything seemed to go smoothly and I walked over to ask Weaver if Whitehead had checked in as I didn't see him in the chow line. Weaver told me he had not, and even though he had another day, I started to feel a little uncomfortable because it shouldn't take that long to get here from Ft. Riley. I joined the other officers to walk back to our tent and they proceeded to point out that Whitehead was probably in Mexico by this time and I would never see him or my car again, which was supposed to be funny but I had a hard time laughing. In a short while, it was time to join the Company for roll call and instructions for the day's activities, which confirmed Whitehead's "absence but accounted for", meaning he was not AWOL (Absent With Out Leave). Even though it was still early, the temperature was starting to climb so calisthenics was omitted from the schedule until we had time to adjust to the heat. Likewise, close-order drill was dropped because the sandy footing made it too difficult to maintain a military bearing, so as we prepared to march to the Motor Park "route step" would be the order, which meant it was not necessary to keep in step. By the time we arrived, in spite of the almost casual pace, most of us were wet with perspiration and I thought the theory that "you don't feel the desert heat so much because it is dry heat" was a lot of baloney. Our coveralls and helmet liner left very little flesh exposed to the burning rays of the sun.

A sergeant from the Desert Training Center came to talk some more about the "dos and don'ts" in the desert. The tanks sitting in the sun are like radiators and can get hot enough to burn you by mid-afternoon, and the air temperature around the tanks in the park could be as much as 15 degrees higher than the official readings, and reach as high as 130 degrees. We were again reminded of the importance of drinking plenty of water and maintaining proper salt levels in our bodies by the timely use of salt tablets. We spent the rest of the morning performing the first echelon of maintenance on the tanks. Every effort was made to acclimate us to the sun and heat and regulated periods of sunning were part of the process. Each afternoon we would strip to the waist, the first day for five minutes, then an additional five minutes each day thereafter.

Following lunch we returned to the Motor Park and each man gingerly took his position in the tank while the driver fired it up. In about fifteen minutes Captain Zillick gave the order to follow his tank maintaining a twenty-yard interval at five miles per hour. We just circled the Motor Park and returned to our starting position, the whole operation taking less than an hour but it was enough to give us an idea of what a full day would be like. In spite of the low speed and the distance between tanks we stirred up quite a bit of dust and realized that we were in for a long, hot, and dusty summer. Even though we were only out for a short period we still had to perform the usual checks of the tanks and equipment required after every operation. Back to the Company area, but before dismissing the men we again cautioned them to check bedding and clothing for scorpions, spiders and other creepy crawly things common to the desert. I then inquired of the First Sergeant if there was any word from Whitehead, which there wasn't. We officers went back to our tent and tried to clean up a little before going to chow. I was relieved to see how smoothly the kitchen was working under these difficult conditions, and Woodward had things under control.

Later I wrote a letter to Gracie then joined the others in a typical army gripe session which covered the heat, the dirt, and as usual, the Captain. It seem we all had an incident involving Zillick. My latest being over Whitehead's absence. If I hadn't let him drive my car he would be here, but I certainly had no reason to think it would turn out this way, and he still had until 2000 hours tomorrow before being considered AWOL. Most officers were not trying to win any popularity contests but it appeared that Captain Zillick wanted to outdo Attila the Hun in the "mean" department.

The next day roll call produced the same results, no Whitehead, and a threat from the Captain to press charges if he is late. Before going to the Motor Park the Captain and the First Sergeant briefed us on the type of activities we could expect as part of the Desert Training Program. There would be numerous road marches during which we would execute various attack formations and some field problems to run through. Some days while in the field we would be subjected to even greater food and water discipline, which created some confusion when we are told to drink plenty of water but on these days limit the amount we use. I had noticed that some would splash water on their faces and we were to conserve the water strictly for drinking. We then spread out and did a few light calisthenics, which we hadn't done since leaving Ft. Riley. The rest of the day was much like the day before, and still no Whitehead. We had just finished our evening chow and were in line to dip our mess gear into the three barrels of boiling water when some of the men started looking in the direction of the public road that went by the camp where a car drew closer and closer to the Battalion area. Yeah, you guessed it, it was Whitehead finally, and wouldn't you know it, my car's grill was all smashed in. After he checked in, Whitehead walked up to explain that he had hit a cow and it took a full day to locate the farmer and straighten out the matter with him, thus justifying my concern about letting a tank driver drive my car. He said he was sorry and would take care of the grill, which he did a few days later when he and Motor Sergeant Phillips, using the Company equipment and material did a really good job putting the grill back together. This was just one of the many incidents that I observed of the ingenuity of the American G.I. I never did hear what the outcome was of his meeting with the Captain but at least he wasn't AWOL.

As the days passed the intensity of our training increased and so did the temperature. On a late afternoon following a long day of simulated combat situations we pulled into the Motor Park and cut the engines. The heat had been terrific and some of the drivers had to literally be lifted from their seats because they were too weak and dehydrated to lift themselves up. When the sweat dried, our coveralls were actually white from the salt from our bodies and we were really dragging. Soon we started making extended drives out in the desert and would bivouac for several days at a time. We were warned that if we did not return to our bivouac area until after dark, to always have a man dismount and lead the tank to where we would bed down for the night. The "scuttle-butt" was that some men had been run over while sleeping, but you never knew how much truth there was to these stories. Nevertheless, it could have happened and we were always very careful to make sure it did not happen to us, which was the purpose of those stories.

Another concern we had was the ever present scorpion and the occasional rattlesnake, and I know for a fact of one officer from "B" Company, Lieutenant Magura, was stung on his neck by a scorpion while riding in the turret of his tank. He became very ill and had to be hospitalized but was able to return to his Company in about a week or ten days.

When we bivouacked we would open our bedrolls and just sleep under the stars, but in the morning we would have to brush the cactus needles off of the bedrolls as we rolled them up. To keep the needles from sticking my hands I would put on some gloves, but it didn't seem to bother those tough young tankers who brushed the needles off with their bare hands, once in a while pulling out a cactus needle accompanied by a barrage of cuss words. Speaking of needles, there was a nearby town of Needles, California where the men could get a cold beer and see something other than tanks, tents and sand. On one of my first visits to Needles I was introduced to the concept of the "water bag" which was merely a burlap bag with a cap on it which you filled with water and hung it on the outside of your car, and as you drove the air would cool the water. In spite of my doubts, I bought one and the next morning I filled it up and hung it on my tank and to my surprise it actually worked, making the water much cooler than what was in my canteen. Also, to provide a little recreation for the men the Division scheduled several trips to Las Vegas, which was just 90 miles from camp, to give them a little taste of city life. I drove up a couple of times and played the nickel slots, which I am sure no longer exist.

The daily activities were rather routine mixing road trips, maneuvers, bivouacs and trips to the ranges to fire the various weapons, but there were a few incidents that I think are worth mentioning. We were heading back to camp after a three-day bivouac when at about 1500 hours it started to get very dark and soon we found ourselves in a cloudburst. Now on the maps we used for our maneuvers were landmarks designated as dry creek or dry lake, which seemed strange to me because they were like craters or gullies in the sand. We pulled up during this downpour near a couple of these so-called dry creeks and dry lakes and after about a half an hour we noticed they were filling up with water. Soon the dry lake was deep enough to submerge a tank and the dry creek became a roaring stream right in the middle of the desert. It was an unbelievable sight and I even wondered if we were going to be caught in a flood. I have never seen, either before or since, such a heavy deluge of rain as that which we experienced that day in the desert. After about two hours it gradually let up, and soon the sun was shining again so we started to move out. We had to pick our way because many of these lakes and streams were too deep to ford. When we had traveled a couple of miles we could actually see the water evaporating from these areas and figured they would be dry lakes and dry streams soon again.

Myself (left) with Sgt. Stanley Barszcz in the Mojave Desert. I wear a sidearm, gas mask, canteen, etc. while the sargeant wears none...he had been in service longer than I.

Me in my tank out in the desert. Some of the crew try to cool off in the shade of the tank. Note my water bag on the side of the turret.

Some of our road trips would take us through little towns where the houses actually had green lawns and trees growing in the yards. What a treat to see green grass and trees after weeks of sand and cactus plants, because our tank trails took us deep into the desert populated by only jack rabbits, rattle snakes and numerous insects. So it was on this particular day we got an early start and hit the tank trail moving at a pretty good clip, destination unknown. Since we were on a trail traveling in a column, we found ourselves eating a lot of dust from the tank ahead, so the ten-minute break each hour was a welcome relief. Finally it was decided that we would leave the trail and go across country where we could stagger the formation so as not to follow immediately behind any tanks in front and avoid much of the dust. We had traveled too far into the desert for the kitchen to reach us making it necessary to use the field rations we carried for lunch. The water in my water bag was actually cold and I marveled at the scientific reason that made this possible.

At about mid afternoon we called off our exercises and were ordered to execute a platoon line formation for the drive back to camp. In about an hour I heard a loud "pop" from the engine compartment and my tank ground to a halt. The crew jumped out and opened the doors to the engine while I radioed to the Captain that I was having engine trouble and dropped out of formation. He told me to try to fix the problem and catch up but if not he would send a maintenance crew to pick us up when he reached the Motor Park. I climbed down from the turret to have a look and saw oil all over the engine compartment and dripping down on the ground. We had obviously blown a cylinder or a gasket or something because it was a real mess and I was puzzled because during the lunch break everything had been checked and all gauges were normal. The records had shown that the engine had not run the usual number of hours for it to be red lined for a major overhaul, but operating under the difficult desert conditions must have caused early "metal fatigue" of some vital part of the engine. It was apparent that we would not be able to repair the damage so we just settled down to wait for our rescue party to pick us up.

It was getting late and I thought if we were still there after dark, it might be a good idea to have a fire. Some evenings can turn a little cool in the desert, also a fire would help to locate us in the dark so I had the men wrestle up some dry brush, tumble weeds, dead cactus, or anything that would burn. As it started to get dark I decided we had better have a guard roster to keep the fire going and watch for anyone coming for us, so I gave them a choice of two one hour hitches or one two hour hitch and they elected the one two hour hitch, and I would check with them from time to time during the night. The first man would be on from 9 to 11, the next 11 to 1, then 1 to 3, and finally 3 to 5, and to avoid any argument I designated who would take which time.

When the sun went down it started to get cool and none of us had any jackets, and not expecting to be out over night we had brought no bedding, so they started a small fire to attract any search party looking for us. As the crew gathered around the fire I climbed up on the rear deck of the tank so they would feel free to engage in the usual G.I. talk. They went on for at least half of the first mans shift on guard, and then one by one they stretched out on the sand to try and catch a little sleep. A little before 2300 I walked over to speak to the two men about to change guard duty and said that it didn't look like we would be picked up before dawn so I gave them my flashlight in case they saw a vehicle. I got very little sleep as I visited each man during his shift, and around 0430 I went back to the man on duty and told him to try to get some rest for another hour or so and I would take over until daylight. I threw some of the brush on the fire and sat there looking at the stars and saw one zipping briefly through the sky and then it was gone. You don't get many opportunities like this to reflect on the past and then ponder the future, two very opposite trains of thought.

Finally, it started to get a little light and the men were beginning to stir, so I put more kindling on to build up the fire so we could heat some water to make coffee. Each of us was able to heat a canteen cup of water and stir in a packet of instant coffee plus an individual box of cereal to which we added a little water so it wouldn't be so dry. We had powdered milk but it was too much trouble to mix with water and it didn't seem to add much to just plain water. We threw the empty cereal boxes and coffee packets on the fire in order to keep the area policed up then sat back to wait to be picked up. By mid morning, I was beginning to feel a little uneasy because they should have come for us the day before and I wondered if they had miscalculated our location. We had heard all the stories of guys being lost in the desert and never found or just their bones were all that remained of them and we never knew if it were true but it gave me something to be concerned about.

Just a little before noon we could see some vehicles off in the distance and shortly Lieutenant James and Sergeant Phillips arrived in a half-track and a tank recovery vehicle. Before I could say anything, James apologized for not coming to get us yesterday but after the Captain finished chewing him and Phillips out for the tank breaking down he wouldn't let them go and bring us in. He said Zillick told him to let us stay out there, that it was a good training experience. I suppose it was but I thought it was a bit unnecessary to leave us out in the middle of the desert unprepared for an overnight stay. Phillips and his men soon had the crane lift the tank, disengaged the gears, and prepared to drag it in. There is a much larger tank recovery vehicle that could winch a tank onto a flatbed and haul it in but this smaller one had to drag the tank. My crew and I rode in the half-track with James and Phillips and his men in the recovery vehicle and we reached camp around 1500. The Company was still in the Motor Park doing after action maintenance on the tanks and weapons following the grueling day we had the day before.

My crew and the maintenance crew went up for something to eat since we had no lunch. James went about his business and I hung with the rest of my platoon until time to go to the Company area where I was greeted by the First Sergeant who informed me that the Captain wanted to see me. Since he had already jumped on James and Phillips, I figured I was in the clear but I couldn't have been more mistaken. He let me have both barrels for letting my tank break down and you would have thought that I deliberately tore my tank up so I could spend a splendid night in the desert. Now an officer is not supposed to argue or make excuses to a senior officer or even offer an explanation unless asked, which I wasn't. By the time I was dismissed I was ready to explode because even though his criticism and accusations were so wrong and unreasonable I just had to stand there and take it.

A rather messy situation developed between Lieutenant DelCampo and the Captain which I did not witness, but Moskowitz and many others did and became the subject of a lot of conversation around the area. It seems that DelCampo either did something or didn't do something that infuriated the Captain to the point where things got out of control, and the Captain actually grabbed the Lieutenant, which is a very serious violation of military regulations. DelCampo immediately reported the incident to the Battalion Commanding Officer who promptly transferred DelCampo out of "A" Company. DelCampo's departure was so sudden that none of us were able to talk to him and the cause of the trouble remains a mystery to this day. I mention this incident because I found myself in a similar situation some time later, which I will describe in the next chapter.

It was early Fall of 1943 while we were out running through some exercises that we were ordered to discontinue all activities and return to camp to await orders. This came as a surprise and as could be expected started a series of rumors that included shipping out to the North African Theater. As soon as I could get to a telephone I called Gracie and told her that it seemed pretty certain that we would be leaving California but no one seemed to have a clue as to where we were headed. Without a moments hesitation Gracie asked me if I could meet her in Las Vegas just as soon as she could make arrangements for the trip. Now it is 2500 miles from Washington to Las Vegas and rail travel at that time was very difficult and I didn't want her spending at least three days on the train under very miserable conditions. As hard as I argued against her coming to Las Vegas, I realized that a team of horses was not going to keep her away, so she said she would let me know what her plans were and when she should arrive in Las Vegas.

The atmosphere around the Company area was one of speculation with rumors of our future running rampant. By now the news was out that the fighting in North Africa had ended thereby eliminating that theater of operations from our "guess list" which left the European Theater or the South Pacific as the future home of the Ninth Armored Division. Since we were presently on the West Coast the latter seemed the most logical choice but an Armored Division does not lend itself too well to island hopping and jungle fighting. Separate Tank Battalions seemed better suited for that type of operation but you never know, so the expert strategists which everyone in the Army was spoke convincingly of their theory concerning our destination and why. Meanwhile the level of preparation for our move kept rising to new heights and we soon were ready for whatever the decision was. Then I received Gracie's letter telling me that she would be leaving that Wednesday and was scheduled to arrive in Las Vegas Friday afternoon where she had made reservations at the Last Frontier Hotel. It worried me that she was going to all this trouble and misery for what could be a very short visit because we were all packed and ready to go on a moments notice.

What happened next was another example of the Good Fortune so frequently bestowed upon me with almost unbelievable results. On the Friday that Gracie was to arrive the official orders came out assigning the Ninth to Camp Polk, Louisiana for additional training and comprehensive maneuvers to be effective the following Monday. Notice of any troop movement was always held until the last minute for security reasons, which accounted for our state of preparedness. This news was greeted by many of us with mixed emotions because we had been training hard for a long time and were Gung-ho to get into combat. Such enthusiasm would be reduced considerably at a later date when the heat of battle would make a tour at Camp Polk very inviting to say the least. Now here is the best part, I would be permitted to drive my car and would receive ten days travel time which meant I could take Gracie and we would have time to find housing near Camp Polk. That Saturday I got a 36-hour pass starting at noon and I arrived at Gracie's hotel about 1400 hours.

I don't know how she knew when I would get there but there she was waiting for me in the lobby and although she must have been dead tired she looked fresh and beautiful. She told me later that she spent over two hours at the hairdressers getting all prettied up for our meeting. I told her I had some wonderful news but since neither of us had eaten I would tell her over lunch. While we waited for our order, I told her first that we were not at this time going overseas, but were transferring to Camp Polk. She heaved a great sigh of relief and whispered a quiet "Thank the Lord" at which time I said that I could take her with me and would pick her up Monday for our drive to Louisiana. Gracie just squealed with delight and kept saying over and over "You mean I can go with you? I can go with you?" I assured her she could. It was a very happy and emotional moment for this little lady who had gone through so much for what she expected would be a farewell visit with her husband. Not knowing what the facilities would be at Camp Polk Gracie wanted to do a little shopping for some "essentials" which might not be available there. These "essentials" consisted mainly of beauty care items such as makeup, shampoo, hair conditioner, and her special brand of soap, which I believe was called "Cashmere Bouquet", and stuff like that. Later we had a nice dinner then went to our room because we both had so much to talk about, past and future, but with all the excitement and recent strenuous activities, fatigue soon caught up to both of us and it was all we could do to get ready for bed and much needed sleep.

The next morning we got up and it being Sunday, went to Mass, had breakfast and returned to the hotel to discuss the trip. I figured I would be able to pick her up between 10:30 and 11:00 the next morning and off we would go. I had decided to go back to camp after we had lunch because I wanted to make a final check on things to make sure I hadn't overlooked anything. All was well and I felt comfortable with the way things were going. The next morning after chow I talked with the Mess Sergeant and as usual he had the situation well in hand. I then walked over to my platoon's tent and it checked out OK. I told Weaver it was a good job and that he would be in charge of the third platoon for the next ten days. Then I headed for the parking lot to get my car and bring it to our tent so I could load it up. On my way I saw Whitehead standing with a group of guys so I walked over to him and said loud enough for them all to hear "Don't even think about it." Well I thought the whole bunch including Whitehead was going to crack up, they just went into hysterics and I felt real good about it. I got my car, loaded it up, told the other officers I would see them at Camp Polk and went to pick up Gracie. She was all ready for me so without delay I took her baggage to the car, checked out of the hotel, said "Farewell, Las Vegas" and we were on our way.

Chapter 6

NEXT STOP, CAMP POLK, LOUISIANA

Wow! What a turn around. Just a few days ago we thought we were preparing for shipment overseas and here I am driving my car from Camp Ibis, California to Camp Polk, Louisiana to spend the winter in the south with Gracie at my side. It was a long enjoyable ride with two overnight stops on the way arriving in De Ridder, Louisiana late afternoon of the third day. We registered at a small hotel there and inquired if they knew of any available housing in the area. I was handed a list of addresses most of which were rooms to rent but a few apartments were also listed. The next day we decided to check out the apartments first and if we did not find something suitable, then we would look for a room. The first place was in a rather rundown neighborhood and so was the house so we didn't even get out of the car. Although we both realized that in our situation we couldn't be too choosy, I knew that Gracie might be alone a lot and I wanted to make sure that she felt safe and comfortable. The next place we drove up to looked old but well kept and just across the street were about a dozen railroad tracks. We were not happy about that but went to have a look anyway. The owners had converted the old house into two apartments. One had a living room, bedroom, kitchen and a tiny bathroom which obviously had been added on. The other had a very small living room, a bedroom with a small refrigerator and a two burner electric hot plate stuck in the corner and a bathroom.

While we were looking a cute young couple came in and we introduced ourselves and immediately hit it off real well. We all decided we would take these apartments. They were Lt. Roy and Betty Ann Lennberg and since we were there first they said we should choose the one we wanted. The one with the kitchen was more expensive but Gracie liked to cook so she chose that one. We felt very lucky to not only find something livable but met a real nice couple who we could enjoy being with. I could see from Roy's patch that he was with the Ninth and was also in the Fourteenth Tank Battalion and if I remember correctly was in "D" Company. The landlord said we could move in the next day so we hurried out to do some shopping for towels and bed linens. Roy had arrived with the troops a few days earlier and Betty Ann had just got in the day before and since they didn't have a car Roy had to ride the bus to camp. On moving day we learned that not only the Miller's and the Lennberg's were at the hotel but the Zillick's and the Moskowitz's were also there. We of course knew Lois Zillick since we lived in the same house in Kansas, but we had never met Florence Moskowitz, a sweet young lady.

Gracie, Betty Ann and I loaded our luggage and purchases in the car and went to set up housekeeping in our "new" homes. It was just a matter of making beds, hanging up clothes, putting towels in the bathroom and we were settled in. I still had a day of travel time left so the following day I took Gracie into camp because I wanted to see how long it took to drive there. I located the Company "A" area where I saw Sid and told him if he could get to my place he could ride to camp with me. He told me he and Florence would look for a room on the weekend and would come by my place. They located a room just about a block away from us and this was the beginning of a close friendship. Each morning Sid, Roy and another man whose name I just can't remember would arrive at our place with their wives and after the men left for camp the ladies would stay for coffee which made it nice for everyone.

In the meantime, I quickly got back into harness resuming most of our usual routine except we didn't have the heat of the desert to contend with and could push the men a little harder. As a matter of fact it was mid-autumn and the weather had turned a little cool and rainy. This required us to learn a new procedure for getting our tanks through some swampy terrain, which was to "corduroy" the road. This involved cutting down small trees or large branches and lay them over the affected area for the tanks to drive on to keep them from bogging down in the mud. We were kept very busy performing various battle exercises and combat problems and it was during one of these exercises that I had a rather serious run-in with Captain Zillick.

We had been ordered to maneuver our tanks into a position to attack some high ground and each platoon was assigned a certain sector from which we would make this attack. I gathered my Tank Commanders and explained the problem in great detail then told my Platoon Sergeant to take charge of the platoon for this problem. I had always wanted to make sure my Sergeants were prepared to take over in the event I would become disabled. I had always felt that Staff Sergeant Weaver was a very capable man and I knew that this move would not be a problem for him. I had also hoped that with him leading the way that from time to time I could have the rest of my Tank Commanders take charge of the platoon for the reason I mentioned above. The Captain came on the radio and gave the order for "A" Company to move out and execute the exercise. Weaver took his position at the front of the platoon and ordered the unit to move forward in right echelon formation on him. I placed my tank in the fourth position so I could more easily observe the rest of the platoon. As we started up the hill he ordered the second section to break off and take a position by a clump of trees to our right. The second section is the last two tanks in the platoon which is where I had placed my tank. So we moved to the nearby clump of trees giving us two positions from which to attack the high ground exactly as we had done a number of times during a similar problem. Then Weaver gave the order for the Third Platoon to advance and take the high ground. I was very pleased with the way things went and when we reached the top of the hill I radioed Weaver and said "Good job, Sergeant."

No sooner had I said that than I received a call from the Captain to report to him "on the double." I dismounted from my tank and ran over to his, where he proceeded to give me the worst "chewing out" I had ever received, for allowing my Sergeant to take charge of the platoon. He informed me that I was the Platoon Leader and he expected me to lead my men and not follow them. His remarks included a lot of profanity that could be heard by most of the men, which was unjustified and humiliating. Regulations provide that a senior officer does not reprimand a subordinate in the presence of his men. I have always believed what I wanted to do would be good experience for my Tank Commanders, but if he didn't approve, all he had to do was say so

Me with Gracie in the back yard of the home we lived in while at De Ridder, Louisiana.

and order me not to do it again and that would have been the end of it. It took a lot of self-restraint to keep from saying something, but I was able to keep my temper under control until I got back to my tank and then I exploded. Inside the tank I called him every name I had ever heard and made up a few of my own.

At the end of the day I went to the Orderly Room and told the First Sergeant I wanted to speak to the Captain, who was in his office. I went in and told him I wanted permission to see the Battalion Commander to request a transfer and he said, "Permission granted." I immediately hurried over to Battalion Headquarters, hoping I would be able to see the Colonel and get this mess over with. On the way I began to wonder if I were doing the right thing because I didn't want to leave my platoon, but I was certain if this type of public humiliation were to continue I would lose the respect of my men. I walked into Headquarters' Orderly Room and told their First Sergeant that I would like to speak to the Colonel, and he pointed toward the office and told me to go on in. I thought this was strange because a visitor to the Colonel is always announced, and I suspected that the Captain had called ahead to tell the Colonel that I was on my way. After following military protocol for addressing the Battalion Commander, I was given permission to speak and proceeded to state my case. I concluded my remarks by stating that I honestly believed that I would not be able to function as an officer at my fullest potential under the conditions I described, so I was requesting an immediate transfer even if it meant an overseas assignment.

I will never forget his response and to this day it stands out very clearly in my memory. This is what he said: "Lieutenant, we are aware of the situation and it will take care of itself at some future date. We do not want to lose you, so I am denying your request, Lieutenant, and ordering you to return to your duties. In the meantime, I will advise the Captain to keep his temper under better control and you can expect conditions to improve. If that is all Lieutenant, you are dismissed." I was absolutely speechless and all I could say was "Thank you, Sir", salute and walk out. I could not believe what had just happened, when I, a Second Lieutenant, was told by my Colonel that he did not want to lose me. Another of the many surprises that happened to me during my military career, and why that Second Lieutenant was proud to be an American soldier who actually enjoyed military life, as these pages have already revealed.

The atmosphere was a little tense for the next few days but I was glad to be with my platoon and kept very busy just doing my job. I never mentioned to anyone about my visit to the Colonel but I had a feeling that there were those in the company, beside the Captain who knew. It may have been my imagination that there seemed to be a little less aggravation as we continued our day to day activities, at least as far as I was concerned. Gracie was not aware of the situation and her presence was an oasis from camp life and had a real calming effect on me. What wasn't so calming was the occasional train whistle during the night as it passed by the house. I mentioned it to Gracie and she couldn't stop laughing explaining that when she and the other girls would sit out on the porch having coffee they would wave to the engineers and they in turn would blow their whistles. I told her that I failed to see the humor in having my sleep interrupted by those engineers' romantic gestures. I really did think it was funny but I had to pretend to be upset which didn't fool Gracie one bit.

The early part of November 1943 we started hearing rumors that we were about to embark on some extensive maneuvers leading to full-scale war games. This would mean a lengthy stay in the field extending beyond Christmas. Since we would not be together, Gracie decided she might as well spend Christmas at home, which certainly made sense. What did worry me was her decision to drive home, which is much farther than she had ever driven before, but she had arranged with the wife of another officer to go with her. Activities at camp again seemed to speed up and we had several sessions at the Post Theater, where an officer from the Army Headquarters explained how war games are conducted and would resemble actual combat as closely as they could make it. Finally we were given a date when we would leave our barracks and move into the field and I received word that at that time I would start attending a seminar to instruct selected officers to be umpires for the coming war games. I could feel the effects of my visit to the Colonel and while I didn't like being away from my platoon, I could see the wisdom of this effort to prevent any further friction with my Company Commander. Also the umpires would be assigned rooms at the Bachelor Officers' Quarters (BOQ) where we would stay until the end of the games which turned out to be a real good deal. With this information Gracie started making plans for her trip home and I mapped out the routes she should take on the way. We spent the evenings going to the movies with the Lennberg's or out to dinner with the Moskowitz's and trying to relax and enjoy the time we had before the maneuvers started. Of course we arranged to keep the apartment so we would have a place to come back to when and if we returned to barracks. Too soon the day arrived when the Division was to move into the field and I had to say goodbye to Gracie and though we had to do this several times in recent months it still wasn't easy. Gracie held up real well though but I suspected it was in an effort to make it a little easier on me.

I went directly to the theater for the first session of the umpires seminar and was immediately made aware of what an enormous undertaking these war games were going to be with three full infantry divisions, some artillery, tank destroyer, and aircraft units to name a few, joining us in this huge operation. We were told time and again how vital our work would be to determine the combat readiness of all of the participants in this action and that we were to be strict but fair in grading the conduct of the unit to which we were assigned. It was also pointed out that we would be working with units in Battalions other than our own in order to avoid any possibility of being inadvertently influenced by personal connections with anyone in that organization. We were also warned to be prepared for many 24-hour continuous observations of how units performed throughout the night, given specific situations. There was a tremendous amount of detail that we had to study from manuals that they gave us which I won't describe here but will come to light as I relate some of the incidents as they occurred during this gigantic military endeavor covering millions of acres, over half of the state of Louisiana.

When the course at the "Umpire School" ended we were taken to the unit we were to work with to acclimate ourselves with the policies and procedures of that organization. Naturally, I was assigned to a tank company with a different Battalion in the Ninth Armored Division and immediately introduced myself to the Company Commander.

He assured me that he had attended the sessions held by Army Headquarters and was familiar with what my connection with his company would be and placed a Peep with a driver at my disposal. His company had been participating in the preliminary exercises and would start another the next day so I decided to tag along just to get a feel of things prior to the start of the war games. My driver picked me up the next morning and we arrived at his company's bivouac area in time for breakfast, which I was able to check on even though I would not be grading them until they started the war games. It was like a dry run for me, giving me an opportunity to practice what I would be doing officially later on. I roamed around the area just observing the activities of the men, where they pitched their tents in order to give them quick and easy access to their tanks, and if they parked their tanks in a way to make a fast exit in an emergency. I spent most of the nights back at the BOQ, but several times I took my bedroll so I could make some nocturnal inspections because we were expected to do some 24-hour checks during the war games.

Just about the middle of December 1943 the official maneuvers finally got under way and I went with the Company Commander to the officer's call where they received the orders of the day which included a move to an assembly area from which they would attack enemy forces. As they lined up the tanks I had my driver park his Peep at the head of the column so I could check the interval between the tanks and the conduct of their crews as they went forward. Since they were not in enemy territory a 25 to 35 yard separation was acceptable while maintaining a speed between 11 and 13 miles per hour. Then the Company Commander brought his tank up to where I was located and backed off the road so he could watch for the same things I was checking. At exactly 0915 he gave the order to move out and his tanks started down the road in column formation. Things went very smoothly that morning and everyone observed the various road march disciplines that were in place for the entire operation. At 50 minute intervals they took a 10 minute break and the smokers moved a proper distance from their tanks and "field stripped" their cigarette butts when they finished. It seemed to be a good day as the men ate field rations for lunch and after reaching their assembly area maintenance was performed on the tanks. Then the men pitched tents and the kitchen truck arrived to provide a hot supper.

There was an officer's call to go over the next days agenda which included first call at 0600, breakfast at 0630, and move out at 0700 to seek and engage the enemy at a position designated on the map. The platoon leaders returned and assembled their men to brief them on the activities of the following day. Security was set up, the men hit the sack and since my barracks were only about an hour away, I decided to go back, shower and shave and get about six hours sleep. Provisions had been made for all the drivers to be housed in a dormitory-type building and I instructed my driver to pick me up at 0530 so we could arrive where the company was camped by 0630 and have breakfast there. The men had struck their tents, no shave, no shower, but did get a hot breakfast and were ready to move out at 0700.

Shortly after leaving the assembly area the tanks crossed their line of departure and although they were not in designated enemy territory the Company Commander suspecting some kind of trickery moved his tanks into various combat formations depending on the terrain and wooded areas. It turned out to be a wise decision because we came to a hill and just before we reached the top he ordered his tanks to halt and had two of his Tank Commanders reconnoiter on foot to determine what might be lurking on the other side. Sure enough they spotted a distant gun emplacement, which he immediately dispatched by waving a red flag and the men at the gun emplacement responded by waving a green flag. I immediately noted this on my report and we proceeded over the hill. After that incident, the Company Commander assumed he was in enemy territory in spite of the fact we had not reached the area indicated on the map and so deployed his tanks accordingly. During the rest of the day several other gun sites were spotted and disposed of. Then upon reaching a large wooded area the men were told to camp there for the night.

These war games were divided into seven phases covering a period of six weeks bringing into play all the units previously referred to in order to simulate artillery and air attacks and in turn employing air and artillery support combined with the use of tank destroyers and other supplemental units. To give a day-by-day account of this activity, while it would be interesting, would be to delay too long getting to the real meat of this story. However, I will relate some of the situations that occurred which should give you an idea of the big picture which these maneuvers presented. For instance, on one of my 24-hour tours, at about 0200, I wanted to see how good their night security was, when I was stopped by one of the guards who commanded "Halt! Who goes there?" I replied "Friendly umpire." He ordered "Advance and be recognized." I stepped forward to be faced with a .45 caliber pistol pointed at me and he looked me over observing the white armband I was wearing indicating I was an umpire then merely said "Pass friendly umpire." I told him "Very good, soldier. Carry on." Normally, I would be a little uneasy staring down the barrel of a Colt 45 but knew the men had been issued weapons but no live ammunition. On another occasion the company had taken cover in a wooded area and I could see a Piper Cub circling around and pretty soon a small bag of flour hit one of the tanks. I notified the Company Commander that one of his tanks was not completely concealed and had been bombed by aircraft and was out of commission.

I had always thought that winter in the south meant nice warm balmy weather but the Louisiana weatherman had other ideas because we experienced rain, low temperatures, snow and a severe ice storm. We were told it was the worst winter in memory of the oldest native. At the time of the ice storm, we were working in close contact with another company whose umpire was a rather robust Texan who was constantly complaining about the cold and rain, which created huge icicles hanging from the trees. "We would never have weather like this in Texas," he declared. "If we were in Texas, it would be nice and warm and sunny," and on and on he went. As a matter of fact, we were operating very close to the Texas-Louisiana line and the map showed that on this particular move we had to cross into Texas. You won't believe this but we no sooner crossed that line when the sun came out, it got very warm and the icicles started falling off of the trees so fast we had to keep our helmets on so we wouldn't be hurt by the falling ice. Well that Texan just would not stop bragging about how Texas brought the good weather as he predicted it would and who could argue with him? We moved back across the line and the weather was still nice but the Texan still gave Texas credit for the change in temperature.

Since we were not too far from the Post during the real bad weather I had my driver take us back to our quarters where we could spend a nice warm night and get a good night's sleep, another benefit of being an umpire.

Christmas came and went with little or no celebration and the maneuvers were winding down. Since I was able to give Gracie an approximate date when it would be over, she had planned to come back between the 15th and 20th of January. When the games ended the Division camped just outside of Camp Polk while the 8th Armored Division prepared to vacate the Post. In the meantime, I returned to BOQ to finish my umpire's reports and attend several critiques of that huge event. I really enjoyed that experience which certainly sharpened my vision of what I might face at a later date little knowing how prophetic it was.

Another perk of being an umpire was the free time I had between those meetings which gave me the opportunity to see Gracie ahead of schedule. After a couple of days of going over reports and discussing the action it was decided that the Commanding Officer wanted a day to read the reports and review the critiques, giving the umpires a day off.

I called Gracie and she came out the next morning to pick me up and spend the day together. It was then she told me about the scary accident she had driving back to Louisiana. She had started across a bridge not knowing it was covered with ice and began fishtailing and banging against the guardrail of the bridge several times before she could bring the car under control. Thank goodness she wasn't hurt but it really shook her up a bit. They stopped for the day at the next motel just to settle her nerves. We had a real nice day together and I took her home that night because I was to stay at BOQ since I had an early meeting the next morning.

Upon completing the debriefing we were told to return to our Battalions for further instructions and I began to wonder if that meant another assignment. I checked in at Battalion and reported to the Colonel who informed me that I would rejoin Company "A" when they returned to garrison the day after tomorrow and he had advised Captain Zillick accordingly. Oh boy, a day and a half to spend with Gracie, what a deal that umpire's job turned out to be. I hurried home to tell Gracie and offered to take her out to dinner but she said she had bought some goodies and would fix a nice meal so we could just relax and enjoy it. I asked Gracie if she would mind riding out to where the company was bivouacked so I could see the guys and pay a courtesy call to the Captain. So the next morning after breakfast we rode out to where the Company was but because the tanks had chewed up the terrain, which was still soggy from the winter precipitation, it was difficult walking so Gracie remained in the car. I immediately went to the Captain's tent to tell him I came by to make sure that I understood the Colonel's instructions correctly and he said that was right and he would see me tomorrow. He also told me that the uniform of the day would be fatigues because the men would be cleaning and performing maintenance on the tanks after over six week in the field. I then walked over to where my platoon was located and visited with the men and Sergeant Weaver for a few minutes, saw the other company officers and told Sid if he got home that night he could ride in with me the next day. As might be expected, the tanks were filthy from the crews climbing in and out with their muddy boots and driving through all that swampy terrain. Then there was maintenance to perform and drawing clean bedding since the barracks had been stripped by the troops of the 8th Armored Division who had just moved out.

The following week we got settled in to our usual training activities with what seemed to me an increasing number of assemblies where officers informed us of current activities overseas. Certain things were said that appeared to imply that preparations were being made for an anticipated invasion of Europe, creating an abundance of rumors around the camp and some even spilling over into town, which of course reached Gracie. She would ask me about them and as is often the case, the civilian population had more details than we in the military. Another thing, our schedule included frequent practices disembarking from a ship down a rope ladder, which was no easy task. Although nothing was said we got the feeling that things were moving faster, that there was an urgency about almost everything we did. Something else we noticed was an increase in the visits from the Colonel and his staff who would even mingle with the men. More barracks inspections by Captain Zillick with greater emphasis on discipline. Even more strict policing of the area was imposed, with the warning that trash left in a combat zone could provide the enemy with valuable information.

We also started a more vigorous schedule of calisthenics and close-order drills. One particular morning, the entire Battalion participated in a period of mass calisthenics where one officer from each Company was selected to conduct a specific exercise for about a thousand men. I was selected for "A" Company and figured I would be the first officer called but instead they started with "D" Company. We were required to mount a high stand and first demonstrate the exercise "by-the-numbers" then have the battalion execute in cadence repeating the exercise twenty times. I was surprised when the first officer did not follow the prescribed procedure for leading the men in calisthenics and those that followed made many of the same mistakes. They did not give the instructions loud enough for the men in the rear ranks to hear and their description and demonstration of the exercise was garbled and not according to the manual. My exercise was the multiple knee-bend, which I had given my platoon many times, and since I always enjoyed drill and exercise, I conducted the drill strictly by the book and the men responded perfectly. As I reached the final series, I stood, raised my right hand, and accentuated the count, which brought the exercise to a halt. I gave the men "At Ease," jumped down off of the stand and was jogging back to my place with the Company. I noticed the Colonel walking toward me down a lane between companies, so I came to a walk to give him a salute and he said, "That was an excellent demonstration, Lieutenant. Congratulations." I said, "Thank you, Sir", saluted and continued on my way but I really felt very pleased.

These types of things certainly aroused a lot of curiosity about whether we would be moving out any time soon. Not ready to push the panic button, Gracie spoke casually about things she heard through the grapevine, some of which were ridiculous and some were rather logical interpretations of what people were hearing. Whether by design or subconsciously Gracie and I were doing more fun things together, having dinner out, going to the movies or just strolling through town. One weekend we drove to Lake Charles intending to spend the night but could not get a room so we returned home. I remember one Saturday afternoon I decided to sun myself so I stretched out on a blanket in the back yard. After I had enough I got up and went inside and Gracie told me that one of the neighbors called her on the phone to tell her that a snake was crawling close to me and Gracie thanked her and said she was sure I would take care of it. I appreciated her confidence in me but I never did see the snake and don't know what I would have done if I had.

The days were passing rapidly and rumors were flying fast and furious and the good citizens of DeRidder were telling Gracie that the 9th was definitely moving very shortly. Still nothing around camp could confirm that but one day Sid said he had been talking to an officer from Battalion Headquarters who had been told to start making arrangements for a "big" move. Of course that could mean a lot of things but to most of us it meant shipment overseas. Then it was June 6, 1944 and the hints made at assemblies became real with the invasion by the Allied Forces at Normandy, France, which left little doubt about the future of the Ninth Armored Division. There even seemed to be an atmosphere of impatience, which I must admit I felt myself. We had trained long and hard and many of us were convinced that we were ready for the "Big Show."

It was about time that Gracie and I have some serious conversation about the possibility of our heading out to sea and so we very calmly discussed just what we would do when we got the word. We had agreed with our landlord to give two weeks notice of our intent to vacate the apartment. Gracie did not want to make that long drive home so at the proper time she would spread the word that our car was for sale. She would also start to ship things home so she wouldn't have too much to carry on the train. I must say she handled the situation beautifully and we were able to really enjoy the remaining time we had together.

At camp excitement started to build and we received a lot of instructions about the customs of the people in the various countries and to show respect and consideration for them. Much was said about our own conduct and that of our men for which we would be held responsible. Then we got into the matter of what to expect in combat which was not a pretty picture reminding us that this would be a war in which people would get hurt and some killed. Of course, there were the pep talks about our heritage, patriotism, and the reputation of greatness to uphold. I realized that all of this talk and activities around camp was helping me cope with the idea of leaving Gracie and how it would affect her and I hoped that she and her lady friends were equally occupied with their preparations preventing concerns for the future. Again it was Gracie's strength that enabled us to have fun during my free time trying to maintain some degree of normalcy whatever that might be in Army life. Also it was becoming more difficult to occupy the men with activities that would keep them from getting restless waiting for what we knew was sure to come. They were asking which direction I thought we would go because some had heard Europe, others had heard the South Pacific. Logic would suggest Europe, which was a good reason for expecting the South Pacific. I told them we could only be sure when we reached our Port of Embarkation (POE) and even that was no guarantee.

At this point the officers of "A" Company were advised that Captain Zillick was ordered to the hospital for a physical checkup. I had known that he was in the service with a waiver for a heart murmur but I thought that meant if that should result in a medical discharge he would not receive compensation. The shocker came a few days later when we heard that he was considered unfit for combat duty and was being immediately discharged. Flashing through my mind was the statement the Colonel made to me "that the matter would take care of itself." Our new Company Commander was Captain George Soumas who seemed to be a likable sort of guy. He was a lawyer from Perry, Iowa, who I soon learned, liked to talk a lot and could be rather amusing at times. A complete opposite of Captain Zillick, he appeared eager to get along with the men and would kid and joke with them. I am not sure it worked and I really thought he over did it but we would see.

July was coming to a close and we were told we should tell our wives we would be leaving in about two weeks but not to mention it to anyone else. That evening when I arrived home Gracie greeted me with the news that the Ninth would be pulling out the second week in August, so much for secrecy. Since we had planned for this situation; we notified the landlord that Gracie would be leaving on the 15th of August; she believed she already had a buyer for the car; she would now buy her train ticket home and ship the rest of her personal belongings home. That being decided we could just relax and wait for the big day to come. Yeah sure. There was a lot of hand holding, some pacing the floor (you would think we were expecting a baby), talk about keeping in touch but a warning about mail service and opportunities to write may often not be available. We were finally advised that our date of departure was August 8, 1944 and we would take the train to our POE. which still was not revealed to us. I wondered if Gracie had that information but she said no one had heard.

On the morning of August 8, Gracie rode to camp with me because I had my duffle bag and musette bag to travel with me. The troops would be trucked to the railroad siding just a short distance away and Gracie followed in our car for one more last goodbye. The other officers stayed on Post the last night so they had said their farewells the morning before. The men quickly boarded the train and we were soon on our way. I was able to get to the door of our car so I could wave to Gracie as the train pulled out and it was then I felt a lump in my throat and hoped that she would hold up okay. Each officer was to ride with his Platoon and had a whole seat for himself, so almost as soon as I reached my seat Sid Moskowitz came by and joined me which was a big help. He had not mentioned it before but he told me Flo was not handling the situation very well. I wondered about Gracie, because it is not easy watching your man ride off to battle.

Chapter 7

ALL ABOARD AND BON VOYAGE!

So here we are on the train heading for Destination Unknown with the window blinds drawn so we can't even see which direction we are going. Most bets are on the East Coast but no one has even heard any "scuttle-butt" on the subject. The routine in this train ride is about the same as when we went to the desert but considerably longer making it necessary to get off for calisthenics. Keep in mind, we are all closed up so we can't see out and so nobody can see in, but the morning of the second day we pulled into the station and we are all ordered off the train for some limbering up exercises for all the world to watch. Now does that make sense. I don't think so. Large numbers of people gathered to watch the men work out and applaud after each routine. Along the walkways beside the tracks were signs saying "Detroit" with arrows pointing to various streets, cabs, parking, etc., and our move was supposed to be "Top Secret." Oh well, I suppose the enemy already had a map showing the route we were taking to our POE. We then boarded our secure train with the window blinds drawn and pulled out of the station to resume our journey to only the enemy knew where. In order to fool the enemy, as we learned later, our train followed a course that would take us up through Canada then to the East Coast unloading us at Camp Kilmer, New Jersey, nearly four days after leaving Camp Polk. By this time we were all pretty stir crazy and really glad to get off of that train and move around a little.

Most of the time at Camp Kilmer was spent making final preparation for going overseas, such as writing Wills, arranging for Power of Attorney, taking out insurance or increasing the amount of existing policies, allotting money to be taken out of pay for a War Bond a month to be sent home, and things of that nature. Then there were the physical exams with booster shots and some new shots for travel abroad. Near the end of a week we were picking up more unconfirmed info about when we were leaving and even the name of a ship was being whispered about. Then we were told that anyone wanting a twelve-hour pass to New York could pick it up the next day and transportation would be provided. Sid and I, and Grimball decided we would go and after we arrived in town several officers from other companies kind of hung with us. We had been let out downtown and told the bus would return to that location at 2300 hours to take us back to camp.

The Empire State Building was on everybody's list to see so up we went to the observation tower where we were enjoying the fabulous view when we noticed all these ships in the Harbor. We asked a nearby Guard which of those ships was the *Queen Mary* because that was the one that we had heard we might be taking. The Guard replied that he was not allowed to identify any of the ships in the harbor but we could see this real huge one that just stood out above the others and knew that it had to be the *Queen Mary*. It was quite exciting to see this great ocean liner knowing that we might soon be sailing on it to Europe. Now it was time to start looking for a place where we could have a nice meal and enjoy a show, so off we went. Soon we came to a well-known nightspot called the Diamond Horseshoe and we all agreed we would have dinner there and catch their early show. When we had been seated, I went to the telephone to call Gracie and told her where I was. She had a million questions, none of which I was permitted to answer but I am sure she realized that this was it. She told me to be careful and come home safely, and also that if there were any pretty girls in the show not to look at them. I told her I would be careful and come home safely but no promises about looking at the showgirls. I was hoping that might cheer her up but I thought I detected a slight quiver in her voice as we said goodbye. The dinner was good and the show was nice and yes, I did look at the pretty showgirls, which I am sure Gracie expected. Afterward we walked back to meet the bus and returned to Kilmer long before our passes expired,

The next morning at roll call we were told to be packed and ready to move at 1100 hours when we would be taken to the POE where we would board our ship for deployment overseas. Boy did that bring out the goose bumps. At last it was really going to happen and we would show those Krauts just who is the "Master Race." Another big shock occurred as we reached the harbor and drew near this gigantic ship which would transport us across the ocean. I got the same sensation as when I first stood beside a tank, its size was breathtaking and almost unbelievable. Yes, this was the *Queen Mary*, truly the Queen of all ocean lines, the sight of which left me speechless and unable to describe just how enormous she was. I had seen many pictures of this Goliath of the Seas, and a distant view from the Empire State Building, but still could not fully comprehend the magnitude of her beauty until this moment. When it was time to go aboard the officers and enlisted men were lined up separately and we were immediately directed to our assigned staterooms. To this day, I brag about going to Europe on the *Queen Mary* in the stateroom for two but what I don't tell is that there were eighteen of us in it.

There were all kinds of instructions and rules to follow during the voyage such as wearing the life jacket, life boat drills, dining shifts, blackout regulations, to name a few, plus the duties of the MP's on board because that was the assignment of the 14th Tank Battalion and we were all given MP armbands which I still have in my possession. The *Queen Mary* had been totally outfitted as a troop ship with dining rooms converted to mess halls, theaters and even the swimming pools were turned into dormitories. No private baths but large latrines and shower rooms and staterooms that contained tiers and rows of hammock-like beds with canvas tarps laced to metal pipes. No Sealy Posturepedic mattresses. Everyone had specific duties, ours as MP's was to patrol certain areas in shifts to assure that all rules were complied with, others had kitchen detail, mess hall, latrine, trash removal, policing the area, etc.

After dark the Magnificent Lady pulled away from her pier and was guided through the Harbor by a pilot boat until we arrived at the open sea. One thing that I was very aware of was the absence of any other ships because my experience at shipping material for the British Army staff taught me that troop ships and freighters always traveled in a convoy escorted by one or more battleships. I found out later that the *Queen Mary* usually went unescorted because its superior speed would permit it to outrun any enemy

My armband issued for M.P. duty during the crossing on the Queen Mary.

craft. I also noticed that there were many anti-aircraft gun emplacements throughout the ship making us fair game for any Nazi u-boats that we might encounter.

My shift for MP duty was 2000 hours to 2400 hours and 1200 hours to 1600, so I was assigned an early seating for my meals. Since the *Queen Mary* was under British command, officers received special treatment and we had our meals served to us in a separate dining room. According to English custom, fish was served as a side dish to our breakfast each morning and even though I wasn't use to fish at breakfast, I really enjoyed it. My first tour as an MP was rather uneventful and for the most part was in the area restricted to the officers on board. I would have liked to visit my people but I didn't know where they were and on this floating city with over 15,000 passengers my chances of finding them were rather slim.

In addition to the Ninth Armored, there were some separate units including the anti-aircraft guys and a contingent of Red Cross personnel, mostly women, which created a situation that I am still reminded of at our company reunions. It seems that the ladies directed most of their attention to the officers on board, showing little interest in the enlisted men, which understandably, they strongly resented. In fairness, the Red Cross group was located in the same section as the officers, which made contact with them easier than with those further removed from their area. Being a married man, I was unable to avail myself of any favors the girls might offer, which most people find hard to believe but it is true.

It seemed to me that the sea was pretty calm but a lot of people were getting sick and I noticed that some of the mess halls were missing a lot of men during the early part of the voyage. Whenever I could, I would go on a tour of the ship and wore my MP armband, which let me in some of the places marked "off limits." The galley was surprisingly clean and orderly considering the thousands of meals they had to prepare each day, and the radio room was just buzzing with conversation. There were daily lifeboat drills although we were never made aware of any threat of attack. I also noticed from the ships wake that the captain assumed a zig-zag course usually during the drill which made me wonder if he was also practicing or had he received a report of any enemy in the area. You do think about such things when you are at war especially if you had a civilian job that was affected by the sinking of one of our supply ships. They had set up a PX on board where you could buy some goodies or necessities, and all things considered, I actually enjoyed the crossing, which terminated on August 25 at Greenock, Scotland.

Early the next morning we disembarked from that Lovely Creature that brought us safely all the way across the Atlantic and as I took a final look at the *Queen Mary* we immediately boarded a train that would transport us to Southern England. As usual, tight security was in order and we again traveled with drawn blinds, which was too bad because we couldn't enjoy seeing the beautiful countryside that was always associated with the British Isles. The trip lasted the rest of the day and throughout the night getting us to Tidworth Barracks the next day where we would be housed in some very old brick buildings, but they were more comfortable than any accommodations we had since leaving Camp Polk. There were a few more sessions to remind us of certain English customs and how we should conduct ourselves so as not to offend the natives and finally we were rejoined with our respective Companies.

We immediately marched to the area of a huge motor park that was designated for "A" Company and found there our brand new Sherman M4A3E8 tanks that we would soon ride into combat. There was a lot of work to be done to prepare these new vehicles and their equipment for action requiring the communications sergeant to see that the radios and intercoms performed perfectly and to show the crews any changes in these sets. The guns had to be cleaned of cosmoline, a lubricant used to prevent rusting and pitting in the gun barrels, and the armorer made sure all weapons were ready to fire. Then we had to road test the tanks to give the drivers the "feel" of the new vehicles so they would be perfectly comfortable at the control of these beauties. Of course we had to go to the firing range to test fire all of the tank guns and spend a great deal of time getting thoroughly familiar with all the new features of the tank some of which were its greater weight, the long barreled 76mm cannon, and the double turret hatches which allowed the loader to fire the 50 caliber machine gun that was mounted on a rotating ring around his turret hatch, permitting the gun to also be positioned for the tank commander to fire.

These were busy times and it wasn't long before we realized that a regular part of our uniform of the day would be our raincoats which we attached to the rear of our pistol belts. There was rarely a day that we didn't have rain in some form, either a shower, a storm, a steady rain, or just a drizzle, but enough to give you a good soaking without your raincoat. It was one of those days that everybody was hard at work when I spotted a man up in the turret of one of my tanks who seemed to be gold-bricking, so I asked him if he didn't have anything to do, and he said that he did and started to chuckle after making a side remark to the other men in the tank. He still didn't start working so I ordered him to dismount and I told him that I wanted to talk to him. He again said something to the others which I was unable to hear. By this time I knew it was Corporal KO Brown who had frequently been in trouble and just recently put in my platoon. They called him KO because he was a prize fighter at one time but had been in the Army quite a while during which time he had been busted several times, that means reduced in rank. When he didn't obey my order I told him to move on the double or he would be busted and his response was to go ahead and that it wouldn't be the first time. Captain Soumas was in the area and I walked over to him and told him I wanted Corporal Brown busted to a Private for insubordination and explained what had happened. Soumas got into his Peep and returned to the Orderly Room to have the First Sergeant draw up Reduction in Rank orders effective immediately. That was the first and only time I busted a man but I felt this was absolutely necessary to prevent any other acts of this nature. Fortunately, he was not only busted but he was removed from my platoon.

A rather unusual experience occurred when we were making one of our road marches and arrived at Stonehenge the Ancient Unsolved Mystery of these huge stone blocks. Not many people can say they visited Stonehenge in a Tank, which I frequently mention in appropriate conversations. Since this was not a guided tour we did not learn much about the history of this unbelievable structure, but the impression it made on me still lingers in my memory.

It was during the third week at Tidworth when I received orders sending me to London to attend a briefing at the British Tank and Tech School where I was to learn the operation of German vehicles and weapons. I still have the tiny notebook I carried and though the pencilled notations have faded, I can still read them and I quote "Wear – class "A" uniform, carry – fatigues, gas mask, steel helmet, note book and necessary toilet articles. Rear Div. Hq. 0815 Sunday." So at 0815 Sunday I arrived at the rear of Division Headquarters along with some other officers to be transported to London where, according to my faithful little notebook we reported to the "Billeting Office at the Washington House." I couldn't help but recall that after leaving Washington, D.C., traveling thousands of miles over more than two years, I am billeted in the Washington House in London. We received our meals at the Casual Officers Mess which was in a huge hall, and as usual, I enjoyed the food there. After breakfast the next morning we were taken to the school and entered a large warehouse type building containing many German vehicles and surprisingly, a couple of American vehicles, one being a Sherman Tank. I would soon learn the reason for that Sherman Tank being a part of the exhibit and to say it caused me some concern would be a gross understatement.

The Sherman Tank was the subject of our opening discussion led by an American officer who called our attention to the two gaping holes, one in the hull, the other in the turret. He stated that the entire crew was wiped out, two killed and three injured, facts that I could have easily done without. Having already ruined my day, he then directed us to the area where the German tanks were located. My notebook reminds me of among other things, that the Panther MV weighed 45 tons, with a 690 HP engine, with a speed of 30 MPH, and here it comes, the Tiger II weighed 66 tons, front armor of 6" and armed with a high velocity 88mm gun which knocked out the Sherman we just saw. There are other features in my little book but the more I knew the worse I felt. The instructor mentioned some of the vulnerable spots of the Panther, the Mark IV, and V and none for the Tiger but it appeared to me its suspension system was almost totally exposed and a shot in that area could possibly disable it. A great deal of the discussion was of a technical nature but very little about how to operate the vehicles, which I thought was the main purpose for our being there. A little later I was to form a different opinion.

At the end of the day we were dropped off at the Officers Mess and had another good dinner. While we were eating, the air raid sirens were sounded and I am wondering where the nearest shelter was when it dawned on me that an air raid shelter symbol was on the front door of the Officers Mess. In a little while the "all clear" sounded and we decided it was time to walk back to the Washington House. As we left we asked an air raid warden if there had been an attack and he told us a "buzz bomb" had passed overhead and landed on the outskirts of town. He also explained that the reason why the Officers Mess was designated as an air raid shelter was because it was downstairs and below grade with several floors above it.

The following day was devoted to discussions of enemy weaponry and ammunition, starting with the smaller caliber guns. He made a point about the 20 mm gun which was belt fed, used only tracer bullets that could not be used in the American 20 mm gun. This was not of particular interest to me since our tanks had no 20 mm guns. When we got to the larger weapons he began to emphasize their capabilities and reminded us that the knocked out Sherman we saw was a victim of their 88 mm and the same fate awaited any Sherman tank that might encounter this deadly weapon.

That night after dinner as we were walking back to our "digs" I spotted a window display and walked over just to satisfy my curiosity. While I was standing there a "Lady of the Evening" approached me and asked if I would like to have a party. Naturally, I declined and was a bit surprised because this wasn't a district where you would normally find that kind of activity. I hurried to catch up to the others who thought the incident was funny.

The next couple of days we kind of repeated the previous two days and I was beginning to get the message, that these were the types of equipment we would soon be faced with and we should be sure our people are aware of it. No effort was made to show us how to operate these instruments of death but only to demonstrate how effective they were. The sessions seemed to be winding down and the final two afternoons we were dismissed early giving us some time to wander about.

I went in this enormous department store which I believed was called Harrods but I am not sure. I went from counter to counter just browsing for nothing in particular when I came to the jewelry section. I felt that I was way out of my element since a Second Lieutenant's salary didn't justify my presence in the jewelry department of this very fine store. Nevertheless, a beautiful pearl necklace caught my eye so I leaned over the showcase to try to read the price tag, which of course was in pounds. After a quick mental conversion to dollars I knew I must have figured wrong because I could afford the amount I came up with. Suddenly a sales lady appeared and asked me if I would like to see that necklace which she was already removing from the case. She placed it on a velvet pad making it look even more beautiful, and I could just picture it around Gracie's neck. I still wasn't certain that I had figured the price right so I asked her and she told me in American dollars, which they would accept. Expressing surprise at the price, I was told that the store had received a number of items to settle an estate and this was a terrific bargain. She said they would be happy to ship it home for me which sounded like a good deal, so Gracie had herself a lovely pearl necklace. I still have it but the last time I saw it, the pearls were lying loose in a jewelry box because the string broke and they were never re-strung. Some day I would like to have them appraised because I have never known whether I was "ripped off" or not.

Friday would be our last day at the school and I would have to say it was very interesting but learning that my tank was not the finest in the world left me with some rather disturbing thoughts. Do our guys want to know that we would be at a serious disadvantage if we had a head to head confrontation with certain weapons and tanks the enemy would be using against us? Depending upon what my orders might be, if I were called upon to conduct a discussion on the subject I would touch on those features which might be considered superior to ours, but the availability of our artillery and air support would more than offset any advantage the enemy might have. I was confident that our training and thorough knowledge of our jobs would guarantee our ability to eliminate any obstacle to the completion of our mission. This was what I truly believed, in spite of the annoying things we were told at this school.

When they came to pick us up Saturday morning we were told that we were going on a quick motor tour of London, which was a real treat. We were able to catch glimpses of Westminster Abbey, Buckingham Palace, and a few other landmarks of that ancient city. Along the way we passed areas that had come under heavy bombing attacks leaving them just huge piles of rubble. You couldn't help but admire the toughness of these people who had endured so much. Later in the day we started our drive back to Tidworth where we would continue our preparation for the move to continental Europe and an uncertain future.

My first day back was filled with lots of questions and a lengthy discussion with Captain Soumas who inquired about what information I had gathered from the course and my opinion of how it might benefit the men. I gave him my thoughts as I have written them here and that the matter should be handled very delicately so as not to add to any stress the men might have about going into combat. An indication of their concern came out when the people came to paint the names on our tanks. Back in the States, the Tank Commanders were permitted to name their tanks, which had to start with the letter "A" because we were "A" Company. I had decided on "Angel Maker" for my tank, the idea being that it would make angels of the enemy. However, now that it was time to put the names on the new tanks, my crew asked me not to name our tank "Angel Maker" for fear it might make angels of them. With combat getting nearer, this type of thinking is obviously present on the minds of many of the men, so naturally, I wanted a comfortable crew so I changed the name of our tank to "At Ease" and they said that was much better. This incident convinced me that the comments I made to the Company Commander were most appropriate. Strangely, there was never anything more said about what we learned at the British Tank Tech School, but I felt that I benefited from it because I learned a new respect for the enemy tanks and weapons, and that is healthy as long as it doesn't create any anxiety.

As our daily routine was designed to fine-tune our readiness to cross the channel, rumors began to circulate as to when we would depart and where we were going. The answer came soon because on September 28 we were told that the next day we would be leaving Tidworth but we still did not know what our destination was. We bid a fond farewell to Tidworth on the 29th, and as we drove our tanks through some quaint little towns, we were greeted by people waving, giving us the victory sign or thumbs up, which reflected the spirit of optimism that was so much a part of these morally strong people. It took nearly the whole day to reach an area near the port of Portland where we camped for the night. The next day was spent loading our tanks on LSTs, which stands for Landing Ship Tanks, where we spent the night sitting in the harbor. On board there were officer's sleeping quarters which the crew turned over to us giving us a very comfortable night's sleep. The ship set sail early the next morning, and as is typical for a crossing of the English Channel, it was very rough and we had to wait for the tide to be right so we could land on the Normandy Beach where that bloody invasion took place nearly four months earlier.

Chapter 8

CLOSER AND CLOSER

As our LST reached the beach, she dropped her loading ramp right at a roadway built by the engineers to unload vehicular cargo. So, at 0230 we drove our tanks down the ramp on to the road and headed inland. Although it was dark we could see some of the shadowy grotesque remains of the destroyed landing craft and equipment from that devastating invasion. When you thought of the great sacrifice made by many of our troops, you almost felt like you were riding over sacred ground. We drove for about 30 minutes when we were led to a very large camping area where we would stay while the division got organized and prepared for a long cross country drive. The weather was miserable, wet and chilly as is usual in the early fall in northern France and living in tents only added to our discomfort. Also, uncharacteristically I developed a severe sore throat, which I endured for several days and then went to the dispensary for some relief. There they swabbed my throat and gave me a small box of Clorets, which was the extent of my treatment for the sore throat. For a while it was extremely painful just to swallow food and water, but it slowly improved and in a few days I felt like I might live after all.

It seemed rather strange that we would spend about twelve days just sitting there, but as we would find out later the allied armies had moved so rapidly after the break-out that they had out-run their supply lines, and had to hold up while they stock-piled enough supplies and replenished their fuel and ammunition dumps before they could move on. We had noticed that the Red Ball Express — that is what they called the fleet of vehicles carrying material to the front — was running day and night and long tank columns on the road would seriously delay those much-needed supplies.

It was about the middle of October when the roads were cleared enough that we could start our drive toward the combat zone. The first day we covered nearly 90 miles in almost twelve hours, frequently checking the new tanks for any malfunction of all the working parts. This was important because although they were road tested while we were in England, this gave us the chance to observe how well they performed over an extended period of time. I believe all of us agreed that our tanks earned a grade of A+ on all counts. Each day we covered between 70 and 90 miles in 10 to 12 hours. One day we saw that our route was to take us into Paris and we all had seen pictures of the greetings the troops before us had received from the grateful Parisians with flowers, cognac, cookies, and hugs and kisses. Unfortunately we arrived in Paris about 2300 hours and the streets were totally deserted and dark, so we moved through town without even slowing down for a friendly wave, which we found a bit disappointing to say the least. They call Paris the city of lights but not that night. Each day brought us a little closer to the enemy lines and we noticed an increasing amount of debris along the roadside as we made our way through central France.

After the fifth day on the road we started to shorten the distances traveled each day to 25 to 50 miles and for some unknown reason we took an irregular course into Luxembourg then back to Belgium and into Luxembourg again. We arrived at a little town of Weiswampach in Luxembourg and set up camp by a wooded area just outside of that small village. This was a short distance from the German lines and we would see an occasional artillery shell land in a nearby field which seemed to excite more than frighten the men. As we neared our destination Sid Moskowitz's tank fired a burst in the direction of Germany at nothing in particular and laid claim to being the first member of the 14th tank battalion to fire on the enemy. He got himself in the record for that and had it been me, I could hear old John Egan calling me a "showoff" again, but Sid didn't hesitate to mention it whenever he could squeeze it into the conversation. Why not!

Each night on the march from the beach we would pitch our tents and the next morning strike them, that means take them down, so by the time we arrived at this area we had become experts and quickly had our tents up before dark. Each platoon had been assigned a specific area in which to bivouac and since we were the third Platoon ours was the furthest from Company Headquarters and the kitchen which made it necessary for us to walk some distance for chow.

Although no one told us, we got the impression that we would remain here for an extended period. Soon the men started digging dugouts or building huts for greater warmth and comfort than the tents provided. My crew decided to build a log hut and told me they would like to go into town to try and find a stove. I didn't know where they thought they would locate a stove but I gave them some money to help them. Sure enough they came back with a neat little stove and a stove pipe and gave me my money back. I had learned not to ask questions when your men manage to obtain an item of necessity, especially since I was to be one of the occupants of Miller's Mansion. I never ceased to be amazed by the ingenuity of the American Soldier, which I may have mentioned before, but the finished product was unbelievable. They had made two built-in double-decker bunks and one single bunk for the Lieutenant, installed the stove with the pipe going out the side and tacked a piece of sheet metal on the wall behind the stove. Then they hung a shelter half, which is half a pup tent, over the doorway to keep out the cold. Once they got started they did all of this in just over a week and it was really quite comfortable, a lot better than sleeping on the ground. The five of us lost no time in moving in. They with their sleeping bags and me with my bedroll. The men carried a sleeping bag, one blanket and a shelter half which combined with their buddy's would make a pup tent that they shared and would each get in his sleeping bag and use the two blankets for cover. My bedroll consisted of the canvas cover, a G.I. comforter, two blankets and a sleeping bag which when rolled up was so big, some people suspected I had brought Gracie along.

Since this activity kept the Company busy for almost two weeks our daily routine called for roll call, breakfast, lunch and mail call, then dinner. After one of the meals each day the Captain would give an informal briefing to the Company during which he would bring us up to date on the War news which seemed to be at a stand-still in the European Theater. He also said that we would be firing our tank guns and told the officers we should brush up on the procedure for indirect fire and calling in a fire mission from a forward observation post. All of the tanks were lined up at the edge of the wooded area near the Company Headquarters and would be fired from their present position. We had several dry runs of a fire mission as a refresher before the actual shooting.

In the meantime, this particular night I had just crawled into my sleeping bag when I felt something move near my feet. Well, I came out of there like I was shot out of a cannon and shook my sleeping bag to get rid of whatever it was. Sure enough it was a little mouse that dropped on the ground and scooted out the doorway. I didn't think much of it but 47 or 48 years later at a reunion I mentioned the incident and a couple of the guys looked at each other and started laughing. During all those years I never once thought of the possibility that some one had put that mouse in my sleeping bag and, of course, when I asked, they knew nothing about it but the laughing continued and I was convinced that was exactly what had happened. My next letter to Gracie contained the story of the mouse in my bedroll but I assured her she had nothing to worry about because the mouse was a male and again I hoped my feeble effort to be funny would amuse her.

One morning we woke up to three inches of snow on the ground which would have been pretty except for the fact we had to trudge a couple of hundred yards to get breakfast. After breakfast the Captain said there would be a fire mission that afternoon so we had the crews mount their tanks to fire up the engines making sure the batteries were fully charged, the radios were operating properly and the gun sights were clean and ready to go. You really had to hold tight while climbing up a snow covered tank because it was so slippery. While this was going on Soumas came up and told me that I was to go up and be the forward observer to call in the fire mission. Officers from one of the Ninth Armored artillery batteries would supervise the firing and be with me at the observation post. After lunch one of the Company Peeps took me to a little village closer to the front line and as we rode along, I couldn't help but admire the beauty of the snow-covered countryside. There was a little church in this village where we stopped and proceeded up the steps to its bell tower.

Now for some time this had been considered a quiet front with an occasional shell dropping in the field near our camp and presumably our artillery fired a round in response, so we didn't want to initiate a major campaign at this point. Imagine my excitement when I looked through my binoculars and saw an encampment of German soldiers less than a mile away. It was time to check the map for the coordinates of our target and determine exactly where we wanted the shell to land. The artillery officers said it would be better to overshoot rather than undershoot because our lack of experience in indirect firing might result in hitting civilians or friendly troops. I then called "Able Company – Fire Mission" and identified the target, gave the map coordinates plus 500 yards, waited 60 seconds and ordered "Fire when ready." Shortly we saw the "hit" beyond the people we had observed who quickly ran for cover and I called "A" Company back, reported "good shot – end of mission – out." In a few minutes, as we were packing up, our location was hit by return fire and we rushed to get out of there in case we would be a target of an enemy barrage. This was to be expected because our location in that bell tower was a typical forward observation post and would often be fired on when a unit was the object of an artillery attack.

The next day I received word that the Catholic Chaplain would visit Company "A" so those of that religious persuasion could attend Mass, and being one of those, I was pleased with this opportunity for a little spiritual support. I was firmly convinced that I needed the help of our Supreme Being if I were to survive this war and would in many situations ask for His protection. He must have been listening or these words might never have been written. About 12 or 15 of us walked over to where the Chaplain was setting up just behind the line of tanks using the hood of his Peep for the altar. His driver was assisting him and just before he started Mass the Chaplain had us all bow our heads while he said a few prayers granting all of us General Absolution which means we could received Communion without going to Confession. As I understand it this is only granted during extreme emergencies. It was about half way through the Mass that I heard a fire mission coming through the radio of the tank right behind us. In a few minutes the directions to the target were transmitted ending with "fire when ready". I said to the Chaplain, "Excuse me Father, they are about to fire the gun of this tank and the concussion could upset the Chalice or the Cruets." His assistant picked up the Cruets and he held the Chalice and soon the gun was fired blowing the Altar Cloth but the heavy Missal kept it from falling off. This was such a wonderful experience and I sure felt good about attending this Mass celebrated in spite of the dark clouds of war hovering all around us.

It has been nearly a month since we made camp in this area and now we are to move to a nearby structure large enough to house our whole company. I guess it had been occupied by someone else when we first arrived at this location, which is why we didn't take it over before. We in the Third Platoon were especially glad because now we wouldn't have that long walk to chow or to work on our tanks and weapons. Also, at this time, the officers had to start censoring the men's outgoing mail and of course, we heard some grumbling about that. We were not permitted to mention location, any action by us or the enemy, or any casualties by either side that we knew of. The officers were required to use a razor blade and actually cut out of the letter any forbidden information. In order to avoid removing any other contents of the letter only one side of the paper could be used.

This building was a huge barn-like structure which had a number of separate rooms on the upper level, with a balcony overlooking a large open area of the first floor. The three platoon leaders occupied one of the rooms, the Captain and James another one and the non-comms took over the remaining rooms leaving the rest of the building for the others to bed down as they saw fit. There was a separate room on the first floor, which had a table and some chairs that the officers used for censoring, eating and writing. We spent whatever free time in this room, which came to be known as the office.

I don't know when they were able to put it together but it was announced that the men were going to put on a show and the officers were invited. The show consisted of some jokes and poems, none of which will be repeated here, some songs accompanied by a combo of a harmonica, the wind section, a ukulele, the string section and a G.I. can, the percussion section. It was interesting the amount of "music" they were able to punch out of those instruments and then there were the humorous skits to express their opinion of officers in general but none in particular, I hope. The guys got a lot of laughs and the affair was a real morale booster in light of the rather monotonous routine of their daily lives.

The officers also decided to play a little and we were invited to a party at the Battalion Headquarters but since I was not interested, I took Officer of the Day so the rest could attend. The party must have been a real "zinger" because some officers that I didn't know brought a very inebriated John Grimball back and dumped him at the doorway. I heard the commotion and went out to find him lying there with his shirt pulled up, exposing his back that was covered with a lot of nasty scratches. The walkway from the road to our building was made of broken rock, which was rough but better than walking through deep mud. They must have dragged Grimball over those rocks and his back was a mess. I managed to get him into our "office," sat him in a chair and leaned him forward to rest his head on the table. I got his shaving kit, a towel and some water, and cleaned off those scratches and just left him there to sleep it off. The next day he was one miserable lieutenant, and Sid was really enjoying John's misery. He was funny I have to admit.

Now it was my turn to enjoy a little change of pace. My Aunt Nettie was one of the aunts who lived with me before I got married and she had a son, General William Kean, a Staff Officer at First Army Headquarters. Whenever Aunt Nettie wrote me she would ask if I had seen Cousin William. She obviously did not know that there was a very wide separation between a General and a Second Lieutenant and my seeing him was a very unlikely event. Well, along comes this letter from dear Aunt Nettie informing me that Cousin William is in Spa, Belgium and he wanted me to make arrangements to visit him. I still wasn't sure that she had it right but I had to check it out. I went to our Battalion Headquarters and explained the situation to Lt. McLaughlin, the Adjutant, who said to hang around and he would try to confirm it. In a short while he said that General Kean was expecting me for lunch the next day and handed me a twelve-hour pass to Spa, Belgium for the 9th of December, which I still have.

At 0800 I set off in a Company Peep with driver and arrived at First Army Headquarters shortly before noon. The Sergeant at the desk was expecting me and told me to have a seat, that the General would be out soon. I knew it was no longer Cousin William but General Kean that I was visiting, so when he came out I stood up, saluted and said "Good morning, General." He returned my salute then extended his hand and we shook hands. He asked how I was doing and had I seen any action. I told him about receiving fire in that bell tower, otherwise the situation was rather quiet. He then introduced me to his Aide who he said would show me around. The Aide was in his freshly pressed uniform, shoes and brass highly polished and here I was just in from the field wearing my combat jacket and not too well pressed O.D. pants and shirt. He showed me where I could wash up and wanted to know about our living conditions. After I told him we managed to keep comfortable and as clean as possible, considering all the mud and limited washing facilities, he told me how lucky I was and wished that he could be with the men in the field. I thought, "come off of it man, you have it made," and I find it hard to believe that he preferred my situation to his. I did say that we all do what we have to do.

We walked into a large kind of reception room that I compared to the "office" we spent our spare time in. There was a telephone in the room and he got a call and I overheard him asking about various brands of liquor. When he finished he said that it was the Quartermaster in Paris calling about an order that the Generals had made. I again thought that this was a great way to fight a war. Finally it was time for lunch and we filed into the dining room which was set for about 25 officers. Cousin William came in and introduced me to several other Generals including General Hodges who was First Army Commander. I expected I would be seated a the very end because I was the only Second Lieutenant there but Cousin William had me sit next to him with his Aide on the other side of me. He said his mother wrote him about my letters to her, which she seemed to enjoy very much. It was mostly idle chatter and he didn't seem to want my ideas on how to win this war in

Some of these Generals were at the lunch that "Cousin William," General William B. Kean invited me to attend. General Kean is barely visible at the far left of the sencond row.

a hurry. When we finished lunch he spent some time showing me around then had to get to a meeting and said he enjoyed seeing me and wished me luck, shook hands and said goodbye. It was really neat having lunch with all that brass and seeing how they managed to survive the rigors of war. I informed the Aide that my pass required me to report back by 2000 hours so I had better be on my way. I thanked him for his help and he said he really enjoyed spending some time with me. We shook hands and I left to look for my driver who was nearby so off we went.

Little did I suspect that one week from that day we would be on the verge of the biggest American battle of the War and we would learn that none of the high ranking officers that I just had lunch with had any knowledge of what was to come, a fact that I found to be a serious breakdown of our intelligence capability. During all that period that we were kind of marking time, the enemy was building up a huge attack force of 20 divisions including eight armored divisions, concentrating on an area which was lightly held by the Allies in the Ardennes Forest.

A few days after my visit with Cousin William, we were told to be prepared to make a move which would take us some distance north of our present location, where we had lived the past six weeks. Many questions were asked about my visit and when I described the lunch and the people who attended there were those who wondered why I came back. I mentioned the officer who said I was lucky to be in the field and everyone within hearing distance volunteered to change places with him, which provided a few humorous moments. On the morning of 13 December 1944 we said "Auf Wiedersehn" to Weiswampach, and started northward on a mission which will long be remembered by the valiant members of Company "A."

Chapter 9

BATTLE OF THE BULGE — PART ONE

As we drove north, we were told that our mission was to proceed to the Roer River Dams above the town of Drieborn, Germany, where we would assist in the capture of those dams in order to prevent the enemy from blowing them up and flooding the valley, creating a geographic obstacle to the planned Spring offensive. The weather was damp and gray and there was a feeling of unrest in the atmosphere. Even the pace we set seemed to create a sense of uncertainty, making us wonder what was going to happen because we only covered about 24 miles the whole first day, according to the Battalion Log. The next day was pretty much the same and although there was no resistance, there was that sensation of danger giving you a chill, making that cold December day even colder.

That was the way things were until December 16 when the Battalion was advised that elements of the 106th Infantry Division, experiencing their first taste of combat, had run into trouble and to move the Battalion into the area of St. Vith, Belgium to aid the embattled troops. Once this was done we would resume our drive to the Roer River Dams and accomplish our original mission, the impression being that this was just a minor delay of no serious moment.

At 0300 hours on the morning of December 17, I was called to an officer's meeting where we were told one officer and a driver from each Company would take the Company Peep forward toward the enemy lines and establish assembly areas for our tanks, which would arrive later in the morning. As I came out of the building where the meeting was held, the sky in the direction of the enemy was just ablaze with flares intended to reveal the location of the troops of the 106th Division. Still, the situation was not seen as one of any magnitude, and the six officers and their drivers set out in their Peeps not knowing what lay ahead.

After about 45 minutes, we encountered a column of vehicles coming toward us but since all reports indicated that the Germans were just testing our defenses we did not assume these were enemy vehicles. Fortunately they were not, so we flagged them down to find out who they were and where were they going. The lead vehicle had a Master Sergeant so we asked him that question and he replied, "Sir, we are moving to the rear" and pointing to seven or eight vehicles behind him, said, "This is all that remains of our Battalion and I am the ranking officer. All the others have been killed, wounded or captured and we are getting out of here." With that he continued down the road, leaving us standing there thinking that the situation was far more serious than anyone had indicated because they simply did not know.

We found it somewhat discomforting that strong enemy forces were just a short distance away and we had six officers and six men armed with .30 caliber carbines to take on the whole German Army. Fortunately our tanks arrived just before dawn and were directed to their respective assembly areas to await further orders.

At 1220 on the 17th of December the first Platoon of "A" Company commanded by Lieutenant Grimball was ordered to support an attack by the infantry on the nearby town of Elcherath. Although he lost two of his five tanks, Grimball and the infantry team inflicted heavy casualties on the German infantry, capturing 87 prisoners. Later in the afternoon I was ordered to take my third Platoon into the town of St. Vith, which was presumed to be still in friendly hands. As always I was in the lead tank and as I approached the town it seemed to be completely deserted with only one person on a motorcycle in view at the far end of town.

I had been told that on the 16th of December the 7th Armored Division had been instructed to move to St. Vith, with its expected time of arrival to be the early morning of the 17th, but it was now nearing evening and they were not there yet. The reason given for their delay was the congested traffic caused by the refugees fleeing the beleaguered town.

While there, I came under a heavy barrage of artillery fire, with buildings collapsing all around causing me more concern about being blocked in by all the debris than being hit by an artillery shell. Finally I received word that elements of the 7th Armored were approaching the city from the other end, and I was ordered to pull out and return to base. I had always assumed that it was enemy fire that I was taking in St. Vith, but I sometimes wondered if that could have been the artillery of the 7th Armored Division laying down a field of fire as they neared the town. I never found out.

Just before dark, we were directed to a nearby wooded area where we might spend the night so we backed our tanks into the woods until just the muzzle of our guns stuck out facing the direction of the enemy. I was hopeful that we might get a little rest since my day started at 0300 that morning. Sleep was out of the question, because the situation was so fluid I wanted to stay on the radio for any orders to make a quick move. It was fortunate I did, because after several hours I heard something in the woods behind us and I yelled "Who goes there?" The response to my challenge was an immediate burst of machine gun or automatic rifle fire. I quickly radioed my Platoon that we were receiving small arms fire from the woods to our rear and to pull out so they could fire back into those woods. My greatest concern, especially at night, was that enemy troops would get close enough to fire their Panzerfausts, which almost all German infantrymen carried. The Panzerfaust was a single-shot weapon similar to our Bazooka, which could easily knock out a Sherman tank, and at night a man could crawl undetected to within range to hit his target. The Platoon responded immediately and began firing blindly into the woods and thwarted that attack against us.

Captain Soumas was some distance away but heard all the shooting and came on the radio to inquire what my situation was. I told him that the enemy had infiltrated the woods to my rear and opened fire on us but because visibility was so poor I could only fire in the general direction of the enemy. I asked for permission to move my tanks back far enough to prevent any more surprise attacks and he agreed. It was total darkness under a moonless, starless sky so we had to move very cautiously to avoid running into a ditch or other types of obstacles. The rest of the night was spent listening to artillery shells whistling over our heads not knowing whether they were coming or going but as long as they didn't stop I was grateful.

Just as it started to get light, "A" Company was ordered to move down the road a short distance just outside of a little town and set up a line of defense. The Captain wanted an inverted wedge with the Platoons on line, the First Platoon on the left, the Third Platoon on the right, the Second Platoon on center and fifty yards to the rear. I couldn't help but remember how often we performed these exercises back in the States and how smoothly we did it under combat conditions. While at that location we received some artillery fire and about mid-day we spotted a small infantry unit that retreated when we opened up on them with our .50 caliber machine guns. I thought they were either on patrol or spotting for their artillery, but whatever their mission, they now knew our position and we could expect some kind of attack. Since we represented a very light defense line with no backup we were ordered to move to another location.

Now let me explain what is the normal lineup for a Tank Company as it moves from place to place. As you know we are made up of three platoons so the First Platoon would lead followed by the Second Platoon with the Third Platoon bringing up the rear and since mine was the Third Platoon we could be the last to leave the area. You have probably figured out that when we are moving back, the unit in the rear is closest to the enemy and it was necessary for me to be alert to any attack from behind.

We had just driven a very short distance when it started to get dark and it was decided to pull to the side of the road hoping we could remain there for the night. I had my tanks turn around to face the direction of the enemy from where we had just come. It was well into the night, which was pitch black and we could hear cannon fire off in the distance but nothing coming in on us when all of a sudden we came under some heavy machine gun and rifle fire and a lot of yelling. I could not see a thing and again my concern was the ever-present Panzerfaust, so I gave my Platoon the order to turn around and move back. Captain Soumas, obviously hearing all the racket, gave the order for "A" Company to proceed down the road and since they were facing in the right direction did not have to turn around as I did. I had ordered my Platoon to turn to the left so we all would be making the same turn and not running into each other trying to get back on the road. As my tank was making its turn we ran into some power lines that caught me right under my chin but I was able to grab them and raise the wires over my head to avoid being hung. As if I weren't having enough trouble with the enemy I had to fight to keep these low hanging wires from lynching me. Along side of the road where we had stopped were the usual power lines and a nearby pole must have been knocked over causing the wires to droop but not visible to me because of the extreme darkness. I was also fortunate that the power had been cut off and these were not live wires or not only could I have been hung, I might have been electrocuted also. Somebody up there was certainly watching over me making this literary effort possible.

By this time I was really getting fed up with these guys sneaking up on me during these very dark nights, which place tankers at a serious disadvantage. The day time action was even worse because of the tremendous numbers being thrown at us forcing us to fight, draw back, regroup, fight and so on creating confusion in the ranks of the enemy. The fact that they were able to build up this attack force of twenty divisions to face a thin defense line of five divisions with the element of surprise in their favor required the allies to execute these delaying tactics while our high command put together a plan for a counter attack. On one occasion, after we had spent a good part of the day at a certain location, "A" Company was ordered to pull out and drop back but the Third Platoon was told to remain in position to cover the Company's withdrawal. I was also told that some of our infantry would be coming out of a wooded area to my right front and I should cover them as well. In a few minutes off in the distance to my left front I picked up what appeared to be a Sherman Tank just cresting a small hill. Since I wasn't sure, I radioed Captain Soumas and asked him to identify that tank for me, and he radioed back that it was a friendly tank. Shortly some of our infantry started pulling out of the woods and to my surprise, that "friendly" tank opened fire on them. I quickly notified the Captain and he repeated "that is a friendly tank, do not open fire". Just at that moment I heard a loud "bang" followed by a much louder explosion from one of my tanks that had been hit by the "friendly" tank and Sergeant Connell in spite of my order to hold fire, returned fire and knocked out the "friendly" tank — problem solved. I never reprimanded Sergeant Connell for disobeying my order because if someone is trying to kill you, you had better take some action and he did. Although he was still able to move, his tank was damaged and had to be pulled off the line for repairs leaving me with four tanks.

There was another situation where "A" Company was ordered to move out and the Third Platoon was again told to remain in position to cover them. The road that we had earlier driven to reach our present location had a sharp curve at just about the place we made our recent stand so I and probably some others trained our guns on that curve in case any enemy vehicles should come around it. Each time we made a move the Germans evidently miscalculated the distance of our withdrawal and would meet up with us earlier than they had anticipated causing them to delay their plan of attack. Apparently that was the case when this German command car came barreling around that curve and was met with a volley of cannon fire from my tank and several others of my platoon. The vehicle completely disintegrated along with its four passengers. The German command car was used by the higher-ranking officers, so at least two of the occupants had to be officers. I will never forget seeing one of the "great coats" they wore fly up into the air and drape itself over the power lines that ran beside the road.

What happened next you won't believe but I am prepared to take an oath on everything that is holy that this is the truth. As I mentioned, my platoon had remained behind to cover the withdrawal of the rest of the Company when after the action I just described I received a radio call from the Captain saying, "We have just run into some trouble up here. The Third Platoon will withdraw and move to the head of the column at two zero miles per hour". You got to be kidding. I stay back to protect their rear and get into a fight with a German command car which offered no resistance and now they run into trouble so I am to take the lead at two zero miles an hour. Now back then two zero miles per hour was the maximum speed for the Sherman tank because driving faster than that puts you in danger of throwing a track especially if you had to turn placing additional stress on the track. This is what I said to my driver, "driver, pull out, move to the head of the column and if you can't get four zero out of this thing get out of there and I will drive". He moved down the road past our tanks at four zero miles per hour.

Shortly after passing the head of the column I saw in the distance a fork in the road causing me to slow down while I decided which way to go. One way was into enemy territory, the other takes me to our rear, either way would require a slight turn so a slow down was necessary. I said a quick Hail Mary then gave the driver the order to bear left, wondering what I might run into. No sooner had we made the turn when I spotted through my binoculars some soldiers lying in the ditch beside the road, their rifles pointed in my direction. We slowed a little more and finally one of the men stood up and waved both hands in a friendly manner. Since my recent experience with a "friendly" tank, I was a little leery of this situation but as I drew closer I knew they were some of our guys from the 27th Armored Infantry Battalion who had pulled back before we did and set up here to fight the same kind of delaying action that I described earlier.

Another situation developed when "A" Company received orders to make our way just outside of a little town nearby where we would meet a unit of the 82nd Airborne Division. It seems they had been driven out of that town the night before and we were to assist them in retaking the town. Captain Soumas called his officers together to discuss his plan of action, which was to approach the town with the First Platoon on the left flank, the Second Platoon on the right flank and the Third Platoon in the center to make the frontal attack. Then he said he had forgotten that the Third Platoon only had four tanks so it would take the right flank and the Second Platoon the center. I mention this situation as an example of how plans are frequently changed on the spur of the moment as you will soon see.

We started out to the place where we would link up with this Company of the 82nd Airborne but our progress was slow because it had snowed pretty hard and it was freezing cold making the road very slippery. Going through a little town the road suddenly went down a rather steep hill and I could see ahead one of the Second Platoon tanks got sideways and slid out of control down the hill and crashed into a stone house, which was built right up to the road as many were. As I passed the tank its crew had dismounted to assess the damage, which apparently was sufficient to disable the vehicle. When descending an icy hill in a tank you put it in low gear and keep a little power on so the tracks will keep rolling and you can steer the tank by gently moving the levers. What the driver of the crashed tank must have done was to pull hard on the levers, locking the tracks making the tank a sled without any steering mechanism.

When we reached our "line of departure" we found the men of the 82nd waiting and the Captain again called us together and said since the Second Platoon had now lost a tank we would revert to Plan "A" which had my platoon making

Troops on the way to Bastogne, December 19, 1944. The wet, dreery conditions are evident in this photo.

the frontal attack with Moskowitz on my right. See what I mean by sudden changes and to me this made no sense at all having one platoon with just four tanks change places with another platoon because it just had four tanks. Go figure. Anyway we got all the tanks in the proper formation and with as many Airborne as we could get on the tanks we started across country down a hill toward the little village ahead. The men that couldn't get on a tank walked behind in attack mode with fixed bayonets. There was a sergeant riding on my tank standing right behind me and said "you get us back in the town. Lieutenant, and we'll hold it this time". I told him that was our intention and wished him good luck. I had planned to lay down a field of fire but there was nothing to shoot at which I found a bit puzzling because we were within 100 yards of some buildings. This is about where we were told to leave them off but remain, to cover their entry into town. I really felt sorry for those guys as I watched them slog through the snow toward an unseen enemy and disappear behind the houses of this little town.

I noticed the other tanks starting to move back but I had not heard any orders to leave so I radioed Soumas to find out if I had missed his order. Using our code names I said "Greek this is Bingo, over" and all I heard was a click. Just then, to my great surprise, at the far end of this town, a tank slowly emerged from behind the buildings moving across my front from left to right. I quickly switched from radio to intercom and said "gunner-tank-A.P. direct front-300 yards-fire". I no sooner said fire than he got off a round, which meant he must have already had a shell in the breach of the gun. I had my glasses on the target and saw that he got a hit, which stopped the tank and I could see some of the crew abandoning it. I knew we had hit the suspension system, which must have disabled it and its electrical system, because it did not catch fire but none of its guns fired nor did its turret move. Because of my trip to London I knew at that moment that again I had received protection from above. There before me was that feared Tiger Tank with its long barreled 88 gun silenced by this miraculous stroke of good fortune because its commander presented its broadside to me, obviously unaware of my presence and the very quick and lucky shot my gunner was able to get off. We couldn't be that good — or could we?

Two American infantrymen in front of a disabled German Tiger tank, Battle of the Bulge.

Now another problem faced me since I was not able to receive any response to my radio call to the Captain. I called again and again all I could hear was a click. We were in a kind of a valley and I wondered if I was in a dead space that interfered with my reception. I thought that click might mean that my calls were getting through but when Soumas pushed his mike button to respond all I got was that click so I called again and said "Greek this is Bingo. I am unable to receive you but believe I hear the click of your mike button. I heard no order to return so if I am to return push the mike button twice if not push it once. Over". Imagine my relief when I heard two clicks signaling me to return to base to which I replied "Greek this is Bingo. I received two clicks so am pulling out. Wilco and out". And we lost no time getting out of there. When we returned to the top of the hill I was able to receive radio messages so I felt that my guess was right about what caused the problem.

I must tell you about another incident that happened so you will understand the many situations that occur when you are in combat. Company "A" had set up a defensive line in an open field with some of our infantry nearby, some using the tanks for cover. A couple of the men dragged a wounded comrade behind my tank to await a medic. I then received a call from Sergeant Weaver who said he had a "stiff G.I." on the rear deck of his tank. I told him I would see if the medics would remove him knowing that the medics do not normally remove the dead. Pretty soon "A" Company was ordered to move back to a new location. All the tanks immediately fired up their engines and the men behind my tank started screaming not to move my tank using several expletives to describe my tank. I yelled back that I would wait till the medics arrived and ordered the Third Platoon to remain in place until the dead and wounded were removed. The medics soon arrived and I told one of them about the man on Weaver's tank and he told me that they weren't supposed to do that but he would take care of it anyway. No wonder they were called "Angels of Mercy" because they sure were. Most of my tanks had some of the "doughs" on them and the two who had helped their wounded buddy climbed on my tank and I gave the order to my platoon to move out and we soon caught up to the rest of the Company.

About the 23rd of December it seemed the whole battalion was on the move with "A" Company bringing up the rear and our progress was very slow as though the lead elements were just feeling their way along. Then it was late in the evening that we started out and again we were bringing up the rear. Some hours later in the night we came to a halt and I could hear a lot of gunfire and see frequent gun flashes at the front of the column. We were pretty much road bound and there wasn't much we could do but sit there and wonder if all that action would get to us. I was visited by one of the men from another platoon and I wondered why he came to me. He asked if there wasn't something we could do to get out of this mess, which had become a hopeless logjam. I told him we were stuck there and wouldn't be able to move until the situation ahead had been cleared up which I knew nothing about. He suggested that we just leave our tanks and walk away from this problem and I told him he better get back to his tank and I would try to forget what he had said. It was quite a while before things quieted down and we could resume our efforts to get out of there. I heard later that the whole 14th Tank Battalion was attempting to disengage itself from the enemy and ran into an unexpected ambush, which caused the leading elements some rather heavy losses. Fortunately "A" Company was far enough back that we didn't get hurt.

The next day during a short break I found out for the first time that a couple of days earlier, Moskowitz's Platoon Sergeant Humphrey had been killed by sniper fire while riding in his tank. Captain Soumas was very upset and he cautioned his Tank Commanders not to ride so high in the turret. I don't believe any of them rode very high because in addition to being dangerous, we were experiencing some tremendously bitter cold, which felt even colder riding up in that turret. The weather had been miserable ever since this battle started back on December 16, which kept the planes grounded leaving us with no air support the entire period.

I can remember early on in the fighting, something happened that indicated how quickly you can become battle hardened. I received a call to come up to this nearby house where Soumas had set up his company headquarters and I had to walk by a small wooded area. There at the edge of the woods lay a dead American soldier and as I glanced down at him I couldn't help but think under normal conditions I would be very upset but I just kept on walking knowing that if you let such things upset you, you would soon lose the mental toughness necessary to carry on.

When I reached the house I found the rest of the "A" Company officers plus some from the Battalion Headquarters Company imbibing in a bit of "bottled courage". Although they knew I didn't drink they offered me some which I declined. The Battalion Surgeon was there and he had some pills that he said would help me stay awake. I told him that with all of the action we were having, staying awake was no problem. My problem was getting some sleep. He kind of chuckled and since there was nothing there for me I returned to my platoon.

This photo shows American infantry entering a Belgian town under the protection of a tank, September, 1944.

Chapter 10

THE BATTLE OF THE BULGE — PART TWO

Still trying to break off contact with the enemy, we traveled all that day and well into the night until we seemed to be out of artillery range. It was dark and we were told to pull to the side of the road to rest a while but stay on the radio. We had not seen our kitchen since December 16 so when possible we would open one of the various rations we had, "C", "D", "K" or whatever. I decided I would try to eat something and yelled to the guys in the turret to hand me a can of "C" rations which happened to be "Beef Stew". You can imagine how delicious a can of cold beef stew tasted with the temperature well below freezing, standing up in the turret of a tank. I opened the can and poured the stew into my canteen cup, which made it a little easier to eat rather than out of the "C" ration can. It actually was so cold it hardly had any flavor but it was nourishment so I ate it. When I finished, not being able to wash the cup, I slipped the canteen back into the cup and returned them to the canteen cover.

I must have been operating on an adrenalin rush for the past eight days because with a little lull in the action I was feeling really beat. I raised the lower seat of the Tank Commander's position, sat down, put my face in my hands and shortly I saw Gracie's face. Then we were watching a movie at the Theater in De Ridder, Louisiana. Was I losing it, having hallucinations, what was happening to me, then I realized just that quickly I had dozed off and started to dream. Standing up again, I shook my head to clear the cobwebs and felt grateful that my mind was clear and I was not having any visions. The radio was quiet and I poked my head out of the turret to listen for any movement. I pulled one earplug out of my ear so I could hear better and noticed it was all bloody and so was my ear. Those of us in the tanks who wore the steel helmet had to use earphones that plugged into our ears. The earphones were connected by a thin metal band that looped over the head from one ear to the other, and when the helmet was put on, it pushed down on the metal band which pushed down on the earplugs, putting pressure on the edge of the ears. For over a week I rarely removed my earplugs even when I had to leave the tank. It was quicker to just unplug the earphone plug from the outlet on the wall of the turret, as a result the constant bouncing up and down caused a severe irritation in my ears finally drawing blood. From then on I put the earplugs in with the headband underneath my chin so that my sore ears could heal.

While I was doing all this I could hear gunfire in the distance to our rear and wondered if the enemy were moving closer. Just as it started to get a little light, our fuel trucks arrived and the men got busy with the much-needed gasoline. Normally the fuel trucks would find a place giving them some cover and the tank crews would have to go get these five-gallon cans and carry them to the tanks but we must have been far enough from the enemy so they could bring the trucks closer to our tanks. When the refueling was finished we got the order to "wind 'em up" and prepare to move out.

I was very relieved that we were moving away from the cannon fire I had heard earlier because I knew that our guys had taken just about all they could handle. Some of them were just shaking all over from the cold and exhaustion that they had endured for so many days. Later in the morning they called for a rest stop to have a smoke or to answer natures call but since I had none of those urges I elected to stay on my radio. In a few minutes I felt a tug on my pants leg and the loader said "Would you like a cup of hot coffee Lieutenant?" Naturally I knew he was kidding and if I said "yes", he would probably say "so would I" or something smart like that so I just said "oh yeah, sure". When he said "well, hand me your canteen cup" I was really worried thinking this man has really lost it but I decided to go along with him rather than risk aggravating his condition so I reached for my canteen cup which still had some residue from my beef stew in it but I figured it wouldn't matter to him. I handed my cup down to him and miracle of miracles in a minute he handed me back a cup of steaming hot coffee. Even now when I tell about the incident, I say it was the best cup of coffee I have ever had even with peas and carrots floating around in it and so hot it burned my throat. I just felt it was Heaven sent.

Now I have to tell you what happened. There is a very strict regulation in the Armored Force that if you want to smoke, you dismount from your tank and move at least ten feet away before lighting up because of the fumes from the high octane gas and all the ammunition carried in the tank creates a real safety hazard. Each tank is equipped with a small Coleman stove to be used if the situation would permit you to get out and heat some "C" rations or whatever. What this man did was light that stove right in the turret of the tank and heat the water for the instant coffee from one of our rations. He could have blown us all up but these guys are so smart that he offered the Lieutenant the first cup so he wouldn't be turned in for breaking the regulations. That is the true story of the best cup of coffee I have ever had.

The rest of the day we kept moving back and I hoped we were putting some distance between ourselves and the enemy. However as it started to get dark we were ordered to pull up to the side of the road but the situation was still fluid enough that we were unable to pitch our tents and set up a bivouac area. While we were able to get a little rest, even before we had full daylight, we got our marching orders so off we went. There were several rest stops and just about noon we were halted and were greeted by a beautiful sight. There was our kitchen truck and the kitchen crew was busy preparing our first hot meal in ten days. The fuel trucks also pulled up and the tankers eagerly refueled the tanks so they would be ready for "Chow Time". I had a chance to talk briefly with the other officers all of whom were as exhausted as I was but also looking forward to a hot dinner. It then dawned on me that Christmas had come and gone unnoticed by most including myself. This was the 26 of December and I realized that I received the best cup of coffee that I ever had, on Christmas day. As the men lined up there seemed to be a renewed spirit among them because they were about to enjoy a wonderful Christmas dinner consisting of turkey with dressing and gravy, mashed potatoes, peas and carrots (not in their coffee), green beans, rolls, coffee (without peas and carrots), and cake. The hot water for washing the mess gear was already prepared so I walked over

Troops of the 9th Armoured Division prepare to evacuate Sherman tanks that had been knocked out in the American counter-attack on the German drive near Bastogne, Belgium.

and dunked my canteen cup to get rid of whatever remained of my beef stew. Being the Mess Officer, I waited until all had gone through the chow line and then I went. The Mess Sergeant was standing behind the servers and I told him what a wonderful meal they had prepared even though I had not had mine yet.

Then a funny thing happened. Since the sun had been out for two full days, the ground was dry and the men could sit there near the kitchen truck and the officers located convenient places to set their mess kits but after I had my mess kit and cup filled, without even thinking, I just kept on walking about fifty feet away from everything and then I sat on the ground alone. I have never been able to explain it even to myself but I sat there looking across the hilly fields, feeling the warmth of this rare sunshine and enjoying this most delicious Christmas dinner on December 26. It just seemed so peaceful and quiet as though somebody had stopped the war just so we could have this wonderful meal without wondering if that next artillery shell had our name on it. I was so grateful for the opportunity to savor the moment that I had to turn my eyes heavenward and say "thank you." When I finished eating, I walked back to face reality and dip my mess gear into the three containers of boiling water but there seemed to be an atmosphere of calm that had overtaken the whole Company. There was much talk about the great meal and how the hot food, the hot coffee and the sun seemed to take away the shivering that the severe cold had inflicted on all of us. The morale level must have jumped twenty points proving the saying that I believe Napoleon made that "an army travels on its stomach."

Captain Soumas said we would be moving further back in about 30 minutes, so I walked over to the kitchen truck where they had already packed up and were ready to move out before the tanks did. I told the crew again what a good job they had done then they took off for a little town about 10 miles away where Soumas had told us we would spend the night in some vacant buildings. Soon we mounted up and headed on down the road hardly believing that we were not getting shot at for the first time since it all started back on December 17.

After arriving at this little village that really appeared to be deserted, we had to wait while assignments to the billets were made by the officers of our Service Company. The men were put into the larger buildings and we three Platoon leaders got this small abandoned house that wasn't much more than a storage shed but it had a roof, four walls and a floor which provided room for our bedrolls. The kitchen had prepared a light meal and then Soumas had a meeting with all the Tank Commanders. He said that the next few days the Battalion would be making short drives stopping at places like this one where we could bed down at night. Apparently no thought had been given to setting up any kind of security and I wasn't about to make the suggestion. He said breakfast was planned for 0630 hours and we would probably leave about 0800 and with that dismissed us so we could get our first nights sleep in a long time. I don't know how long I had been asleep when I was suddenly awakened by the unmistakable creaking of tank tracks, and wondered if they were ours or enemy tanks. Then I thought the heck with it and I just laid there unable to go back to sleep. I found out the next morning that those were fresh troops moving to the front replacing those of us who had borne the brunt of that massive German offensive.

Soumas was right about the short drives as one of them was only eight miles for one hour from 1630 hours to 1730 hours. I got the impression that we were just keeping out of the way of the units moving forward so as not to create any traffic problems that might slow down their advance. A rather pleasant event occurred when we met up with one of the Red Cross Clubmobiles and the column halted to permit the men to grab some donuts and hot coffee. I got some too and it was the only time we would ever see one of those trailer trucks.

It was New Years Eve when we reached the outskirts of a little village and we parked our tanks on the side of a hill just across the road from a house that the Captain took over for his headquarters. Naturally, he had the kitchen set up right next to the house and we were able to eat inside. Soumas announced that a few days earlier the kitchen had butchered a cow and the Company would have steak for New Years Day dinner. He also said he had invited the Battalion Staff Officers to join us, ever the politician looking to make points with the brass.

New Years Day we had mail call for the first time since before the attack and many of us received packages intended for Christmas and of course there was one from Gracie. The box was badly beat up but the contents were in pretty good shape which included the traditional fruit cake, several boxes of cookies, some candy canes and the usual razor blades, soap, toothpaste and shaving cream. There was also a letter in the box dated December 1, 1944 and more recent letters at that mail call. She told me how much she enjoyed my letters and was glad to know that I was safe and in no danger. I was glad she did not know what the last two weeks were like but she would find out soon enough if she didn't already know. At breakfast I noticed that a rather large pit had been dug near the kitchen truck so I asked Woodward what it was for. He told me that was how they were going to cook the steaks and showed me this large piece of heavy metal mesh to grill the steaks on. He would use these briquettes, which were blocks of compressed coal, to cook them over and in spite of my curiosity I didn't ask how he acquired this stuff. I did know that many people in that part of the Country used those briquettes for cooking and heating so they were easily available.

Plans for the meal were to have the guests from Headquarters come at 1300 hours for a drink (or two), then get the meal from the makeshift grill and return to the house to eat. The Company Officers would use their mess gear but the guests would be given plates and cups. The men would have their chow time at 1400 hours so as not to be bothered with having the Battalion brass around.

Every time there was something different in the food department Sergeant Woodward came off with flying colors. He had it all figured out to have the men start through the lines getting the steak last. They would have been on the grill about four minutes turning them over after two minutes and ready to serve as the men reached the grill. The grill would hold about twenty-five steaks and as each one was taken off another was put in its place. I was able to watch the whole process since I didn't drink. I skipped that part to see the crew getting set up and starting the steaks for the officers. After I ate I went back out while the men lined up and saw that everything went like clockwork. Some of the men would call out "I like mine medium" and "I'll have rare" or "well done" but of course they took what they got and were one happy bunch of Tankers.

Shortly I went back inside to join the others, and Soumas must have explained my absence because I was the Mess Officer. All of the guests came up and congratulated me for the excellent meal. I assured them I had absolutely nothing to do with it and that all the credit should go to the Mess Sergeant and his crew and maybe they could tell him.

Captain Stackhouse, the Battalion Surgeon was there so I walked over to him and said "Doc. Look at my fingernails, they have all these little purple polka dots on them." Then he said, "They have been frost bitten" and I said "my toenails are the same" and he replied "well they are frost bitten too so come down to the dispensary in the morning and I will give you something to ease the pain and you will also get a Purple Heart." I felt a little uncomfortable about that even though I knew the regulations provided that if you incurred an injury in combat you were entitled to a Purple Heart. The injury did not have to be inflicted by the enemy, just while in combat with the enemy. I knew of a man who got cut climbing over a barbed wire fence while under fire and received a Purple Heart. Our Company Commander closed a turret hatch on his hand and smashed a couple of fingers and he received a Purple Heart. Still I didn't feel right about it and didn't know what I should do. I didn't have to make the decision about the Purple Heart and I didn't get anything for my frost bite either because just before dawn, we received orders to move out which surprised me since I thought we were out of range from any enemy attack. We only moved a short distance so there must not have been any threat that caused the move but maybe some new units needed that space where we had been, who knows?

We stayed put for a few days then about the sixth or seventh of January 1945 we really took off leaving Belgium, crossing into France covering a total of about 130 miles moving in a southeasterly direction. A couple of days later another big hop of nearly 90 miles to Verdun, France, where we were billeted in an old Army barracks and received our first shower in weeks. The next few days we took rather short trips of 25 and 42 miles reaching the area of Metz, France, "A" Company settling down in the little village of Althoff.

Since our part in that vicious conflict seemed to have reached its conclusion I would like to take a moment to recap what we had just accomplished. Let the records show that this was the biggest, the bloodiest, the most costly American battle of the entire War with 80,000 American casualties, 19,000 killed and a loss of 800 tanks. Although I have mentioned here how much we were involved in the fiercest part of the battle, the 9th Armored Division received little notice for its heroic stand at and around St. Vith because elements of the 9th were so frequently broken up and attached to other units that it became known by the enemy as the "Phantom Nine." At one point we had moved so far north that we were in the British Army sector under the command of Field Marshall Montgomery for over 24 hours. Most accounts of the Battle of the Bulge fail to include the action of the 9th Armored Division. Not until 57 years later in 2002 did the Army check the records and discovered what a tremendous contribution we made by delaying the German attack and wrecking their campaign. The German High Command twice officially declared the Ninth Armored Division completely destroyed only to again face segments of the Division when they least expected it. Our Combat Command "B" was finally awarded the Presidential Unit Citation "for extraordinary heroism in combat in the vicinity of St. Vith, Belgium," a copy of which is repproduced herein.

Now I would like for a moment to direct your attention to the map of the Battle of the Bulge showing the location of the Allied front on December 16, 1944. Then you will note that by December 20 the line had a rather large bend where the Germans had pushed through nearly thirty miles but at St. Vith where we were fighting the line barely moved. What made that situation so bad was, as you can see, the Germans had driven past our position which meant we had enemy troops to our front and both flanks so we were ordered to move back on December 23.

Thus ends the saga of "A" Company's heroic and epic stand during the Battle of the Ardennes Forest in the vicinity of St. Vith, Belgium, which the writer looks back on with justifiable pride.

We were now at a point where we must stop and replace vehicles and personnel lost in that great conflict in preparation for the rumored spring offensive.

Map showing the German advance during the Battle of the Bulge. One star (✪) shows the town of St. Vith and the pocket that formed around us. The other star marks the town of Aachen where we were sent after the Battle of the Bulge and prior to our advence to the Rhine River.

By virtue of the authority vested in me as President of the United States and as Commander in Chief of the Armed Forces of the United States, I have today awarded

THE PRESIDENTIAL UNIT CITATION (ARMY)
FOR EXTRAORDINARY HEROISM
TO
COMBAT COMMAND B, 9TH ARMORED DIVISION

Combat Command B, 9th Armored Division is cited for extraordinary heroism in combat in the vicinity of St. Vith, Belgium from December 17 to December 23, 1944. Combat Command B, 9th Armored Division was subjected to repeated tank and infantry attacks, which grew in intensity as German forces attempted to destroy the stubborn defenses that were denying them the use of the key communication center at St. Vith. By the second day, the flanks were constantly threatened by enemy forces that had bypassed the St. Vith area and pushed far to the rear in an effort to encircle the command east of the Salm River. The attacking forces were repeatedly thrown back by the gallant troops who rose from their fox holes and fought in fierce hand-to-hand combat to stop the penetrations and inflict heavy losses on the numerically superior foe. As the command continued to deny the important St. Vith highway and railroad center to the Germans, the entire offensive lost its initial impetus and their supply columns became immobilized. By 21 December, the German timetable was so disrupted that the enemy was forced to divert a corps to the capture of St. Vith. Under extreme pressure from overwhelming forces, Combat Command B, which for 7 days had held the St. Vith area so gallantly, was ordered to withdraw west of the Salm River. By their epic stand, without prepared defenses and despite heavy casualties, Combat Command B, 9th Armored Division, inflicted crippling losses and imposed great delay upon the enemy by a masterful and grimly determined defense in keeping with the highest traditions of the Army of the United States.

Chapter 11

RECOVERY AND REPLACEMENT

The Battalion advance party had arrived several days ahead of us to provide billeting in the homes of people living in the area. Company "A" took over this little village of Althoff and each tank crew was assigned a house where one room would be its quarters for the duration of our stay there. The occupants of these homes were very friendly and hospitable and did not seem to object to this intrusion on their property. They were people of very modest means living off the land and the house we three platoon leaders shared had a small connecting barn which housed a cow and a few chickens which gave the air in our room a very special fragrance. There was a bed in the room, which Grimball commandeered since he was the senior officer and Sid and I slept on the floor in our bedrolls. Even that seemed like a luxury because we were not being shot at for which we were most grateful. Soumas took a house near the center of the village and had the kitchen truck set up right in front, which made it easy for the men to reach at chow time. A nearby open field was selected as an improvised Motor Park where we parked the tanks. I still have in my little notebook a diagram of the village locating the various tank crews, the Command Post and the Motor Park.

Although nothing had been said, it was quite obvious to me, and an absolute necessity, that the demands on the men were being eased to permit them to recover from the nerve wracking stress that combat imposes on both mind and body. Some routine formations were required for roll call, daily visits to the Motor Park to fire up the tanks because it was still winter and bitter cold and the need to maintain constant security precautions. The word was that English speaking Germans wearing American uniforms riding in American vehicles were trying to penetrate the Allied lines reminding us that we were very much in a war zone. The password used to challenge anyone you did not know was changed daily along with a counter password. A lot of pages from my little notebook had to be torn out but one page has a couple of password counter password combinations that should be ok to release now. They were "WINCH – PULLEY", and "NIGHT – ATTACK" so when you challenged someone you would order "HALT – GIVE THE PASSWORD" and if that person answered "WINCH" he would also say "GIVE THE COUNTER PASSWORD" then you would answer "PULLEY." We frequently had to go through this procedure because we were in reserve status in the Third Army sector under General George Patton and many unfamiliar people passed through our area, some of whom, I was sure, were to test us to see that we were observing orders.

A nice break occurred when a convoy was made up to take us into Metz, France, to attend a show at the Wagner Opera House named after the famous composer who had given many concerts there in his time. When we arrived at the theater we saw that the Red Cross had set up a kind of Canteen in the lobby where we got sandwiches, donuts and coffee. It was a welcome escape from reality and did much for the morale of men and officers alike.

In a few days we started having mail call and I received a number of letters that had accumulated since the last one. Most of the letters were from Gracie and one from Aunt Nettie saying she had heard from Cousin William who told her that he was able to learn that I was all right. Easy for him to say but of course I was OK thanks to the Good Lord although I was still trying to get my head on straight.

The men started some letter writing of their own after a stern warning that we were under very strict censorship and their remarks would be limited to their health, requests for goodies, and some words of affection. I remember one man wrote to his Mother saying; "I am well and very lucky to be alive." I had to cut out the "very lucky to be alive" because it implied that he had been in some very heavy fighting and no reference to combat was permitted.

It was interesting to notice that the men were starting to come around and the horseplay and good-natured hassling were on the increase. Officers were trained to be on the alert for the man or men who were very quiet, very little communication and whose mind appeared elsewhere giving the impression that he might be thinking of ways to get away from all this such as "going over the hill," self inflicted wounds or fake illness. We saw no signs of that among our men and I was really relieved to hear the typical G.I. language picking up again.

Also we started to get better organized by scheduling certain activities at specific times and performing some details such as cleaning weapons, first echelon of maintenance of the tanks and other Company vehicles in case we might be ordered back into combat.

In the meantime we received some new replacements and even though I had not lost any in the battle, a couple of my men were transferred to other platoons so that the new men could be evenly distributed to each platoon. These guys had never tasted combat and had not received nearly the amount of training we had before coming overseas. I felt kind of sorry for them because they were joining a bunch of men who had been together for several years and they had to feel a little strange, but G.I's have a way of mixing so it didn't take long for the new ones to fit right in with the old.

Things were gradually getting back to "normal," if there is such a thing in the Army, and I began to feel that cohesiveness in my platoon that provides the teamwork displayed during the recent fighting. As the men worked at whatever the assignment was that day, I made sure they were aware of my presence by discussing with them the condition of their gun barrels, was the head-space of the gun a problem or did combat or the cold have any permanent effect on their health. Not to pry, or to exert authority, but to convey a sincere interest in the man and his job. I had talked briefly with the new men in the platoon and discussed with Sergeant Weaver their progress and his opinion of them. He informed me that he thought they needed a lot of work and he would see that they got it and I knew he would.

About the middle of February I received another letter from Aunt Nettie telling me that Cousin William (General Kean) suggested that I make arrangements to have lunch with him again. I supposed he was curious to see how we reacted to combat since we had experienced very little at the time of our last meeting. So I again go to Battalion Headquarters and explained the situation to the Adjutant who contacted First Army Headquarters and learned the General would see me for lunch the next day. We were about 30 miles further away than the last time so I was given a sixteen hour pass from 0800 to Midnight to drive about 100 miles to visit with cousin William, have lunch, then drive back that 100 miles by midnight. I had told Captain Soumas about my Aunts letter and asked if I could go to Battalion to make arrangements. He couldn't very well say no and when I told him I would be going the next day he said, "Well goodbye, it has been nice knowing you" as though I wouldn't be back. I don't think he was too pleased and I believe he resented the fact that one of his officers was related to a General.

Before we left I had to go get the password and counter password for the day expecting we would receive numerous challenges on the way. The trip was uneventful and to my surprise, we were not stopped once until we arrived at First Army Headquarters where an MP asked to see our passes as we drove into the compound. I again had to show my pass at the door of the building where I was to meet Cousin William. No one called for the password and I thought that security here where some of the top brass were located should be much tighter but again nobody asked me. The procedure upon my arrival was pretty much the same as last time except I was escorted into his office and after following military protocol he extended his hand and offered me a chair beside his desk. He again mentioned his correspondence with his Mother who consistently asked if he heard anything from me. I told him that Aunt Nettie apparently was unfamiliar with the restrictions combat placed on social contacts. He laughed and said that certainly was the case and he tried to put her at ease regarding my situation. If she only knew.

He then said that while he was kept informed as to the "big picture" he was interested in the action of my Company. I told him we were in the 14th Tank Battalion, which was part of Combat Command "B" of the 9th Armored. His immediate response was "oh, then you were in the St. Vith area, a real hot spot, vital to the success of the German offensive." I assured him that was exactly where we were and yes, it certainly was. He was really warming up to the discussion of my involvement and had a number of questions, which I was proud to answer. Suddenly he glanced at his watch and said he had a couple of things to do before lunch so he called his Aide and told him to show me where I could wash up and he would join us at lunch.

Lunch was very pleasant and his questions provided me the opportunity to describe some of the situations I found myself in during the recent fighting. Since I had not talked much to his Aide before lunch he seemed very interested in what I had to say and asked a few questions of his own. I had told the General that my pass required me to report back by midnight so after a short conversation following lunch he said that he guessed I wanted to get on the road to avoid being late. I thanked him for the lunch and said I enjoyed our talk and he said it was his pleasure and he would get a letter off to his Mother telling her of our meeting including my good health. With that I saluted, shook hands and bid him and his Aide goodbye.

My driver was ready for me so away we went on our return to Althoff which was uneventful until we came upon a Battalion out-post where we were halted and ordered to give the password. I immediately gave the password and called for the counter password which one of the guards gave and told us to pass. We drove on and just as it started to get dark we were almost at Althoff when we were again halted by a couple of soldiers I recognized who asked for the password and after we gave the counter password I said, "good work men," they saluted and we drove into the Company area.

I was very pleased because every day we were reminded of the continuing German efforts to penetrate our lines and both Battalion and Company "A" were on the alert. I checked in at Battalion then at Company where I saw Captain Soumas and told him about his guards stopping us. We had not eaten so I asked Woodward to have something thrown together for my driver and me, which with some hot coffee really hit the spot. It was still February and the Peeps have no heat so a hot meal with coffee was mighty welcome. Soumas told me that he had received word that we could expect a move within the next week or ten days and to make sure my platoon was ready.

For the next few days time was spent checking and rechecking the tank equipment and repacking musette and duffle bags with new items of clothing replacing what the men claimed were "lost in combat." Normally such items had to be "salvaged," which meant turning in a worn item in order to receive a new one, but claiming it was "lost in combat" got them a new one without turning in the old. Those guys never missed a trick. The guessing game of where and when was in full swing with much wishful thinking being offered such as "duty in Paris" or some "R&R" (rest and recuperation) at some plush location. They would soon find out how badly they had missed the mark when we finally got our orders.

I could not make up my mind whether or not to pack my officers Field Coat, which I had worn all through the Bulge. The coat was blanket lined and quite warm but very bulky compared to the Combat Suit I had. The Combat Suit consisted of a jacket, pants, and cap, which were also blanket lined but the pants went from the ankles up to the chest with shoulder straps something like a farmer's bib overalls. The reason why I chose the Field Coat rather than the Combat Pants was when nature called those pants were the devil to get out of. I did wear the jacket and cap, which covered my ears over my radio ear plugs, long johns, O.D. pants and shirt, and the Field Coat, but still got cold and the frost-bitten fingers and toes. For now I decided I would not wear the coat but would keep it handy in case we encountered some more bitter cold weather.

I spent a lot of time just mingling with the men while at work and during some off time in order to determine their level of morale and frequently got the question "when are we going home, Lieutenant?" and all I could tell them was "When this thing is over" and "we still have a good way to go yet." Of course this wasn't the answer they wanted but I knew it was what they expected. In spite of the prospect of more combat, they seemed to be in good spirits with the normal grumbling and griping so typical of the American "G.I."

It was the last week in February 1945 when we received orders to pull out and head north toward the German town of Aachen, which was already occupied by American troops. This move would cover about 175 miles staying out of range of enemy guns, stopping each day before dark and allowing the kitchen to feed the men. I could hear a lot of cannon fire on the way which I assumed was our own artillery and wondered if they were softening up the enemy for a large scale Allied attack. From time to time I would hear a comment about our Spring Offensive but this was still winter.

It was now February 27, 1945 when we arrived at the outskirts of Aachen, once a major city of Germany but now a vast area of rubble and devastation. Captain Soumas called the officers together and told us we would camp at that location for the night. He said he had to attend a Company Commanders meeting after supper and he would brief us in the morning at 0730 hours. He seemed very sober and serious avoiding his usual light hearted attitude and left little doubt about what was in store in our immediate future.

Aunt Nettie, who facilitated my lunches with General Kean.

Chapter 12

THE DRIVE TO THE RHINE

We had slept in our tents and woke up on February 28 to a rather gray overcast morning but the kitchen had prepared breakfast and the hot coffee took some of the chill off of the atmosphere. It was now time to join Captain Soumas and the other officers to learn what our mission would be. He told us that our objective would be the Rhine River, some 54 miles away at which time we should get a break while the very complicated problem of getting across that wide span of water was being resolved. He then informed us that the First Platoon had been given the new Pershing Tank and would not be accompanying us on this mission.

It seems that the Pershing was a much heavier tank than the Sherman, weighing over 40 tons compared to our 32 to 35 tons and had a much wider track which created a problem. When a tank unit is on the attack, the retreating forces would always destroy any bridges along the way in order to slow down the advancing tanks. Therefore it was necessary for our Engineers to follow at a reasonable distance so they could be called up to lay down some bridging material to replace the blown up span permitting the tanks to proceed across. The standard bridging equipment would not accommodate the heavier Pershing Tanks with the much wider tracks.

May I remind you that a Tank Company consists of three platoons of five tanks each and a Headquarters Section of two tanks, so now we are left with just the two platoons, Sid's and mine while John's platoon would have to take a different route where reconnaissance had determined there were no bridges to worry about. John would join another unit of this task force, which was under the command of our Battalion Commander Colonel Engeman.

Then Soumas said we would move out at 0830 hours with the Third Platoon in the lead — hey wait a minute! How come Third is first, I thought one was first, two was second and three was third, at least it was when I went to school, but the Captain must have gone to a different school so Third would be first. Also this Miller guy was a naughty Lieutenant because he always rode in the lead tank in his Platoon even though it was a violation of S.O.P. (Standard Operating Procedure) which stated that an officer may not ride in the leading vehicle in combat. My Company Commander knew I rode in the leading tank and he would sometimes say, "you know you are not supposed to be up there," but he never gave me an order not to, so that is where I rode. I figured I would be up front for maybe four or five hours and then we would rotate so at 0830 hours off we went in the direction of the Rhine River with the Third Platoon first.

After a while we reached the Roer River where the Engineers had built a pontoon bridge to replace the one that the retreating Germans had blown up. Crossing these pontoon bridges in a tank is a rather delicate procedure because the treadway was just as wide as the tank track and the weight of the tank would make it bob up and down. We took it very slowly and soon made it across at which time we were in enemy territory.

You could almost feel a change in the atmosphere and we soon started receiving some sporadic artillery shelling and small arms fire sometimes referred to as light resistance. I never appreciated that being described as "light" resistance because it was my feeling that if you were killed by a .30 caliber rifle shot you were just as dead as if an artillery shell hit you but that was how they classified it. We were slowed while our own artillery responded and blasted the enemy positions with a heavy barrage eliminating the problem.

As we continued moving forward I began to realize that I had been up there for six hours, then eight hours and now ten hours. Had they forgotten the policy of rotation and would keep me in the lead until the war ended? Just a little later I came to a stream where the bridge had been blown up so I dispersed my tanks along the bank of the stream to wait for the Engineers to come to provide a way for me to get across. It had now been close to twelve hours and darkness was setting in which meant we would probably have to spend the night at this position.

We definitely were within rifle and machine gun range so the Engineers could not use lights while working during the night. We were frequently fired on in the darkness and our random return fire was intended to keep the Germans from creeping up close enough to fire their Panzerfausts at our tanks so this kept us busy the entire night.

At first light some Engineers came up to survey the situation and determine the materials necessary to do the job. They called back to their base and left to meet up with the unit bringing the equipment and guide them to our location. I really didn't feel too comfortable just sitting there because the Germans knew we were there since we had exchanged gunfire all through the night. I told my men to be on the alert so as not to get picked off by sniper fire. The Engineers came and were hard at work all morning while we provided cover for them. It was almost mid-afternoon when we got the word that they had completed the job and we should line up and prepare to move out.

By this time I had been up there 33 hours and I was getting pretty edgy from that constant exposure to enemy fire when Captain Soumas ordered the Second and Third Platoons to switch positions. Sid Moskowitz moved his tanks around mine, and the Second Platoon would now take the lead. Having been given the order to move out we proceeded on our way toward our objective but after about 20 minutes we came to a halt. The Captain radioed Sid to ask what the problem was saying that we were running behind schedule and had to keep moving. Sid called back and said "We are under fire." Soumas told him to "take care of it and let's get going because we are behind schedule." Sid responded "we are under fire and trying to locate—." That was the end of his transmission, his tank was hit, Sid was killed and two other tanks in his platoon were knocked out after 20 minutes being up there. I am there 33 hours and Sid gets killed after 20 minutes. How do you explain things like that? The "fortunes of war" I guess.

I have to tell you something I did which is an example of how you can almost become "brain dead" from the stress of being under fire in the heat of battle. After the radio message from Sid to the Captain was cut off in the middle of a sentence I saw smoke up ahead of me and a man running in my direction limping badly. Thinking that must be Sid, I jumped down from my tank and ran toward him to see if I could help. Upon reaching him I grabbed him and we both ran a few steps toward the rear when I realized that "this isn't Sid," so I turned him loose and told him to keep going. I again turned to look for Sid when I began to hear my men screaming at me "Lieutenant get back here," and my brain started to get back in gear making me aware of what a stupid thing I had just done. I felt completely drained and could only walk back to my tank, climb up and practically dropped through my turret hatch. Not a word was said but I noticed a couple of the guys shake their heads as if to say that wasn't a very bright thing to do.

We obviously had run into a very strongly defended enemy area and had to hold up there until their guns could be neutralized by our own artillery and air support. We dispersed our tanks around this large open field where there were numerous haystacks. When nightfall came we started to receive machine gun fire using some tracer bullets, which set the haystacks on fire. These fires would silhouette our tanks and draw artillery fire which required us to move away from the burning haystacks keeping us busy most of the night. By morning things had quieted down but we received the bad news that the Second Platoon had lost three tanks with most of the crews wounded and several killed. We also heard that the First Platoon had run into the same defense line, which must have covered a broad front including the sector they were in. They lost one of the Pershings, killing Staff Sergeant Key the First Platoon Sergeant. This was a very disastrous battle for "A" Company, which was weakened considerably by its losses.

While we waited for our orders, I received a call from Staff Sergeant Weaver who said "Lieutenant I have a man here who is losing it. He is going to pieces and I don't know what to do with him." Not sure how to handle the situation I told Weaver to send him over to me and I told my bow gunner to go over to Weaver's tank and I put his man in my bow gunners position. I wondered what would happen because when we are on the move, Weaver's tank is the fourth tank back and now he will be riding in the lead tank. It was pretty late in the morning when Soumas radioed me to line up and be prepared to move out. With Sid killed and the First Platoon off in another direction I was all that was left so I had to take the lead again. Soumas also told me to stay off the road until we had passed the disabled tanks keeping at least 200 yards to the left. The reason for our late start was to permit the removal of the dead and wounded and I could see in the distance some maintenance vehicles and what I presumed to be our maintenance personnel. When I got about a thousand yards past them I moved over to the road where I could pick up the speed a little which over cross-country was kept to a minimum.

Soon we were to discover what had caused all the trouble when we reached the long line of German 88 millimeter cannons stretched out as far as the eye could see and they were dug in at ground level. Also these guns were painted tan to blend in with the soil around them, which was why Sid couldn't find them. From what I could see most of them were badly damaged either from direct hits or by the Germans themselves as they were forced from their emplacements. As we drove on we again experienced that so-called "light resistance" but it was enough to slow our progress so as to avoid another disaster like the day before. To my surprise, it was just mid afternoon when I was ordered to halt and cut our engines. There was no explanation for our stopping at this time and I could only guess that they may have learned of some larger forces ahead or they were busy mopping up some of the "light resistance" I had passed through. Whatever it was I was grateful for the break, as I was pretty up tight over Sid getting hit and could use this opportunity to relax a little.

We stayed at that location the rest of the day and the next morning we just traveled a short distance to a little town where we again were told to cut our engines. Whenever we cut our engines the men would hop out to grab a smoke or relieve themselves, or just walk around to loosen up a little. At such times as these we would disperse our tanks in such a manner as to cover all approaches to the little town in the event of a counter attack. It was less than an hour since we arrived at this place when the town received a barrage of artillery fire and because of the nearby buildings, we closed our hatches to avoid flying debris or shrapnel which are fragments of an HE, high explosive shell. The shelling only lasted about ten minutes then all was quiet and I thought it was OK to open my hatch. Just as I started to look around from up in my turret, I received a radio call from one of my other tanks telling me that my driver had been over there during the shelling and was killed.

Wilbur Rouse was my driver and while he was out of his tank he apparently decided to walk over and talk to some of his buddies in another tank. Most of the men were pretty close because they had trained together for at least several years so when they had the chance they would visit for a few minutes of G.I. conversation. To me the Tank Driver had the toughest job in the tank and I always had a special appreciation for the work they did but now I have to decide what my next move would be in light of this tragic development. The condition of the man Weaver sent me for my bow gunner had not improved and when I first told Soumas about him he said for me to hold on until we got our break at the Rhine not anticipating the situation I now faced.

I radioed Soumas and told him my driver had been killed and I needed an immediate replacement. He said he would call Company Headquarters to send up a man who would drive my tank and I remember being very concerned about getting a man who could really do the job. It must have taken the First Sergeant a while to decide which man would be most suitable to drive my tank, but finally selected Melvin Gustwiler who had been driving one of the Company trucks. I really did not know Gustwiler and I was uncomfortable with the fact that he wasn't a Tank Driver but I had no choice. The First Sergeant must have thought this would be a good opportunity to get the Morning Report signed by the Company Commander so he would ride along when they brought up my driver. The Morning Report has to be sent by each Company to Battalion every day and contains all the activities of the Company the previous day.

Shortly after Gustwiler reported to me we encountered more shelling and I later received word that the First Sergeant had been hit and was seriously wounded which later proved fatal. When we first entered this little town I noticed a church on the side of a nearby hill and a church steeple is always a good spot for a forward observer to call in a fire mission for the enemy artillery. Looking through my glasses I thought I saw some movement up in that steeple so I had my gunner fire a couple of rounds into the steeple. I have often wondered if that could have been a minister or a priest that I saw but since we received no more shelling I am sure it must have been a German Forward Observer bringing the artillery fire in on us.

Later in the afternoon I was ordered to move my platoon a short distance to the outskirts of another little village where some of our infantry was being pinned down by some machine gun and rifle fire from the enemy that was dug in. Many of these little villages are only two or three hundred yards apart so we reached the area quickly and I had my platoon form a line on me and we started moving slowly across the area sweeping the field with our machine guns. I had been riding pretty low in the turret to avoid getting picked off by a rifleman but I did want to get a better view of the situation so I stood up a little higher and looked to my left to see someone walking beside my tank. At first glance I dismissed it with the thought it was one of our infantrymen that had been pinned down but a second look revealed it was a General walking along with his pistol drawn and firing at some of the enemy we had flushed out of their foxholes. It was quite a surprise for me riding in a tank in the front lines and here was a General just walking along beside my tank. I found out later that the General had just lost his Aide who was riding with him in his Peep and he was so mad he was determined to get somebody for killing his Aide and I am sure he did.

We completed the job of clearing the area of the enemy, most of whom took off as soon as the tanks arrived so we returned to rejoin the rest of the Company, but not before I saw a Peep pick up the General and speed off to the rear where he belonged.

We remained at that location until the next day when a strange situation developed that caused me some concern. Captain Soumas called me on the radio and told me to come over to his tank, that he needed to talk to me. I jumped down from my tank and trotted over to where he was and he told me that he wasn't feeling well and may have to go to the Hospital. If that should happen he wanted me to take over the Company but I strongly protested saying that I would do anything he wanted but I would hope he would tough it out and I would cover for him whenever it was necessary. It wasn't long before he took me up on it because that afternoon a Peep came up to my tank and the driver said the Captain wanted me to go to a meeting for him so I took my little notebook, jumped into the Peep and off we went. Just a short distance later we observed what appeared to be a pile of clothes lying in the road ahead but as we drove around it the driver screamed, "My God Lieutenant that was a G.I.," to which I responded "yeah, I know." I believe I mentioned before that it is so important to keep your composure in these situations because it happens so often it would get to you and you would be like the man Weaver sent over to me.

We came to this building which I soon learned was the Battalion Headquarters and I went in and reported to the Colonel saying I was representing Captain Soumas of "A" Company who wasn't feeling well. The meeting got underway and the Colonel gave a briefing of what the Battalion losses were since leaving Aachen and needless to say "A" Company was not the only Company that got hurt. He then stated that our mission remained unchanged that we were to reach the Rhine as soon as possible and we should get a break when we did. I was very aware that he seemed to make eye contact with each Captain but seemed to avoid me and I get the impression that he was somewhat displeased that Soumas wasn't there. He also mentioned that the enemy resistance had been more than expected but hoped we could pick it up a notch from here on in. Having said that he dismissed us and I returned to the Company and went directly to the Captain's tank and gave him the information I got from the meeting including the Colonel's belief that the rest of the drive might not be as rough as it had been.

Now it is the morning of the seventh day of this drive and the Third Platoon has been out in front the whole time except for the twenty minutes that the Second Platoon was there with such disastrous results. No sleep, no hot food, no showers and constantly exposed to enemy gun fire caused me to worry about our physical and mental condition, having already lost Sergeant Weaver's man from "Combat Fatigue," our Company Commander showing signs of caving in and I was afraid I might be getting a little punchy myself. As the previous day was drawing to a close we were still on the move and I had been looking through my binoculars, scanning the area ahead to make sure there was no enemy within view that could create a problem at nightfall. I let the glasses hang from the strap around my neck and looked toward the distance ahead when there appeared a vision of Gracie's face with a rather sad expression. It only lasted for a second or two but enough to wonder if the situation was getting to me. These were the things that were going through my mind as we started another day, the same as we had for nearly a week and there would be more.

Shortly before noon we arrived at another little village where we halted for a short rest to grab something to eat. In a few minutes Sergeant Goodson, the Tank Commander of my number 2 tank, climbed up on my tank and started asking how long we were going to keep leading the attack. At that moment the village started taking some artillery fire and, remembering my drivers fate, I told Goodson he had better get back to his tank. His response to me was, "what's the use Lieutenant, they are going to keep us up front here until we get it anyway." I told him "Speedy, we are supposed to get a break when we reach the Rhine which can't be too far away so get back to your tank and just hang in there." He climbed down from my tank and just kind of shuffled off in the direction of his tank. It is when men get that kind of an attitude that they get careless and put themselves and their buddies at risk, which is why I said I was getting worried.

There was no damage from the recent shelling and we took off again hoping we would soon reach the Rhine River, that great natural barrier that would give us that much-needed rest. Fortunately, the only direct fire we encountered was from rifles and machine guns, but that sporadic artillery shelling was both nerve wracking and a constant threat to our well-being. Later in the afternoon I spotted what appeared to be a town so I halted to get a better look and it seem to me it was larger than most of the villages we had been passing through. I radioed back to Soumas what I had seen and he told me it was probably the town of Stadt Meckenheim where we were to meet up with the First Platoon and spend the night. He said that Battalion had determined it was not heavily defended and to get a little closer to see if we would draw fire. As I said earlier, I was getting a little edgy and an order like that wasn't exactly what I needed but of course I went on hoping the Battalion report was accurate. It did seem reasonably quiet with an occasional far off rattle of a machine gun or automatic rifle so we drew near the town and Soumas radioed for me to stop where I was. He told me we would wait for the First Platoon to arrive and a billeting party would come up to assign houses where we would spend the night, which was music to my ears.

There was a line of trees along the road into town and I always liked to use trees for cover whenever I could so I pulled up under the nearest one to me. All of a sudden there was this ear splitting explosion and I felt a stinging sensation all over my face so I yelled through my intercom that we had been hit and to dismount. I wasn't going to burn up in my tank like Sid did and out I went diving head first off the side of the tank onto the slope of a ditch beside the road which probably kept me from breaking my neck. After I landed I crawled to the top of the ditch and saw that my tank had not yet caught fire. I was afraid to touch my face thinking it was half blown away so I asked the man lying next to me if my face was bleeding badly. He said "no, but it is very red." The tank seemed to be ok so I told the men to mount up and I very sheepishly climbed back into my turret.

I looked at the tree beside me and realized what had happened. Apparently an A.P. (Armor Piercing) shell fired at me hit the tree splattering splinters all over my face. The shell hitting that close made a terrific sound causing me to think the tank had been hit and that I was covered by steel splinters from my tank. Another indication, that I was getting "gun shy" from the constant exposure to gunfire. I knew I had to write about this incident because if I didn't my daughter would and she would make it worse. Even today when I give a talk, my daughter insists that I tell that story because she likes to see how embarrassed it makes me.

It was getting late when I received the order to move into the town and I was guided to a group of buildings where "A" Company would stay. Soumas came up to assign the sites where our respective platoons would stay. Most of these buildings were severely damaged by air and artillery shelling. He showed us where he would be and where there would be an officers call at 1900 hours. Then he suggested that we grab some of our rations and return for the officers meeting at the appointed time. Returning to my tank I gathered my men and told them to eat something and I would get with them later to tell them what the officers call was all about. All that was left of the building we were assigned was the basement, but there were no complaints as this would be the first night in a week that we would be able to lie down and sleep. I opened a can of "C" rations which was "corned beef hash" and a box of "K" rations giving me some cheese and a biscuit and then I rounded out my four course dinner with a "D" ration chocolate bar for desert. It may not sound like a very fancy meal but to be able to sit down on an old wooden box and quietly eat that meal seemed like a feast for a king.

It was nearly time to walk over for the meeting and I looked for Grimball and Yoho but I guessed they had already gone. The location was the basement of a bombed out house and it surprised me that the Colonel didn't have it much better than we did. There were lots of German Marks scattered all over the floor. I reached down and stuffed some in my pocket remembering that after World War I it took a wheelbarrow full of German money to buy a loaf of bread because it was so worthless, but I thought these would make a nice souvenir.

Colonel Engeman walked in and ordered "at ease" and started the briefing of the next days battle plan. He said that we had to get to the Rhine River, which was twelve miles away and he would be the Task Force Commander, which consisted of the 14th Tank Battalion, Company "A" of the 27th Armored Infantry Battalion, a platoon of Tank Destroyers and various other supporting units. The leading element would be the Infantry Company who would ride in their halftracks until it was necessary to deploy. They would be supported by Lieutenant Grimballs' Tank Platoon, which he said he had not been able to use during the drive due to the weight of the Pershing tanks and the width of their tracks but he felt the Germans were really afraid of them. Needless to say I was very relieved to hear this and I was glad I could tell my platoon we would not be in the lead for a change. Our flanks would be covered by other Task Forces, and reconnaissance planes had reported very few enemy between our position and the river. The colonel then advised us that our kitchens were on the way and we should have hot breakfasts in the morning. He suggested that First Call be at 0600 hours, breakfast 0630 and be prepared to move out at 0700 hours and with that he said "good luck" and dismissed us.

On the way out Soumas told us that the Colonel's suggestion would be our schedule and he had been in touch with our kitchen to confirm the arrangements. He also said that we would have hot cakes for breakfast and I knew this would please the men because that was their favorite. It is the nature of the typical G.I. to complain about Army food but when our guys got hot cakes you never heard a single gripe except there wasn't enough. So I returned to my platoon where they were waiting to hear what I had learned at the meeting. I told them that after a week of the Third Platoon being in the lead, the First Platoon would be in front as the support group for the Company of Infantry heading the attack. Among the responses I heard were "finally," "it's about time," "at last," and "What took em so long?" with a few others I won't repeat here. Then I said "The kitchen is going to catch up with us and we will have hot cakes for breakfast" and with that they let out a cheer that could be heard in Berlin. I told them we would have First Call at 0600, breakfast at 0630 and prepare to move out at 0700.

I was really beat so I splashed some water on my face and didn't bother to shave my whiskers, which had grown enough to make me look like a real bum. My bedroll was on the floor so I unrolled it but didn't open it and just flopped down and closed my eyes for the first time in a week.

It was still dark when I woke up and I looked at my watch which said 0530 so I decided to get up and was going over to the kitchen when the runner came in and yelled "it is 0555 we are moving out at 0630." Hey! How come! What happened to breakfast? Where are the hot cakes? Of course, I knew the answer as I said to myself "this is war man, this is war." It seemed awfully cruel to promise these men who had been through so much for so long, that they would have a hot breakfast and not give it to them. You can be sure there were a lot of unprintable comments from all of the men as they hurried to roll up their sleeping bags, took care of a few necessities and stumbled out to their tanks to ready them for the drive. The order came to "wind 'em up and get in formation" which my guys had already done and then a strange thing happened. Without a word the men started jumping out of their tanks running over to the kitchen with their mess kits grabbing some hot cakes and dashing back to their tanks. It looked almost like it was planned because the kitchen crew was waiting for them and dumped a pile of hot cakes in the mess kit slapped on a glob of butter and poured some syrup right on top of them and off the guys went to their tanks. It looked like a cross-country race with these men charging across the field getting their hot cakes and charging back again. Oh yes, my crew got theirs too with both gunner and loader climbing out of the loaders turret hatch which they couldn't have done with the old tanks that had no loaders turret hatch. They offered me some but I wouldn't think of taking any from these people who needed this so badly. I just said thanks but I would get some later knowing full well that "later" would never come.

We started to move and I radioed my platoon to report each crew present to make sure we would not leave anybody at the chow line. In less than ten minutes we came to a halt but I did not hear any gunfire and I wondered what the delay was. Then I got a call to send my dozer tank up to help remove a huge roadblock. Usually a roadblock is covered by enemy fire but the Germans must have taken off as they often did when they saw the tanks. We were held up a considerable length of time and I couldn't help but think that this time could have been used eating breakfast if they had known about this roadblock earlier. It took at least an hour to clear enough room for the tanks to get through and again we got under way. Although we were far from rested most of my platoon were a little more relaxed from a short nights sleep, a bit of a breakfast and, more important the fact we were not in the lead for the first time in eight days except for that disastrous twenty minutes when the Second Platoon was up front. One thing that did keep us on edge was the familiar sporadic artillery shelling and the distant sound of machine gun bursts and rifle shots causing some brief delays, which I imagined was the infantry clearing out those gun emplacements. I know of one instance when I got close enough to watch where we were approaching a thick wooded area on both sides of the road. Knowing that the Germans usually hid in the woods and would use their Panzerfausts to knock off the tanks as they rolled by, our infantry dismounted from their halftracks and flushed out both woods. As usual they did a good job and took a number of prisoners, which they marched passed our tanks on the way to our rear positions. It was getting close to noon as we resumed our drive and after a while we came over the crest of a hill and again the column stopped but this time it was for a different reason.

Off in the distant valley was the majestic Rhine River and this is where we would get our promised and much needed break which hopefully would raise the spirits of these very tired and weary men. But hold on here — looking through the haze of this gray, damp day we could see a bridge still standing with German troops streaming across it. We were sure it would be blown up as soon as all of their people were safely on the other side. The question now was do we fire on the bridge, and trap the escaping enemy or do we make a dash to try and capture it in the unlikely event it was not destroyed. Those answers would have to come from at least the Battalion level so we would wait for orders, which were quick in coming.

"The Rhine Barrier" showing the 25 bridges across the Rhine. All but the train bridge at Remagen were destroyed by the retreating Germans.

Chapter 13

CAPTURE & CROSSING THE BRIDGE AT REMAGEN

We viewed this bridge with mixed emotions. While knowing what a prize it would be we would also be deprived of our break. The Ludendorf Bridge, named after a World War I German General, was built shortly after that war and was a two way railroad bridge with a tunnel that ran through a high rocky cliff on the east side of the River. Also on the east side was the little town of Erpel that would figure prominently later on as events started to unfold. It might be worthy of note that the Rhine River had not been crossed by an invading army since Napoleon's conquest of that part of the European continent.

As expected, after a very short period the order came for the lead elements to proceed into the town. The lead elements consisted of Company "A" of the 27th Armored Infantry Battalion and the First Platoon of Company "A" of the 14th Tank Battalion and in close support would be the remainder of the Tank Company. The tanks were told not to fire at the bridge with our big guns so as not to damage it obviously hoping to capture the bridge intact which was an extremely unlikely consequence of our action.

The column moved rather cautiously into Remagen and started to receive some artillery and machine gun fire as it slowly made its way in the direction of the bridge. All of a sudden there was a huge explosion ahead of us and our immediate reaction was "there she blows and now we get our break" but that vision was short lived. The bridge was not blown up. Instead, a large crater was blown in the approach to the span but none of the other charges on the structure were detonated. The front of our column had now reached the bridge and my dozer tank was called up to help fill in that deep crater. I lined up my platoon of tanks along the bank of the river to give me a clear shot at any action I saw on the other side. All that I observed at that moment was a motorcycle driving through Erpel. We fired a burst from our .50 caliber machine gun as he disappeared behind some houses.

We had arrived at Remagen at just about 1500 which was the time some of the prisoners had said the bridge was scheduled to be destroyed, but we knew that this one explosion wasn't intended to blow up the bridge and that the worst was yet to come. The crater was finally filled in and we were wondering what was next when we received word that the Infantry would attempt a crossing under covering fire from our tanks. This was a very risky mission because it was felt that the main charges on the bridge would be set off momentarily, dropping the troops on the bridge into the river, and leaving those that might make it across stranded on the other side.

Just as the Infantry was preparing to make their dash, another even greater explosion went off right on the bridge. Certainly this would be the end of that structure as huge billows of smoke, dust and debris totally obliterated it from our view and we were sure that now we would get our break. Not so fast, because when the smoke and dust cleared, much to our surprise, there stood that old railroad bridge that simply refused to die. The Task Force Commander soon repeated his order for the Infantry to take the bridge and move to the other side under cover of the tanks' firepower. So in spite of the tremendous odds against a safe crossing, the men of Company "A," 27 AIB started their dash along the 1200-foot heavily charged span to a fate only time could tell. Along with the Infantry went a unit of Engineers tearing out wiring and tossing explosives into the river as they made their way toward the opposite end of the bridge.

I was always aware of the danger that I was in during the times I led the attack on the drive for the Rhine but I at least had the protection of 32 tons of steel wrapped around me. These men as

The Ludendorf Bridge at Remagen, Germany, as it appeared before World War 2.

The bridge at Remagen showing damage prior to its collapse.

Another view of the bridge showing more damage.

they zigzagged against enemy fire were protected only by their GI shirt, which did little to stop a German bullet. Bravery is not the absence of fear, but the willingness to face danger in spite of that fear. These guys were brave and got the job done as they reached their objective without a single casualty. Soon we saw a stream of German prisoners walking back across the bridge from the tunnel where they had taken cover when they saw the Americans arriving at Remagen.

Now we have the bridge, which has been secured by the removal of the hundreds of explosives that had been wired to it and the next step is to make it usable for vehicular traffic especially the tanks. Again the Engineers were pressed into service to lay planking along the railroad tracks and cross ties to give some semblance of a road so we could travel over it. You can imagine the Herculean task it was to bring up enough material to cover about 1200 feet of railroad track and get it in passable condition.

In the meantime I was instructing my platoon to zero in on certain targets across the river and record their gunsight readings so we could fire on the targets after dark in the event of an expected counter attack. It was getting late and all this activity continued long after dark when at around 2100 hours I was summoned to an officers' call in the basement of another bombed-out house.

The Colonel was still in charge of this operation and called us together to give us our orders for the next action. I invite you to read carefully this perfect example of how in combat the best-laid plans can go terribly wrong. The Colonel told us that it was absolutely imperative that tanks get across the bridge to reinforce the Infantry in the event of a counterattack by the enemy. Along the river on the other side ran a railroad track that had to be blown up to prevent the Germans from bringing in troops by rail. At exactly midnight, the Engineers would set off a charge blowing up the railroad track and that would be the signal for the tanks to start across the bridge. Also they will have strung engineers' tape to guide us and keep us from falling into the river because the planking only covered the one track and there were these gaping holes all along the other track. If we should stray beyond those tapes and fall through one of those holes we would find ourselves at the bottom of the Rhine River. After the tanks reached the other side they were to make a clover-leaf under the bridge and head north to the edge of this little town of Erpel. There they were to rendezvous with the Infantry at a roadblock set up to provide security for the tanks during the rest of the night. This plan also included a platoon of Tank Destroyers, which would cross soon after the tanks and Infantry were settled in.

It was now time to decide who was to do what and the Colonel turned to the Captain and said "Soumas, I want "A" Company to go across the bridge." Well my first reaction to that would have been to remind the Colonel that there were two other Tank Companies in our Battalion and "A" Company was pretty beat up. But I guess he already knew that and it would not have been very wise for me to say anything, which of course, I had no intention of doing anyway.

As he closed the meeting the Colonel said, "be sure you keep your men awake and alert because we don't know what is over there and you could run into trouble," and with that cheerful remark he dismissed us. Captain Soumas was sitting near the door so there was no way I could sneak past him. Sure enough, as I approached him he said "Miller, I want your platoon to be in the lead crossing the bridge." Now why didn't that surprise me? But he did say this: "And I think you should put one of your tanks in front of you." As I have mentioned before, he and I had discussed this but he never really gave me an order so I was about to go out the door when the Colonel said in a loud voice, "Miller, come back here." He was still sitting at the table where he had given us the plans and it seems he overheard what Soumas had said to me. Shaking his finger at me he again raised his voice and said, "You will have a tank in front of you tonight and from now on, and that is an order." Like I tell the folks in my talks, you do not want to be guilty of insubordination in the face of the enemy. It could result in an immediate Court Martial and execution and that was something I really didn't want to happen. Insubordination is disobeying a direct order from a superior officer, which under any circumstances is a serious matter but in the face of the enemy it is totally unacceptable.

With the Colonel's stern admonition burning deeply in my mind I walked out to tell the tank commander of my number two tank, "Speedy" Goodson, that he and I were going to have to change places that night and he would be in the lead. His only response was "How come I get this honor?", which I totally ignored and was glad it wasn't any worse than that. I told all my tank commanders what the plan was and they were to be very careful because of the extreme darkness and not to get separated from the rest. I explained to my guys, as I had done before, that the Third Platoon had to lead because the Pershings of the First Platoon were too heavy to put on the bridge that had been severely weakened by the efforts to blow it up and because the Second Platoon was reduced to just two tanks by the shelling it received so we were all that was left.

As the witching hour of midnight approached, I placed my tanks in position to go when we received the signal to move across the bridge. While I was waiting I decided to have a look at what was to guide us along the way so I dismounted and walked over to check it out. I had to get almost on top of that tape before I could see it because of the total darkness of this moonless, starless night and I wondered how I would be able to see it from my position nearly 12 feet up in the turret of my tank. The answer, of course, was I couldn't so for me the use of that tape to guide me was SNAFU number one. While the Tank Driver is seated much lower and would be closer to the tape he would be "buttoned up," meaning his hatch is closed, and would have to look through his periscope sight which provided a very limited visual range making it virtually impossible to see that tape. I also noticed that the tapes were placed on either side of the planking, which was just the width of the tank leaving absolutely no margin for error. When I returned to my tank I wanted to again warn my people about how dangerous and narrow the roadbed was but we were observing radio silence until we got underway.

Here it was now midnight and I was straining my ears to hear the explosion that would be our signal to move out, but there was none. SNAFU number two. Then the Colonel came on the air and gave the order for the tanks to proceed in accordance with his instructions. Now I could talk to my platoon and I told them to take it slow and easy and be very careful to stay within that small invisible tape to avoid a sudden shower in the river. I am sure my guys failed to see any humor in my warnings but I hope you do.

We were moving at a pace set between two and four miles an hour and I couldn't see Speedy because I couldn't even see the end of my arm. I radioed him to take it easy and not to get too far ahead of me. He called back to ask if I had just felt a bump, which I had and he replied, "Well that was your tank bumping mine so I am not very far ahead of you." All I could say was "Roger and out." Although the bridge was roughly 1200 feet long somebody must have stretched it to about five miles that night because it was a long way across. We finally made it without any serious problems. Some may ask why I put my five tanks at one time on a bridge whose strength was unknown but I gave it a lot of thought and because I knew from the machine gun fire that there were some Germans over there and, always fearful, especially at night, of their use of the Panzerfaust, I did not want tanks to cross one at a time and be picked off like sitting ducks. If we were in close formation and the lead tank got hit, the tank following could spray the area with its machine guns either killing or chasing the enemy off so there would be no damage to the remaining tanks. Upon reaching the other side we made the "clover leaf" under the bridge and headed toward the northern end of Erpel where we would rendezvous with our Infantry at the roadblock they were to have set up. As I mentioned, this is where we would spend the rest of the night with the Infantry providing security for the tanks and themselves.

It seemed that I was going a little farther than I expected when all of a sudden I was being fired on. That certainly wasn't my Infantry, there was no roadblock, and I found myself in a firefight. SNAFU number three. When the Germans attacked at night they would often yell and scream and call "Comrade!" which is supposed to confuse and maybe stop your firing to take prisoners. As always I was aware of the possibility of getting hit with a Panzerfaust so I dropped a grenade out of my turret and heard at least one other go off so some of my guys were doing the same thing. I wasn't about to get out of my tank in the dark so I radioed back to Battalion. I reported to the Colonel that there was no Infantry or roadblock and I was engaged with the enemy and to send me some Infantry to take prisoners. His response was: "You will hold your position until the last tank is shot out from under you." Now that wasn't exactly what I wanted to hear. I didn't ask him if I could go somewhere, although I would rather have been watching a movie or having a soda at the corner drug store. I just asked for the Infantry that I had been told would be there and wasn't.

After another sleepless night interspersed with distant machine gun fire and the occasional "swoosh" of an artillery shell coming and going we began to see the light of day which again was gray, damp and dreary. Through the early morning haze I saw a boat like the ones used to push and pull the barges up and down the Rhine. My tanks were pretty close to the water's edge and the boat was very near me moving up river toward the bridge. I yelled as loud as I could "Stop that boat. Stop that boat" then "Halt" but it kept coming ever so slowly. My Loader hearing me yelling came up through his turret hatch to man the .50 caliber machine gun and I told him to put a couple of bursts at the boat's water line. He did just that and the boat immediately dropped anchor. I decided to report what I had done and found I was still on Battalion frequency so I talked to one of the Staff Officers and said I had my guns trained on the boat ready to sink it. He said to hold my fire unless somebody started shooting at me and he would send a boarding party to take people off of the boat. In less than a half an hour a small craft arrived with just three men on it and approached the German vessel. One of the Americans called out "Kommen sie aus! Kommen sie aus! Mit hands uber kopf." I yelled over to them "I gotcha covered" just as some German soldiers came up from the cabin with their hands over their heads, the first man waving a white cloth. One of the Americans climbed aboard and went inside and soon returned with a civilian, apparently the boat's pilot. They all boarded the American craft and I noticed one GI sat at the front and the other aft with their rifles trained on their prisoners.

A little later an ambulance drove past my tank and disappeared around the corner behind some houses. I heard some machine gun fire and in a few seconds the ambulance came tearing back

Sign placed on one of the bridge towers.

around the corner and I could see a number of bullet holes in it. I radioed this incident to Captain Soumas who informed me that all units were to remain in place as reinforcements were already crossing the bridge. I now found out that SNAFU number four occurred when the first Tank Destroyer to start across the bridge last night fell into one of those holes along side of the planking but did not go all the way through and just hung there. They tried to back it off but couldn't because one track was suspended and they couldn't get traction so they tried to push it into the river because it was holding up traffic but it would not budge. It was not until 0530 that they managed to dislodge it and traffic could move across the bridge. So there I was from midnight until 0530, no Infantry, no tracks blown up, no roadblock, no Tank Destroyers and I am in a firefight all by myself. What did I tell you about those well-laid plans? SNAFU!

This photo showes the planking over the railroad tracks and the tape intended to guide the tanks and keep them from falling into holes during the midnight crossing. The bridge collapsed four hours after this photo was recorded.

Just moments after the bridge collapsed, killing 28 Engineers.

It is now around 0800 and I am up in my turret eating a box of cereal from our 10 in 1 rations when a Peep came past me headed toward that corner where the ambulance had gone a little earlier, and I let out a yell that echoed through the Rhine valley to "get that Peep back here." The driver slammed on his brakes, turned around and stopped at my tank. "What's the problem Lieutenant?" inquired the Lieutenant Colonel riding in the passenger's seat and I told him about the ambulance and that this area was under fire. He ordered his driver to go back and did not say anything about the disrespectful way I yelled at him. I didn't know it was a Colonel and it wasn't anyone I knew, but I would have acted the same regardless of who it was.

I was very glad to hear the news from Soumas that reinforcements were on the way because we only had one nights sleep in over a week and the bridge crossing and the other action during the night left my platoon really wrung out and badly in need of some relief. It was late in the morning when Soumas called me and said I was to attend an officers meeting at a house just beyond my last tank. I wondered who could be there because we only had one platoon leader across the bridge, so I walked up to the house and saw Soumas and a bunch of other officers I did not know. Soumas told me that my platoon was being attached to a Company of the 78th Infantry Division because their tanks hadn't arrived yet. I felt like killing him but all I could do was shake my head and wonder what he thought my men were made of. We walked over to where the others were gathered and Soumas introduced me to the Captain who was the commander of the Infantry Company. Soumas said he was sending me one of the two remaining tanks from the Second Platoon and I should let it lead the Platoon for a while. I was really worried that we were being pushed beyond the limits of human endurance and that we might be approaching the breaking point. I dreaded having to tell those very weary guys that we were going to continue the fight. It was enough that we didn't get the break we thought we would when we reached the Rhine and now to have to keep going seemed like a little too much to me.

German prisoners being escorted across the bridge.

Chapter 14

EXPANDING THE BRIDGEHEAD — THE WAR GOES ON

The Infantry Captain told us that the order of march would be one Infantry platoon in the lead with the tanks in close support, followed by the rest of the Infantry Company. I told him about the gunfire around the corner from my position and he said he had heard about that and if the resistance was too strong he would bring up my tanks to clear the way. The plan was at 1330 to move the Infantry to where I was located and have the lead platoon form up in front of me prepared to go forward at 1400. It was then about 1230 and I wanted to get back to my tanks and explain to the Tank Commanders what we were going to do knowing that they were going to be some very unhappy people. They wanted to know how long this would last and all I could tell them was probably until the Infantry Divisions could get their own tanks across the bridge to rejoin them. Pretty soon the foot troops came up and a lieutenant with his platoon walked by my tank to deploy just beyond the tanks. I had put the tank I had received from the Second Platoon in the lead with Sergeant Connell's tank next. I was behind him, then Speedy, then Jewell who had taken over Weaver's tank when Weaver became First Sergeant. A few days after Sid had been killed I got Soumas' permission to offer Weaver a Battlefield Commission but Weaver turned it down saying, "you can stay up front there Lieutenant, I'll stay back where I am." Then our First Sergeant got hit and Weaver agreed to take that job leaving me without a Platoon Sergeant so Sergeant Connell was made my Platoon Sergeant.

At 1400 hours the Infantry Captain gave the order to move out and I had told my platoon to stay close to the "doughs" because of the shooting we had heard earlier around that corner. Initially we maintained a 25 yard interval but after we had negotiated that corner without incident I had them open up to 50 yards in the event we had to open fire we would not be too close to the Infantry or each other. Also, tanks maintain a safe interval to avoid more than one tank being damaged by a single bomb or mortar shell. As we headed North artillery shelling seemed a little more intense, forcing the foot soldiers to dive for cover more often. We were nearing the town of Unkel when we changed directions and started in a more easterly heading to deepen the bridgehead, which by now had been expanded approximately two miles north and South of the bridge.

The afternoon was closing and we received orders to halt in place and the doughs to dig in for the night. Soon a truck drove up with some hot food containers to feed the Infantry guys but nothing for the tankers and I asked their Lieutenant if they weren't supposed to feed us. He said that there were only enough rations to feed his Company and that having us was a last minute decision and there wasn't enough time to order extra rations and he was sorry. Needless to say I was very displeased, not that my guys would go hungry because they always saw that they had more rations than they needed, but for them to watch those men eating hot food while they dug into a "C" ration can of cold beans seemed unfair. I guess the saying "all's fair in love and war" applied here.

We settled in for the night and my crew decided to sleep on the ground, some even partially under the tank. I sat on the deck of the tank leaning up against the turret so I could occasionally switch on my radio which we earlier had orders to shut down. Even though I was dead tired I only dozed off once in a while because I was not sure what our next move would be. Shortly after dawn I was again visited by a messenger from the Infantry C.O. who said he was to escort me to a meeting with the officers of our attack force. We walked back just a short distance to a barn close to the road where the Captain had set up his headquarters. I walked in and was offered a cup of coffee by the Captain who was seated at a table with a map spread out on it. Soon all the officers were there and he had us gather around the table so we could see the map. He drew a circle on the map saying that town would be our next objective, which was roughly three miles away and we should take the town before noon. Then he said "There are three ways we can attack this problem: number one, we can have the tanks charge the town at top speed with guns blazing creating chaos among the defenders; number two, the tanks could advance in line with our infantry riding on them; or number three, the tanks could move in cautiously with the infantry following on foot using the tanks as cover. I will decide which plan we will use once we are close enough to make an evaluation of the situation. We will have air reconnaissance to keep us informed of enemy strength and movements." He then said that our order of march would be the same as before and the line of departure would be where my lead tank was located, and we should be in position in one hour. The time at that moment was 0730 and we synchronized our watches with his, after which we were dismissed.

I returned to my tanks and gathered my Tank Commanders to brief them on the plans for the morning. I was careful to give them the three methods of attacking the town, resulting in some very spirited responses and even a few chuckles. It was obvious that the Captain wanted to get our tanks involved but wasn't quite sure how to go about it. The men asked "What was plan four?" They must have gotten a little rest because they appeared in better spirits.

It turns out that Soumas had given me both of the two remaining tanks of the Second Platoon so I put the other one in the lead with Jewell's tank next, then mine, next Goodson, Connell, then the other tank from the Second Platoon. Sergeant Swayne's dozer tank was not with me, probably kept back for any clean up work wherever needed.

The "doughs" began to assemble around the tanks and one platoon moved in front to take the lead according to the formation of the previous day. One thing that was different was a Medic Peep fell in between the tanks and the leading Infantry platoon in order to reach any injured troops a little more quickly. In spite of the emphasis that the Captain placed on the use of the tanks, I had a keen respect for these men who were out there protected only by a G.I. Shirt. They started out at 0830 right on schedule and after about a fifteen minute interval I gave my tanks the order to move out, leaving us a thousand yards behind the lead element, but at even five miles per hour we would soon be closer to them than desired. I had told the Tank Commander of the lead tank to keep moving if the doughs stopped, in case they would run into something and needed our help. Incoming artillery was almost a fact of life when tanks were involved. That is why we tried to keep a substantial distance between ourselves and the foot soldiers. We were reasonably unaffected by artillery fire, except for a direct hit, as long as the guys kept their hatches closed, which I insisted upon when there was a threat of enemy fire.

I was constantly using my binoculars to observe the efficient manner in which those Infantrymen went about their business. As they approached a hill a couple of scouts ran forward then crawled to the crest to check for any machine gun nests that might be in the area. If they came to a wooded area, a squad of men would systematically work their way through and should there be a lot of gunfire another squad would quickly dash over to give support. That kind of teamwork usually results in the success of the operation.

Suddenly I saw my lead tank had stopped but Jewell's tank kept on going, giving me the impression that the lead tank was having mechanical problems and I wasn't very happy about that. As I pulled up along side of the "disabled" tank I saw a man on the ground and I yelled "What's the problem?" One of them said "Mounts got hit." Mounts was the driver of that Second Platoon tank, and apparently was not buttoned up and was hit either by shrapnel or sniper. I radioed ahead for Jewell to move up to the Medics' Peep and have them send someone back to attend to Mounts, and Jewell radioed back that he was already on the way. I had to keep moving but shortly the Medics came up to render aid to Mounts. In spite of their efforts they were unable to save him, as Henry Mounts' wounds proved to be fatal.

It was nearly noon when we came to a halt and the Captain's runner came to my tank. He said that the objective was reported to be undefended and it looked like it would be a house-to-house operation. I was to deploy my tanks at this position and wait for further orders. No sooner had I gotten my tanks in place when the Captain arrived in his Peep and asked if I had any questions. I told him I had received his message "loud and clear." He then motioned to the rest of his Company to come through and be ready to approach the town. He told me to have my tanks in a state of readiness, in case things in the town were not as had been reported to him and if he met stiffer resistance than expected. Also he thought the presence of the tanks may have caused any enemy troops to pull out and he would send a runner back with a situation report after they had cleared the town. Seeing our tanks on this side of the Rhine must have had a shock effect on the Germans because the River was supposed to be an insurmountable obstacle to the allied offensive and the present situation certainly reduced their morale to a new low. We never did establish radio contact with the Infantry, but of course I had communication with my tanks and passed along this information to them.

The Captain then took off and followed his men as they neared the town, and from my vantage point through my glasses I could see in the distance some of the action as it unfolded. There was some scattered rifle fire and I couldn't tell if they saw something or if it were just precautionary to flush out anybody who may have hung back. Again I marveled at how they methodically approached the problem by forming units to secure a building with some surrounding it, the others entering the door. They gradually disappeared from my view, and now I had to turn my attention to a problem of my own.

I was dangerously low on fuel and it was obvious to me that no one was assuming the responsibility of providing it for me so I could keep on going. I had not heard from anybody in "A" Company since I had been attached to this Infantry Company and I wondered if I were out of range of our radios so I called Soumas, "Calling Greek, this is Bingo. Over". Nothing but silence. Again "Greek this is Bingo. Over." Then "Bingo this is Gopher Headquarters, go ahead. Over." Gopher was Colonel Engeman's code name since he was from Minnesota. I said "Gopher this is Bingo. I am desperately in need of fuel and feel it would be unwise for me to move from my present position. Over." "Bingo this is Gopher, we read your message and will see what we can do. Out." It sounded like they were not making any promises, and I had the uneasy feeling that my needs were very low on Battalion's list of priorities but all I could do was wait and hope.

At this point there would be an amazing chain of events that started back when we were still in the Metz area the previous month. There was this wild Lieutenant named Morrison who I believe was in "C" Company of our Battalion. He loved to gamble and was always in a poker game if the situation permitted. Everybody liked "Morey," which we all called him, and one day during a lull in his card playing, "Morey" decided to try to make a swagger stick out of a German 50 caliber shell. As he tried to open the shell the powder somehow exploded, inflicting some pretty bad burns on "Morey's" upper legs and he was taken to the hospital. While he was there, the Ninth Armored received its orders to move North, and when Morey heard about it he told his doctors that he had to get out so he could be with his outfit, but the doctors told him his wounds hadn't healed yet and they could not discharge him. "Morey" persuaded the doctors to let him ride in an ambulance under the watchful eye of the Battalion Surgeon Captain Stackhouse and so he was able to stay with the Ninth.

So here I am with my tanks sitting out in an open field with an occasional artillery shell fired at our position and worrying how I can get fuel for the tanks. I am looking through my glasses hoping I might see some help coming when way off to the rear I see a truck heading in my direction and I breathe a little prayer that it is my fuel. Believing that it is I was trying to locate a safe spot where the truck could unload its cargo and I noticed it was getting closer to us putting it in danger of getting hit by the artillery. Well it kept coming and coming until I could see that the driver was Lieutenant Morrison and he pulled up right behind my tank. I said "Morey, what are you doing? Your are going to get us all killed." He hobbled down from the cab and said "Hurry up and get your gas." The men were already running up to get these five-gallon cans of fuel and carry them back to their tanks. We were standing at the rear of my tank when there was some shelling. "Morey" and I both dove under my tank, and I swear "Morey" was laughing like it was a big joke, while I was wondering if this was the end. He was actually enjoying being under fire and when the shelling finally stopped the men finished refueling so "Morey" could get out of there. Later, when I was able to tell my fellow officers about that incident, it was said he probably wanted to get killed because he had three wives back in Texas and had not divorced any of them. He eventually did get killed riding in his tank when a Panzerfaust hit him.

I could see how exhausted my men were and what an effort it was to carry those five-gallon cans to gas up their tanks. It began to trouble me when they seemed almost oblivious to the danger of the artillery fire that we had been receiving every day for ten days with practically no rest and only their cold rations to eat. This kind of indifference could get them hurt so I got on the radio and told my platoon not to take any chances and I was sure we would soon be pulled back, although I had no idea when that might happen.

As the evening wore on things seemed to quiet down a bit and I assumed that the Infantry guys were going to spend the night in the town that they had spent most of the day clearing and probably concluded it was now secured. I told my guys to try and get some rest but keep one man on the .50 caliber at all times. Since I wanted to stay on my radio I let my crew relax and hopefully get a little sleep. Our machine gun was within my reach in case I needed it, but as I have said before, back then we did not have night vision scopes and could do very little in the dark. I must admit that several times during the night I caught myself dozing off and would suddenly awaken and tried shaking my head and twisting my body to speed up circulation. Total fatigue was starting to overtake me. I kept trying to think of ways that I could avoid losing control of my faculties, so I stooped down in the turret and shook the loader, and told him to open his hatch and come up to talk to me. Since this was the man that fixed me that cup of coffee during the Battle of the Bulge, we talked about that and could laugh a little thinking what could have happened to us. I told him that as much as I needed it now, I didn't want him to ever do that again. This really helped me, and I chomped on a chocolate bar and gulped down some water to try to build a little energy.

The next morning the Infantry Captain rode up in his Peep and told me that he would be moving his Company out of the town later in the morning and when he did I should enter the town and remain until further orders. He said that he had received word that some of the tanks from the Battalion, which was attached to the 78th Infantry Division, had come across the bridge and when they got organized he would be able to turn me loose. I told him that was good news because I was afraid my men, and I as well, were beginning to suffer the effects of the prolonged exposure to enemy fire. I radioed this information to my platoon and gave them the line of march toward the town which would be Connell, Miller, Goodson, Jewell and the tank from the Second Platoon which may have been commanded by Sergeant Herder.

By late morning I had the tanks line up and we started rolling toward the area that the Infantry was evacuating and we were able to take over. When we arrived their rear guard was just clearing the last couple of buildings in that end of town so we deployed at strategic positions in order to best observe the entire situation. I had stopped my tank right beside a house and knowing that the doughs had cleared all buildings, I still thought I should look around. With my carbine at the "ready" I went inside and checked each room, and being careful of "booby traps," finally reached the kitchen. The place was pretty much a mess from the job the other guys did but I opened a cabinet and saw a loaf of black bread and a jar of cherry preserves that they must have missed. We had often been warned against eating any food left around because of the possibility it could be poisoned or booby-trapped but this looked so good I thought I would take a chance. I found a knife, cut off a slice of bread and spread some of the preserves on it and it was delicious. I had read that the Germans complained so much about not having any white bread and had to eat this black bread, which I though was great. Since I felt no ill effects, I even fixed myself another piece but I did not drink this water using my canteen instead. I was really enjoying those few minutes of relaxation when one of my men came in and said the Company was calling for us to return. This was the message I was waiting for, so I told the man that the bread and preserves were good and he could take them. I hastened as best I could back to my tank. I radioed Soumas calling "Greek this is Bingo. Over." The response was "Bingo this is Greek Headquarters, go ahead. Over." "Greek this is Bingo, I received a message that I am to return to base. Will you confirm? Over." "Bingo, Greek Headquarters, message is confirmed. Return to base and report to Battalion Headquarters. Over." "Greek this is Bingo. Roger-Wilco and out."

We lost no time in gathering our forces to prepare to return to our own Company but I wondered why I was to report to Battalion. Certainly they didn't have another mission for me because we just could not take any more without a break, and I was ready to tell them that. We were about 13 or 14 miles from Erpel and we arrived back there in less than two hours, going first to the house where my platoon was to be billeted, then I trudged up the street to Battalion Headquarters. There were some people standing around and I just said that I was Lieutenant Miller and I had orders to report here. With that an officer, who I believe was Captain Roberts, stepped up and said, "Here, you better have a seat, Lieutenant," and he took my arm and had me sit in a chair then walked back to the others. I just sat there almost in a daze and I heard somebody say, "Those guys are really beat. Just look at Miller over there." That did not do much for my ego but I can imagine that I looked pretty awful. The Captain came back after a while, and told me the Colonel was out but would talk to me later about what happened while I was with that Infantry unit. He suggested I go back to my Company and he would tell the Colonel I had been there. So back I went, hoping to get some time to lie down and get a little sleep.

Someone had brought my bedroll and duffle bag in and placed them in one of the rooms on the first floor. This house was what we called Colonial style back home. It had a center entrance to a small foyer with what would be a living room on the right, a dining room on the left and the kitchen to the rear. From the foyer was the stairway leading to the second floor containing three bedrooms and a bath. My things were in the living room area and the rest of the platoon was scattered in the other rooms. I described this house because of an incident that took place, which I will relate to you in the next chapter so don't go away.

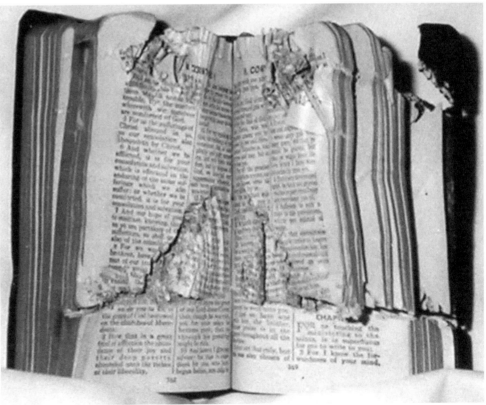

A recent photo of Thomas (Jack) Ward of Company "A" and a close up of his shredded prayer book. On March 1, 1945, this prayer book saved his life when his tank was hit and he received several wounds. The piece of shrapnel that tore through this book would have pierced Ward's heart. Luckily Ward carried this in his left shirt pocket where the book's metal cover (now badly dented) stopped the shrapnel.

Chapter 15

SOME R & R AND NONE TOO SOON

It seems that while the Third Platoon was involved with the 78th, the remaining people of "A" Company were taking it kind of easy except for maintenance on the tanks and weapons. The First Platoon still had not crossed the river because they had to wait for the engineers to improvise a ferry to bring those Pershing Tanks over one at a time. Those staying on the west side of the river were being subjected to some heavy artillery fire, and since the town of Erpel was situated at the base of a very high cliff which provided some protection, the Headquarters of both the Battalion and CCB lost no time in setting up in Erpel.

I stretched out on my bedroll for a while and Soumas came in to ask how I was. I really did not know what to tell him because I just did not know, so I could only shrug my shoulders in response. He said the kitchen was here and chow would be in about 30 minutes and he would see me then. The kitchen had been set up behind the houses very close to the cliff, which gave it more cover from enemy fire. As tired as I was, I was still anxious to get some hot food in me and it did help. Soumas and I were the only officers there because Grimball stayed back with his tanks and I guess Lieutenant Yoho was with him. Soumas said he heard about Henry Mounts and another man getting it the same day and he wanted to know what else took place during those three days. He also told me that when he was asked for some tanks he had no choice but to send me, but I still felt he could have suggested using another Company. I suppose he thought that would not be proper so I got the short straw. He said to give my men a day to relax but the tanks and guns should be serviced as soon as possible. Most of the men were back at the house when I got back, and I told them what the Captain had said and to try and rest up.

When I finally "hit the sack" I was convinced that I would not wake up for a week, but combat creates some unbreakable habits so as dawn broke I opened my eyes, ready to get up to start the new day. Immediately I arose and went up to shave and clean up for the first time in two weeks, which had a very refreshing effect on both my mind and body. I pulled some clean clothes out of my duffle bag, all of which made me feel like a "new" man, a far cry from the "old" man that "crashed" just the night before. You can imagine how great breakfast was, another first after those devastating two weeks that had cost "A" Company so much. I tried so hard to flush those horrible thoughts out of my mind because there was more fighting to be done and such thinking is a deterrent to the aggressive attitude necessary to carry on.

Remember the floor plan of the house as I described it previously? Because following breakfast, I was standing in the foyer talking with several of my men when there was a tremendous explosion over our heads, and we knew that the house had been hit with something big. In a matter of seconds we saw this skinny little man as white as a sheet, covered with plaster dust, come charging down the steps with his pants down around his knees, dashing past our group and "mooning" us as he tore through the front door, which fortunately was open. He had been upstairs in the bathroom sitting on the "throne" when this huge shell came through the roof just above where he was sitting and he lost no time in vacating the premises, cutting loose with a stream of cuss words that would have made any old soldier proud. The man was Richard Lively who told me many years later that he weighed 115 pounds at the time of this incident, which could have and should have been a terrible tragedy but resulted in what I call one of the funniest situations to come out of the war. Richard is still with us and comes to our Company reunions where the subject always comes up. We even had a ceremony where he was crowned our

"Richard the Lion-Hearted" and was restored to his "throne." It had to have been a mortar shell because the house was too close to the cliff for artillery to hit it.

At one point we heard an enormous amount of firing outside so we stepped out to see what it was all about. There was a whole battery of antiaircraft guns firing at a German fighter-bomber that was trying to get through to bomb the bridge but our guns got a hit and I saw the pilot bail out, landing right in the middle of the Rhine River. I don't believe he made it to shore. I will have to say we were all pretty jumpy and this kind of action didn't do much to settle our nerves.

Meanwhile, the Engineers were hard at work, some building a pontoon bridge across the river, others trying to reinforce and strengthen the badly damaged old railroad bridge. Artillery was a constant threat to these men, who labored feverishly to get the job done in order to provide bridging for the additional forces needed to further expand the bridgehead and continue the assault on central Europe. Often I saw them run for their lives when the shelling got so heavy they had to abandon their work to dash for shelter on the banks of the river.

As the day drew to a close, a couple of good things happened to me. The mail clerk arrived with some letters from Gracie and an order to report to Battalion the next day at 0800 with clothing and accessories sufficient for a seven day leave in Paris. I had not received any mail since before we left Aachen nearly two weeks ago, so I was really eager to read what Gracie had to say. I remember that she said she felt some relief by the reports that things seemed to be going our way but trouble was expected when we reached the Rhine River. Reports were that the Germans were building up their forces to prevent the Allied Armies from crossing the river and a major battle was anticipated at that time. She obviously had not heard about our capture of the bridge when she wrote her last letter, and I wanted to let her know I had made it but it was too soon to refer to any action in our letters.

My appearance when I reported to Battalion Headquarters must have made someone realize that I had taken a rather severe physical and emotional beating while leading the drive for the Rhine, crossing the bridge, and continuing the attack while attached to the 78th Division. They apparently thought I was in serious need for some rest and recuperation and decided to give me a break for a few days. Although I was feeling a lot better after some hot food and a little rest, I wasn't about to refuse this trip to Paris. I was concerned about being away from my platoon but indications were that they would be staying in Erpel for at least several more days.

I had put on clean clothes so I packed the soiled things, hoping there would be some facilities for having them cleaned. The next morning I again got up early to shave, wash up and have some breakfast before heading to Battalion. I had told my guys where I was going, that I would see them in a week and to stay out of trouble, which was asking a lot of those war-weary men.

At Battalion there were others to go also, so we mounted a truck and were soon on our way. We were to cross back over the bridge, which still was one-way so we had to be escorted by an MP while traffic was stopped on the opposite side. After we got across, the driver had to weave in and out because we were one of a very few vehicles going in our direction and there still was a lot of debris along the road. An officer rode up with the driver and I got the impression that they had made this trip a number of times before. When there was a stretch of clear road the driver really stepped on it, and I am thinking that I got through all of that combat only to be killed in a truck wreck. We had to travel about 250 miles, so I guess he wanted to be sure we would get there before dark. Somewhere between 1200 and 1300 we came to an encampment with a mess tent set up and we were fed a hot lunch, a luxury I was beginning to get used to. Except for being bumpy the ride was uneventful and we arrived in Paris late in the afternoon. The officers were dropped off at one hotel and the others were taken to another one nearby. The hotel was run by the Red Cross, where coffee and donuts were available at all times. I was assigned a room and given directions to the Officers' Mess, which also was open day and night. A couple of the other officers and I agreed we would wash up, take a little rest then meet to walk over together for chow. It hardly seemed possible that we could move around so freely without the threat of some kind of enemy attack. After a nice meal we all walked back to the hotel, and each of us seemed anxious to grab a magazine from the rack and retire to our rooms where we could "crash" and relax completely. It wasn't long before I slipped off into the arms of Morpheus for the first night of a sound sleep that I had in weeks.

Because I have a built-in alarm clock, I was able to wake up and get one of the two bathrooms on my floor before anyone else. It had a shower stall and the other two essential pieces of equipment, which enabled me to take care of all my needs. They had put towels in my room and since this hotel was for men only I could move from the bath to my room draped only in my towel. I got dressed, made my bed, straightened the room and filled out the laundry list and put it and my clothes in the laundry bag that was in my room. Then I went downstairs and gave my laundry to the man at the desk and walked over to have some breakfast. I decided to take a little stroll around the area and immediately became aware that rationing here was much stricter than we had at home, as evidenced by the limited vehicular traffic on the streets. What there was of it was mostly military and hundreds of bicycles, including one ridden by a nun, which I had never seen before but would see many times during my visit to Paris. It was such a nice day I just roamed through the streets and peeked into some of the shops which seemed to be low on stock, once again the result of tight rationing.

Since it was getting close to noon I started working my way to the Officers Mess where I saw one of the guys I rode with, so we had some lunch together. I told him what I had been doing that morning, and he said that he had slept late and just had some doughnuts and coffee at the hotel. Those of us who came together did not spend much time together so I can't remember any names. It seems that we all wanted to use that time trying to get our heads back on straight, and being alone would be the best way to do that. Together our conversation would certainly lead to discussions of what we had just been through which could defeat the purpose of the break. As we walked back to the hotel I told him that I had brought along the latest letters from Gracie and wanted to read them over again to see just how many of her inquiries I could answer.

At the hotel they had some tables in the lobby with paper and pencils, so I got Gracie's letters and sat down to try to respond without violating any censorship regulations. I always start out by saying I am fine, but this time I had to add that I was very tired and had been sent to Paris for a little rest. I told her to pay attention to the date of this letter and the dates of certain news reports so she would know that I was ok as of this date. It was too soon to tell her about the bridge incident and I certainly could not tell her about Sid because of the restrictions against mentioning casualties on either side. The fact that I didn't even mention Sid's name might have been a clue that something had happened to him. I told her how I had spent that morning, especially about the nun riding a bicycle because she had always attended Catholic schools and back then, all the teachers were nuns and the thought of a nun riding a bicycle was unheard of.

Each day I would take a leisurely walk to one of the city's landmarks, which included the Eiffel Tower where I was only permitted to go up to the first landing, the Arc de Triomphe with its Eternal Flame, or a walk along the Seine River. I noticed that there were no pleasure craft, just working boats hauling various materials. I had planned to go to Mass at the Cathedral of Notre Dame on Sunday and it wasn't until I got there that I found out it was Palm Sunday. When I walked into the church I was suddenly aware of a sacred aura about the place, and a huge choir of blended voices started singing a hymn, softly at first and as I walked up the aisle toward the altar they appeared to gradually increase the volume until the tremendous power of their voices almost shook the walls of that holy building. For Palm they handed out these tiny branches with little green leaves on them and I wondered if this was customary in Europe or was the type of Palm I was used to just wasn't available. I placed that little piece of greenery in my prayer book that I always kept in the left hand pocket of my GI shirt, and it remained there until just a few years ago when it either just deteriorated or it fell out on one of the many times I displayed it during one of my talks. The front cover of that prayer book was metal and many of the men carried one just as I did, and I found out later one actually saved the life of a man in Sid's platoon. The Mass was just beautiful and the atmosphere there had sort of a cleansing effect on me for just being there. It was truly an uplifting experience, renewing the strength and determination I needed to go back and finish the job that I had started.

Now the hour was approaching when I would have to bid a fond au revoir to the not-so-gay Paree and return to the business of dodging enemy bullets. Although it was early spring, the weather was rather warm and by mid-afternoon after inhaling a lot of dust we all were pretty thirsty. We arrived at a little town where there was a small beer hall so we stopped hoping to get something cold to drink. Most of the guys ordered these frosted mugs of cold beer, but since I was a non-drinker I declined and asked for a soft drink. To my dismay, I was told they only served beer so since it was cold and wet I ordered a mug, but just one swallow convinced me I would never be a beer drinker.

It wasn't long before we reached the Rhine River and I thought how different this drive to the Rhine was compared to the one just a few short weeks before. We crossed somewhere north of Remagen on a pontoon bridge and drove south and east, finally reaching the Battalion area only about fifteen miles from Remagen. I reported in to Battalion and Company, then located where I was to bed down before heading for chow. Grimball told me progress had been slow due to several minefields and roadblocks that had to be cleared by the Engineers. Enemy resistance had been comparatively light but was expected to increase as we penetrated deeper into enemy territory. It seems that I got back just in time for some rough going — how lucky can you get? I don't think many people believed that I didn't get drunk while in Paris or that my activities there were of such a subdued nature. They seemed to lose sight of the fact that my reasons for going were more therapeutic than recreational.

At the officers call that evening we were told that the major mission of the First Army, which we were a part of, was to contact the Russians at the Elbe River, a distance of approximately 500 miles. We should expect to encounter more minefields and roadblocks plus pockets of heavy resistance. Our air and artillery support would be increased and there could be some lengthy drives if the enemy started running. As usual we would receive a supply of maps for the territory we would be covering, and it was hoped that the tanks would shut down at night but no promises.

Because of the short distances the Battalion had traveled, the kitchens kept pretty close to their Companies so we had breakfast the next morning and things seemed to move at a more relaxed pace compared to the fury and intensity of the drive for the Rhine. As predicted our advance was slowed at first while a stretch of landmines was cleared, and later on a roadblock held us up. Fortunately neither of these obstacles was covered by enemy fire as was the case early on.

During one of these delays I started reading some of my mail that was handed to me on my return from Paris and I was shocked into disbelief by one of the letters from Gracie dated March 8, 1945. In it she wrote:

> The strangest thing happened last night that left me filled with all kinds of emotions such as confusion, fear, joy, amazement and wonder. I don't know how long I had been asleep but I suddenly awakened and sat straight up to see a bright light shining on your picture which was on my dresser. I could not cry out or get up, all I could do was just stare at this phenomenon and wonder what message it was trying to convey. Did something happen to you? Were you in trouble? Are you all right? The light on your picture slowly dimmed until it was gone and my room was left in total darkness. I lay back on my pillow trying to determine what meaning I could attach to this awesome experience which left me totally drained but mysteriously calm and assured that all was well, permitting me to fall back into a deep sleep for the rest of the night.

Of course that letter referred to an incident that occurred at the exact moment I was crossing that bridge which was accomplished only by the Grace of God who was telling Gracie that he was watching over her husband at a time of great peril to himself and his men. At the first opportunity I wrote Gracie that I was not able to tell her what happened that night but to remember that date and I would try to clear up the mystery for her at a later date. As it turned out, the newspaper reporters reached her before I did. They wanted a photo of me to run with an interview a reporter from the Associated Press had with Colonel Engeman in which he related the story of the capture and crossing of the bridge at Remagen. In that interview the Colonel recounted the conversation he and I had when I radioed that I was under attack and to send me some infantry to take prisoners and this is what he said:

Lieutenant Miller had hollered a couple of times for some "doughs" to take prisoners. The Germans were hanging around wanting to surrender but we have found it wasn't healthy to get out of a tank in a situation like that. I told him to stay there until the last tank was shot up. He came back with a 'Roger' and I didn't hear any more from him.

This article was run in the *Washington Star* on March 18, 1945 and Gracie got a copy of that paper. In my talks I tell people that after reading that story she went directly to the Veterans Administration to collect my insurance, which of course isn't true. I am sure she was "shook" up as the Colonel's closing remark certainly did sound menacing and final and naturally gave Gracie cause for some concern.

On the night that I crossed the bridge at Remagen, my wife Gracie awoke to see a light shining on this picture

Chapter 16

RENDEZVOUS WITH RUSSKY AT THE ELBE RIVER

The early days of this drive were painfully slow due to more mines, roadblocks and frequent artillery shelling. Then there was the ever-present Panzerfaust, which fortunately is not very accurate beyond fifty yards, although we did hear that Lieutenant Morrison of "C" Company caught one right in the chest that killed him. Also we sometimes waited for a psychological warfare tank to come up with its huge amplifiers and warn the town's-people to put out white flags or be subjected to our artillery barrages.

At one point we ran into a heavy concentration of enemy artillery and we had an air-ground liaison officer in one of our tanks. Soumas radioed that the he was going to call for air support and for us to make sure we had the correct identification panel on our tanks. Shortly, three fighter-bombers zoomed low over our column and I could see off in the distance where they would dive behind this high hill and then a big cloud of smoke would rise above that hill. After they had made several passes at that position they came on the radio and said, "Mission accomplished, we're heading home." You can imagine how we felt having to continue the battle while they go back to a hot meal, a shower and a warm bed. But the air-ground liaison officer radioed back, "Before you go, how about giving the boys a show?" and sure enough they did all kinds of rolls and loops and really put on a show for us right in combat. Then they took off and we hated their guts. Not really because as always our Air Force guys did a fantastic job for us.

Pretty soon we started to pick up the pace, driving 28 miles one day, 68 miles another day and so on and the lead element was rotated frequently because we had most of our Battalion with us. One day as we were moving along, I heard a terrific explosion to my rear and I saw a huge cloud of smoke and flames then a number of smaller explosions, and I wondered if that could have been a large bomb, but found out later that we had by-passed a gigantic ammunition dump that one of the units following us had blown up. It was a relief to know that the enemy had not launched another huge bomb at us, as we hoped he no longer had that capability.

On the fifth of April some of us were pulled off the line and driven a pretty good distance to the rear. There we were lined up and General Leonard, the Commanding General of the 9th Armored Division, stepped forward to address us. He told us that we were gathered there to receive recognition for our part in the capture and crossing of the bridge at Remagen, and praised us for the courage and toughness we displayed in that great accomplishment. He also said he decided to do this at that time just to make sure we did receive these decorations. I wondered if he was suggesting we might not be around at a later date. He then walked down the line pinning the Distinguished Service Cross on each of us. I remember after he pinned mine on he shook my hand and said, "Congratulations Lieutenant. Keep up the good work." I replied, "I intend to sir." And I wanted to add, "if these Germans will let me," but I didn't. Grimball, Soumas and Goodson were the others in our Company who received them. After the ceremony, we were dismissed and were back on the firing line in about an hour.

The war-weary Germans were surrendering in increasing numbers, but there were always those fanatics who were still taking a toll on the advancing Americans. Those wanting to surrender were ordered to drop their weapons, remove their helmets and any other instruments of combat including daggers, binoculars, compasses, cameras, etc, place their hands on their heads and move to our rear. We watched carefully as they passed us to make sure they had removed all of such items. At

Our Division Commander, General Leonard, congratulating me after pinning the Distinguished Service Cross on me. Captain George Soumas, my Commanding Officer, is seen in background. April 5, 1945.

My Distinguished Service Cross.

> The President of the United States of America, authorized by Act of Congress, July 9, 1918, has awarded the Distinguished Service Cross to
>
> FIRST LIEUTENANT CHARLES W. MILLER, USA
>
> for extraordinary heroism in military operations against an armed enemy:
>
> First Lieutenant Charles W. Miller, 01016389, 14th Tank Battalion, United States Army, for extraordinary heroism in action against the enemy on 7 March 1945, in Germany. Upon approaching the Ludendorf railroad bridge across the Rhine River, First Lieutenant Miller immediately placed his tank platoon in a commanding position and directed effective fire upon hostile emplacements on the opposite bank, covering the crossing of friendly infantry and engineer units. That night, despite the extreme darkness and the fact that the strength of the bridge was unknown, First Lieutenant Miller, in the face of intense machine gun and artillery fire, personally led his platoon across the span. By his daring courage and unhesitating action, First Lieutenant Miller succeeded in leading the first American armor across the Rhine River, providing invaluable support for the foot troops on the opposite bank.

Citation for my Distinguished Service Cross.

one point I noticed a lone German officer walking in my direction who had something hanging around his neck so I decided to dismount and check it out. I had my carbine at the ready and ordered him to halt. As I approached him I noticed that it was a camera, which I immediately relieved him of and after looking him over, motioned him to continue towards the rear where our intelligence people would pick him up for interrogation. I returned to my tank and stuck the camera in my musette bag and wondered if it or I would survive to ever use it. Fortunately, we both did and I still have it, which I have put to good use.

Shortly after we had crossed the Rhine, and while I was away in Paris, there was a change in command. We were now designated as Combat Command "A" but Colonel Harrold was Commander and General Hoge who had been in command of CCB was given an Armored Division. You wonder, when there is a command change, if there would be a change in strategy and tactics but I did not notice any difference as we continued the attack on the enemy.

A situation occurred that I probably shouldn't write about but in order to maintain the integrity of this account I feel compelled to include it. Another tank company with some infantry was in the lead when we approached a town that appeared badly shot up. Although there were no white flags displayed, it appeared that the place was deserted and no resistance was anticipated so we moved on in. When we were in the town it was break time and the men dismounted and lit up or whatever. As I often did, I remained in my tank to keep the radio open. It so happened that where my tanks stopped there was a jewelry store that was pretty well damaged. When the break was over the men climbed aboard and one of my crew said, "Lieutenant do you want a watch?" and he had about a half a dozen little foil boxes each with just the works and face of a watch in it. I took one and thought that was the least these guys deserved after all they had been through so I didn't say anything. After all they were just "liberating" those things even though some might call it looting. I still have the watch but I had to have a case and bracelet made for it.

Our advance continued at a rather irregular pace and I suspected that the observation planes overhead would spot some heavy gun emplacements causing us to pull up while they were neutralized. At one point we had stopped and while we waited to resume our march, a line of surrendering Germans walked past and one man did not have his hands on his head. I noticed he really looked old and beat, which I guess all of us did and as he stumbled along, Lively, who was in the tank just in front of mine, jumped out with his .30 caliber machine gun which we called a "grease gun" because that is what it looked like. He walked over to this guy and pointed his gun at him and I thought he was going to shoot him. I yelled at Lively to take it easy and get back in his tank but before he did he grabbed this man's two hands and roughly jammed them on his head almost knocking the poor guy down. Lively was really mad and I couldn't help thinking that a day or two earlier that German would have killed both of us if he had the opportunity.

The next day something happened that almost made me wish Lively had shot the man. We were nearing a town and could see in the distance that the people had their "laundry" out indicating that the town was undefended so we moved on in. The people were all lined up along the side of the street and as my platoon was just in the center of the town there was an explosion right in front of me. Sergeant Connell's tank had been hit and he and his crew bailed out. I stopped my tank and ran toward them as they were carrying one of the men into a house. Their tank was still moving down the street without a crew and at that moment Whitehead, the driver, took off after his tank and was able to climb on and bring it to a stop. In the meantime I saw a squad of infantry guys take off in the direction of a man who had fired a Panzerfaust from his position just back away from the street we were on. Our people soon returned and I heard one of them say, "Yeah, we got the SOB." An elderly woman standing at the street suffered burns from the flash from the weapon and she was taken away to be treated. I went into the house where they had taken the injured man. He had been hit in the legs but did not seem to be in a lot of pain. I told him I was sorry and he said, "Don't be sorry for me Lieutenant. I am going home and you guys have to stay and fight some more." I shook his hand, wished him luck and went back to my tank. Connell's tank had a hole in the hull just above the drive sprocket but could still be driven. Since we had been shutting down at suppertime most days I told Connell to try to stay with us until then and maintenance would take over, which he was able to do.

It was just a week after the medal ceremony with the General when a Peep pulled along side of my tank during a break on our drive toward the Elbe River. A Lieutenant on the passenger side yelled something to me that I didn't understand so I yelled back to say it again. "The President has died," he said, "President Roosevelt is dead," then he drove on. My first reaction was shock and disbelief because we were not aware that he was even ill. Current events take a while to reach the front lines. Then I started to wonder what effect this would have on the war. Would there be a change in tactics and strategy, would this lift the morale of the enemy and lower that of the allied forces? Soon I started thinking more intelligently and realized that plans had to be in place for the conduct of the war well into the future. We had lost a great and much respected leader and he would be sorely missed, so now it was time for his successor, President Truman to step up to carry on this gigantic endeavor that still lay ahead.

Although we were frequently under fire it seemed like our attack was proceeding in a more orderly fashion than we experienced in its early stages. Our reconnaissance, both air and ground, appeared to be more effective because the resistance we encountered was located and dealt with more quickly and completely than before. Furthermore, as soon as the enemy was engaged they promptly threw down their weapons and abandoned their guns to join the lengthening line of surrendering Germans. Unfortunately there often were those who were determined to fight to the bitter end. I have not described each and every encounter with the enemy that we experienced along the way because it would be so repetitious that I am fearful it might become boring. It is sufficient to say that we were in constant danger with little or no opportunity to relax, with the enemy gunfire being the order of each and every day. That is the way it is with a tanker who must constantly be alert for those kinds of attacks designed to knock out a tank and its crew.

To keep any delays to a minimum we would often skirt the edges of a town and take a course that would give us a rear view of the houses and other buildings in the areas. On one occasion when we did that, I noticed a line of high fences enclosing the back yards of the row of houses. From my position up in the turret I could see over those fences and what I saw in each of those yards sent a chill up and down my spine. There in full view, all ready to go was a German 88 cannon needing only a gunner and to have that fence pushed down, and this story would never have been written. Fortunately the guns had been abandoned and had never fired a shot. Otherwise they could have really played havoc with the advancing allies.

One day found us on the famous Autobahn, the pride and joy of the German automotive world and we were able to maintain our maximum speed of twenty miles an hour. As a result we covered a good bit of ground and it seemed like the enemy must have been forbidden to fire at anything on their beloved Autobahn and we met with no resistance the entire time.

Unfortunately we had to soon leave that stretch of road to pursue a more direct route to our objective, the Elbe River. Finally about April 16, 1945, with my platoon in the lead we came to a river where the bridge had been blown up. A glance at my map revealed that this was the Mulde River so we kept driving northward hoping to find a bridge intact ala Remagen but there was no such luck. I was ordered to hold up and not fire my big gun beyond the river for fear an overshot might hit some Russian troops approaching the Elbe River, a distance of 1500 yards. I learned later that the distance was more like five miles but I guess they were playing it safe.

A familiar scene took place when an ambulance went past my tanks and around a curve only a few hundred yards away. I heard some machine gun fire and the ambulance came roaring back riddled with bullets. In a little while just as it was getting dark, several vehicles went by, one carrying a row boat, and stopped before rounding that curve. Barely visible up that road I saw some men dismount from the vehicles and huddle behind them to discuss a plan. It now became obvious to me that whoever shot up that ambulance was on the other side of the river and our guys were making plans to cross that river and go after the culprits. I have spoken before of my admiration for our "doughs" for the manner in which they go about their business. They really know what they are doing.

Before long total darkness set in and I could no longer observe their actions, but I could imagine what they were about to do. It was very quiet for some time and then I heard the "burp" of a German sub-machine gun followed by the rattle of automatic rifles, which lasted a good ten minutes. Then there was silence broken occasionally by a short burst of rifle fire and I just hoped that all was going well for our guys. Soon I could hear voices from up the road and in a little while the vehicles came past my tanks obviously returning to their base. I learned the next day that a small group of candidates from a nearby SS training school was determined to fight to the death for the Fatherland and that is what most of them did. Our men were able to capture one of those boys alive and brought him back for interrogation.

A call from Captain Soumas informed me that we were not going to advance further. An infantry outfit passed through us, crossed the Mulde, and moved on to the Elbe for the planned rendezvous with the Russians. I suppose some of the Ninth Armored Commanders were disappointed that we didn't get that privilege but it was OK with me. We took over a few houses for a couple of days then moved back a short distance for another couple of days. According to the Battalion log, our next move was back about 21 miles where we set up for what would be an eight day stay, during which we were issued new clothing and got the impression we might soon be marching down Broadway.

We were not far from First Army Headquarters and I wondered if I would see General Kean, but it didn't happen. Also there was one of those notorious German concentration camps close by and we were offered the opportunity to visit to observe the atrocities that had been inflicted on those unfortunate prisoners. I had no desire to go and after I heard how horrible it was, I was glad I declined.

We have accomplished the First Army's mission, meeting the Russians at the Elbe River and now we can start thinking about going home — or can we? It seems that this guy named George Patton is still fighting down in Czechoslovakia and wants some additional tanks in his Third Army Sector and guess who got the call. Yeah, you got that right; it was the 14th Tank Battalion. So we pack up and again hit the road for the long trek to Czechoslovakia.

Some of the souvenirs I gathered along the way. The camera (top, center) is the one I took from a German officer. Many of the photos in this book were taken with this camera.

Chapter 17

ARE WE THERE YET? — NO, BUT SOON

Being fully aware of General Patton's passion for speed, our commanders lost no time in getting us on the road and on our way to Czechoslovakia. Since we were traveling on land we had previously taken, we met no opposition and were able to cover a good amount of ground each day. According to the Battalion log we drove nearly 75 miles the first day and over 105 miles the second day, taking a couple of days break in between each travel day. Soon after crossing the border into Czechoslovakia, we were once more into enemy territory where we were greeted by a volley of artillery shells. Now it is time to put on that invisible cloak that cannot be penetrated by any human emotion: no fear, nor compassion, no grief or joy, no pain, nor hunger, no anger, just completely without feeling. We again must push on, shooting at whatever appears to be a threat and threatening to shoot those wanting to surrender, more of whom were very old or very young wearing only an arm band for a uniform in accordance with the rules of the Geneva Convention. The return to this horrible life style had the effect of making violent men out of what once were relatively gentle people. The ear splitting sounds of war were all too familiar but which you could never get used to, causing you to grind and clinch your teeth until your jaws ached. How much longer can the body and mind endure this abuse?

Our progress had been slowed with the stiffening of the resistance but whenever we drew close to the enemy gunners, the shooting stopped and more and more prisoners were taken. At one point we drove along the bottom of a high cliff, which was a stupid place for tanks to be because any enemy troops on top of that cliff could drop grenades or shoot Panzerfausts down on us, which caused me some real concern. This was some of the worst tank country I had ever experienced and I wondered if we would ever make it through. We were lucky and did not run into any difficulty at that point. I thought "A" Company had survived this new mission without casualties but I would later learn that I was mistaken. Because of the urgency of keeping the attack going we remained with our tanks throughout each night.

Then one morning we got an early start and our artillery was already busy clearing the way for us. Our objective once again was to keep going until we met up with the Russians. So far the morning was pretty quiet and we were able to maintain a slow but steady pace. Around mid morning it seemed like an eerie quiet descended on us and while I was trying to figure out what was going on a Peep pulled along side my tank and an officer yelled something at me. I ordered my driver to stop and the officer in the Peep yelled, "It's all over. Hold up for further orders." I wasn't sure I heard him correctly so I asked him to repeat what he just said. I radioed my platoon to halt and called my Tank Commanders to my tank and gave them the message. A little later, our company Peep came up and told me that the kitchen would set up in the field nearby and chow would be at 1300 hours. Now I had seen pictures of American and Russian soldiers meeting here and at the Elbe River, showing them shaking hands, hugging, dancing and sharing a bottle of Vodka, but there was none of that kind of celebrating among our guys who still seemed almost emotionless, probably not sure that this thing was really over.

I too felt kind of numb as I stumbled over to where the chow line was forming and received the horrible news that Sergeant Swayne had been killed by sniper fire late the day before. Swayne had been with me ever since I joined the Ninth, and although he had been transferred to the Second Platoon while I was in Paris I still felt like he was one of my men. When Moskowitz and the

Second Platoon got shot up, the Platoon Sergeant was one of those wounded and, like when they took my Sergeant Weaver to replace our First Sergeant, they took Swayne to replace the Second Platoon Sergeant. I hated to lose these men but I was proud that they were selected to move up in rank. This news seemed to arouse me from my stupor and I became terribly angry that this should happen even as the War was coming to an end. After chow was over, we were assigned houses to take over for as long as we remained at this location. I sent a party of my men to the house to advise any occupants to leave because we would be billeted there while we were in the area. Shortly one of the men returned and said some ladies in the house told him there was a man upstairs who was sick in bed and couldn't be moved. I was already very angry about the news of Swayne's death, and now I was ready to explode as I charged up the stairs where this man lay in bed while the women stood there wringing their hands. I removed my carbine from my shoulder, held it at the ready and ordered my man to tell those women if that man wasn't out of there in five minutes I would shoot him. I don't know if he was really sick or not, but I was in no mood to argue and the women hurriedly escorted the man out of the house. As it turned out he was fully dressed under the covers but he did seem elderly and feeble, so I have never been sure whether I was being cruel or just refused to be fooled; in either event it didn't really matter. We took over the house and after getting settled in, returned to the tanks to perform the usual maintenance procedures.

The next day about mid-morning the Third Platoon was again selected for another juicy assignment. There were reports that a few German stragglers were heading down the main road to surrender, and I was told to take my platoon up the road to intercept them and hold them until a truck could come and pick them up for processing. So up I go to find an appropriate place to assemble these "few" German soldiers and soon I saw a large open field beside the road that seemed to be suited for the job. I placed my tanks so they straddled the road and prepared my men for what sounded like a simple mission to halt these people, disarm them, and wait for them to be picked up. But as I looked off in the distance I could see what appeared to be a column of combat vehicles plus a long line of soldiers on foot. I quickly called my Tank Commanders back to revise the plan, which included directing all vehicles into the field to form a motor park, making sure combat vehicles' guns were unloaded and their crews were disarmed and all weapons placed in an orderly pile. The line now extended down the road as far as I could see and I knew that this was more than I could handle by myself. I called Company Headquarters to advise them of the magnitude of the situation, which resulted in the use of our whole Company including some personnel from other units of the Battalion. It seems that most of the German troops in the area wanted to avoid capture by the Russians, preferring to surrender to the Americans. So it was necessary to set up a huge encampment to accommodate an estimated 20,000 men and 2000 vehicles which included armored cars, half-tracks, self propelled guns and trucks of various types. I remembered the camera that I had impounded and got it out of my musette bag to take the first picture since I obtained it. Some days later when I had the film that was already in the camera developed, this was the first photo I sent home to Gracie with an explanation on the back, and I still have that photo.

Since our tanks were positioned to surround the enclosure we had to keep them there all night while other men patrolled the area on foot, even though we did not expect anyone would try to leave. The German officers very efficiently organized units within the compound to perform various services such as medical, feeding and the like but avoiding the impression of a prisoner of war camp. However the next day a nasty situation was narrowly avoided when several men at the far side of the encampment tried to make a break for it. It so happened that I was in my tank where I had spent the night and standing nearby was our Combat Commander, Colonel Harold (he may have been made General by then) talking to a German General when the incident occurred. Seeing what was happening Harold said to the German General, "If you don't stop those men I will have the Lieutenant here open fire." Well those men were just too far away for the General to do anything so Harold said, "Lieutenant open fire." I replied, "Yes sir" and turned to the man who was manning the .50 caliber machine gun and told him to fire a burst over their heads, which effectively brought them to a halt. It seems that some British prisoners of war had just been released from a camp not far away. As they passed some of the Germans, they told them they were being held for the Russians. It was a tale made up to vent their anger for the treatment they received from their former captors. The situation was brought under control and there were no further incidents while we were there. Later in the day we were relieved by an MP Battalion and a Military Government unit.

Another duty given to me was to investigate a claim that an American soldier had molested a German girl, which I noted in my little notebook. She claimed the soldier with pistol in hand walked into the house and threatened to shoot if he did not get what he wanted. She told me her two sisters-in-law and a man I understood to be her father, were present but were ordered to leave. The girl gave me a pretty detailed description of what took place, which I have in my little notebook, which I prefer not to write about except to say that the soldier did not carry out his threat. I turned my report over to Battalion and never heard any more about it. The reason I mention this incident is to show the various types of details I was assigned. Why I got this one is a mystery to me because there are people in Battalion Headquarters who are supposed to handle such matters.

Soon we received orders to pack up because we would shortly be leaving the area. We moved out and spent a couple of days on the road, arriving at the pretty little town of Burgkunstadt, Germany, in Bavaria. It was obvious that Burgkunstadt had escaped the ravages of the war and our stay there could be a pleasant experience, which anything would be after what we had been through.

This photo shows the line of vehicles and personnel fleeing the Russian forces in order to surrender to the Americans, May 8, 1945. I had been ordered to move my platoon into a possition to intercept "a few stragglers." Before the day was over I had the whole Company helping to disarm nearly 20,000 men and 2,000 vehicles. Notice amid the pile of confiscated weapons, the number of Panzerfausts (long tubes with large warhead). My tank is visible in the background on the right. This is the first photo I took with my captured camera.

Chapter 18

POST-WAR DUTY IN BURGKUNSTADT, GERMANY

When we reached Burgkunstadt, we were directed to a large open field near the edge of town where we could move our tanks and other Company vehicles in a kind of makeshift motor-park. Adjacent to this field was a large shoe factory still in operation but at a much reduced capacity due to the shortage of manpower. Included in the compound was a dormitory which had housed the factory workers and would now provide sleeping quarters, bathing facilities and a kitchen and dining area for the men in Company "A," the likes of which they had not enjoyed for many months. It certainly did my heart good to know that these war-weary soldiers would be able to live an almost-normal life in these comfortable accommodations. Also nearby was a three-story residence containing an apartment on each floor, in which the factory superintendent and his family resided. We would soon learn that he and his wife were taken into custody due to his strong ties with the Nazi Party, leaving their four young children in the care of their Nanny who herself seemed little more than a child. The officers took over that building, but rather than uproot those little children, they and their Nanny could remain in the lower apartment and the officers would move into the two upper units, each having three bedrooms, a living room, kitchen and bath, giving each of us a private bedroom. I find it difficult to describe how it felt to live in such luxury.

Some rather strange personnel changes took place during our move from Czechoslovakia, which found Captain Soumas transferred to an unknown location since he said nothing to anybody about leaving and just disappeared. I have never been able to understand that, because we had been through so much together and he leaves without a word. Then we acquired a First Lieutenant, Guy Copeland, a neat guy who came to us from either "D" Company or Service Company but was not too familiar with our tanks. Also we picked up a man named Mr. Reisner, who claimed to be a British subject from South Africa and had been "posted" in Germany before the War and was trapped when the War started. He spoke fluent German and was a tremendous help as our interpreter, so he was given a GI uniform, without any insignia of course, and he was billeted with us. At that time no one questioned his story and we were able to make valuable use of his service.

Although the War was over it was still necessary to perform the usual maintenance procedures on the tanks and weapons, so when the tanks were in place the men immediately went about their jobs in the efficient manner to which they were accustomed. When they had finished, they were lined up and marched to the dormitory to get settled in. Woodward had his kitchen all set up and was preparing a hot evening meal. He showed me to a balcony overlooking the yard between the dorm and the building where the officers stayed, on which he had set up a table with a sheet on it and eight chairs, which was where the officers would have their meals. Although there were only five officers and Reisner, the extra chairs were there in the event we should have company, which we later did.

Burgkunstadt was a quaint little town, which somehow had escaped the ravages of the War and showed no visible signs of any gunfire. It had a church and some shops, including one where I could have the film from my camera developed and buy additional film. Traffic consisted mainly of the two or four-legged variety except for an occasional military vehicle, and order was maintained by a police force of one, identified by a white armband emblazoned with the word 'Polizei.'

The second day there the men were to spend the morning disassembling and cleaning all weapons, and as I walked among them I became abundantly aware of a drastic change in the atmosphere surrounding them. Their conversations seemed to be at a much-reduced volume level, and the frequency of the profane and obscene words was considerably less than had once been considered normal. Their conduct was almost subdued, and I knew then that these people had come to this place as young flamboyant boys, but through the inhuman experience of the world's bloodiest, most vicious, unmerciful acts of man's inhumanity to man in the history of the universe, they had emerged as the complete men that I observed before me. Yes, they knew full well the terrible price that was paid to get them to this point, since each one had suffered the loss of many of their buddies, and now they had the time and opportunity to grieve over those losses. I decided not to linger too long in their presence because I knew that they thought that an officer just didn't understand. If only they realized that I too had experienced the same tragedies that they did and in that regard we stood on common ground.

That afternoon would be devoted to recreation and sports of their choosing, but I was to take a driver and a Company Peep out through the country side to seek out any German soldiers who might be unaware the War was over, or who refused to give up and wanted to continue the fight and if need be die for the Fuehrer. Except for that remote possibility, I looked forward to seeing more of the area and the beautiful hills of Bavaria. We drove up many dirt roads to get to the wooded areas where we could call out: "Der Krieg ist ueber. Komen Zie aus. (The War is over. Come out.)" My driver and I both had carbines but tried to keep them out of sight so no one would be fearful that they might be harmed.

If we came to a village or town, we entered very slowly and would stop just to look around as we sat in the car. Usually in a short time the Buergermeister would come up and politely ask if he could help, often in pretty good English. I slowly explained our mission and asked if there were any uniformed or armed soldiers in the area. On those rare occasions when there were, I inquired if they were SS troops or members of the Nazi Party, and of course I was told they were not but I made a note of the town and Mayor in case Battalion wanted to follow up. This became an almost daily routine, and the word must have gotten around because we soon were being greeted by the Buergermeister who brought eggs, fruit, cookies etc., which I accepted not knowing if this violated the rules against fraternization. To be honest, I didn't care because these were items we had not received too much of in a long time. When we first were given fresh eggs, I had one of our housekeepers fry up a whole dozen that evening and I proceeded to eat them all, which was a real treat.

On another one of our jaunts we had ventured a good distance out, and during our return trip I noticed ahead of us a girl limping along the road in her bare feet. We pulled up beside her and motioned to her to come over, but she seemed frightened and hesitated so I got out of the Peep and again beckoned her to come forward. She very timidly approached us, and I could see that her feet were bleeding and she really looked beat. I asked her where she was going, and she replied she was trying to get home and she started to cry. I asked where she lived, and I was surprised when she said Burgkunstadt because I felt she would never make it in her condition. Again I thought about the fraternization restriction but I just could not let this poor frightened girl, who was in a lot of pain, continue to drag herself for at least another ten miles. I told her to get in the back of the Peep and she nodded "no" as though she were afraid, but I said we were just going to take her home because we also were staying in Burgkunstadt. Finally she slowly climbed into the back of the Peep and we headed on down the road. When we reached town, I asked her which way and she pointed further down the street we were on. We came to a line of houses and she indicated which one was hers, so we stopped and let her out. She went in the house and I told the driver we would wait a few minutes to make sure she was ok.

Pretty soon a priest came out of the house and said her family was almost hysterical over her return, and wanted us to come in to share in the celebration over a glass of wine. I told him thank you but it was against regulations, and he told me that the girl had been forced to perform domestic services for some high ranking Germans and she ran away in the middle of the night when the Americans arrived, which is why she had no shoes. The priest vigorously shook my hand, thanked us again and we took off for our Company area. I felt really good about what we had done and my driver also said how glad he was that we helped that young lady.

Downtown Burgkunstadt.

Tank driver Whitehead (left) who smashed-up my Mercury. Sgt. Vario (right) was wounded when Sid was killed.

Ed Weaver, my former platoon sergeant wearing the master sergeant stripes he received when our first sergeant was killed.

(L to R) Myself, Copeland, Yoho, and Grimball.

Company "A" men cleaning tank weapons. My tank "At Ease" is the one on the right, Goodson's tank is on the left.

Local civilians and Company "A" men at Church in Burgkunstadt; Mass just let out.

*Dormitory where the men stayed.
Our tanks are parked in back. I took this photo from the officers' apartment.*

One morning we were down with the tanks when a Peep drives up with a Lt. Colonel, who stepped out and introduced himself as Lt. Colonel Rodden who had been attached to the 14th Tank Battalion as an assistant to the Battalion Commander. We told him that the men were performing the daily checks on the vehicles and weapons and were just about ready to break for chow. As Mess Officer, I asked if he would join us for lunch and he said he would like that very much. I excused myself and hurried up to the kitchen to tell Sergeant Woodward to set another place for the Colonel. Not surprisingly, he said it was already done because the Colonel had stopped there before coming down to the Motor Park. With a Mess Sergeant like Woodward, who needs a Mess Officer? When the others arrived, we washed up then went out on the porch to wait until the men went through the chow line. Suddenly here comes Woodward with several of his kitchen crew carrying bowls of food and a complete setting for the Colonel. The rest of us had our mess kits and after Woodward served the Colonel the food was passed around for us to help ourselves. I thanked the Sergeant and his men and complimented them for a good job. The Colonel said I should be complimented since I was the Mess Officer, but I assured him it was all Sergeant Woodward's doing and he deserved the credit.

Then the Colonel dropped a bomb when he said that, although he wanted to visit "A" Company, the main reason for coming was to thank Lieutenant Miller for saving his life. It seems that he was the Colonel I yelled at the morning after we had crossed the Rhine when his Peep passed my tank heading around a turn where an ambulance had been shot up a little earlier. That very morning he went to Colonel Engeman to ask who the officer of the lead tank platoon was, and told him what had happened. He said he wanted to thank me ever since that day, but I had been attached to that Infantry unit and then sent to Paris, and he just couldn't catch up to me until now. I couldn't believe a Colonel would try so hard to find and thank a man who had so disrespectfully screamed at him, and I told him so and we all had a good laugh. I took a picture of the group at the table, which I sent home to Gracie, and I still have it.

I was starting to make good use of the camera, taking lots of pictures of the men all around Burgkunstadt and also of those four little kids with their young Nanny. I couldn't help but notice how

This is the porch where the officers ate. (Clockwise from left) Grimball, Yoho, Nash (he took Sid's platoon), Reisner (barely visible), Copeland, and Lt. Col. Rodden who came to thank me for saving his life.

hard that Nanny worked: taking care of the four children, doing the large laundry consisting of among other things a huge number of diapers, and keeping their house clean. Back then people used cloth diapers, which they washed and reused until they wore out. The children seemed to like having their pictures taken, especially when I had some candy bars that I received with my cigarette rations, which I could put to good use since I didn't smoke. The Nanny would have no part of the picture taking, either covering her face or turning her back when I tried to snap her. In one photo she was running up to retrieve the little ones who had come up to get some goodies from me, and another was of her back as she leaned over to brush off the steps up to the house, which I must confess was a classic G.I. view of a young lady. After some time she started to become a little less unfriendly, and finally accepted a chocolate candy bar, which she told me the next day had made her sick to her stomach because it had been so long since she had eaten any chocolate candy.

At one point I was told to visit the studio of a local artist for a sitting for a portrait of all the "A" Company officers who were at Remagen. As it turned out he was doing a mural for a victory celebration to be held in the auditorium of the shoe factory right there in Burgkunstadt. Battalion Headquarters hosted a very nice party for all of the officers in the Battalion, where the champagne flowed freely and we were all covered with con-

The German nanny and her charges.

fetti and streamers. The mural had me riding astride a bottle holding a glass of the bubbly in one hand and a pistol in the other. I took a picture of it and sent it to Gracie, assuring her that I still did not drink but the artist just assumed everyone did. It was the first time most of us had worn our blouse and pinks since leaving the States, not even when I visited General Kean. Speaking of the General, Colonel Engeman asked me if I had visited him just before we were ordered to Czechoslovakia, because every time I went to see the General we found ourselves involved in some serious fighting. I pled not guilty and we were able to laugh about that strange coincidence.

I wanted to look into the possibility of procuring a pair of tank boots from the shoe factory so, armed with several packs of cigarettes, I told the supervisor what I wanted. He said he would be glad to have them made especially for me and measured my feet and ankles in about six different places, and said he would have them ready the next day. I gave him the cigarettes and you would have thought they were gold. He was one happy man and asked if I needed anything else, so I mentioned that the shoes of the Nanny were badly worn and would he know her size. He said he knew "Elizabeth" very well and could make a pretty good guess the size she wore, and he brought a nice but plain pair of shoes he thought she would like. She seemed to be almost in shock when I gave them to her and the next time I saw her out in the yard, she called my attention to them and I was glad to know that they fit her. No, I did not get and did not want any special favors from her. We

A detail (of me) from the mural that was painted for the party. (Right) me and Yoho at the party.

had two housekeepers who kept our quarters neat and clean and did any cooking that we might want. Of course our laundry was handled by Battalion so there was nothing I needed. Incidentally, they made me not one but two pairs of beautiful tank boots, which are still in my possession.

Catholic Mass was celebrated in the Church right there in Burgkunstadt, but the Americans had to sit in an area sectioned off for them and we were not permitted to take Communion from the German priest. If we wanted Communion and to hear Mass in English, we would have to go to another Church in a nearby town where one of our Chaplains would say Mass. When there were enough men who wanted to go there, I could get a truck to transport us. I did not understand why we couldn't get Communion at the German Mass, unless it was felt we would have to co-mingle with the congregation and that would be fraternizing. It didn't make much sense because the men mixed with the others outside the Church after Mass.

Our daily activities were rather routine and were performed without any pressure or urgency but almost leisurely, just as it should have been to permit these fine men to get themselves back to normal. It was nearing the middle of August 1945 when we started hearing talk of the 9th Armored Division splitting up and its people being re-deployed. General Leonard, the Division Commander, had already left for his new assignment, General Hoge, our Combat Commander, was long gone, and General Harrold was the temporary Division Commander. So it did not come as a complete surprise when I received orders to report to a Replacement Depot, which we called a "Repo Depo," that was located in Chateau-Thierry less than fifty miles from Paris. I was given a few days, so there was no big hurry to get ready and I was able to casually say my good-byes, which I rather dreaded. I made sure I did not get sentimental when I notified the men, and it wound up with a lot of "See you Lieutenant" and "Good luck Lieutenant" or "Take care Lieutenant" and that was it. What did surprise me was the reaction of "Elizabeth," who actually cried when I told her I would be leaving soon. Here was a young lady who early on tried very hard to keep me from taking a picture of her, and now presented me with a very nice posed picture of herself and a couple other photos of when she was younger. I guess I was able to show her that I was not such a bad guy after all.

In a few days, a truck came by to pick me up plus about five other officers from various units of the division, closing out our association with the 9th Armored Division. I knew two of the officers; Lieutenants Magura and Hamilton, who I believe were with "B" Company in our Battalion, which made our departure a little easier.

The Repo Depo in Chateau-Thierry was called "The 6960 Replacement Depot," which served as a collection station for personnel who were eligible for shipment to the South Pacific where our military were still hotly engaged with the Japanese. It was a huge "tent-city" where we would wait until there was a need for men of our qualifications, which were a pulse and a warm body. The three of us were assigned the same tent with about three other officers. These were very large tents which had, in addition to the cots, racks to hang our clothing and two big tables with long benches where we could sit and write or read or whatever. They also had electricity and flooring which made them very comfortable.

Not too much was happening there except for one incident that I think is worth mentioning. I was stretched out on my cot reading *Yank* or *Stars and Stripes* while Magura was standing nearby cleaning a pistol that he must have taken from a surrendering German. When he finished, as is customary, he pulled back the chamber, cocking the gun and pointing toward the floor, pulled the trigger. Much to our surprise the gun went off and the spent round, after hitting the concrete floor ended up in a two-by four bracing the tent just above my head. I was pretty mad about it but I thought Magura was going to break down, realizing what he had done was absolutely inexcusable. He had left the ammunition clip in the gun, so when he cocked it a round went into the chamber and it was loaded. Fortunately he had followed standard procedures and pointed the gun down, so it lost most of its force when it ricocheted in my direction. He was even more upset than I was, which was plenty because he had violated the most important rule of gun handling by not removing the clip and making sure it was unloaded as the first step when cleaning a weapon. It could have been disastrous but fortunately there was no harm done.

We were able to arrange a couple of trips to Paris and I took many pictures with my liberated camera. On our first visit, which was still late August, we managed to get passes to the exclusive Racing Club of Paris, which claims to have introduced the bikini bathing suit. I was able to shoot some of the ladies in their bikinis and sent a couple of the prints home to Gracie, which may not have been a great idea. During another trip, we took in some of the nightlife of Paris and I got some shots there, which I did not send home to Gracie.

Then we received the news that a terrific bomb equal to 20,000 tons of dynamite was dropped on the Japanese city of Hiroshima leveling most of the buildings and killing thousands. This seemed to signal the end of the War but they still wouldn't surrender, so another bomb was dropped on Nagasaki and thank the Lord, they gave up. Now I could breathe easier that I wouldn't be shipped over there for more fighting and could start thinking about going home. Not so fast, because the Army came up with a point system to determine who was eligible to return to the States. You were awarded points for the number of years in the service, for the number of months you were overseas, for the number of major campaigns you fought in, and for each decoration you received. I came up short by just five points, which I would have received from the Purple Heart I did not get and did not want for the frostbite, so I could expect to receive an assignment returning me to Germany until they lowered the points required. Just where that would be I would soon find out when I received orders to move to another camp in the area, which was designated Camp San Francisco. I was attached to the 80th Battalion, which had the responsibility of assigning personnel to various locations where there was a specific need. There I met a couple of Lieutenants with whom I would share a tent and who turned out to be a lot of fun to be with. The name of one was Wilson Hall and the other's last name was Ransom, but I don't remember his first name. Hall and I took a couple of trips to Paris but Ransom had been there many times and had seen enough. We really seemed to enjoy each other's company and get along real well but never exchanged home addresses so I lost touch.

The anticipated orders came the latter part of October sending Ransom home, me to Marburg, Germany, and I believe Hall became an Aide to one of the Generals. I wonder how he did that because I had a cousin who was a general and all I got was a couple of free lunches. Again I had to say some goodbyes but I guess you learn to accept them without too much emotion, but I did hate to leave a couple of fun guys.

While at the Repo. Depots

(Right) Tent city at the 6960 Replacement Depot.

(Below) Photos while at Camp San Francisco; bikini's at the Racing Club of Paris; myself, Ranson, and Wilson Hall outside of our tent.

Chapter 19

ONE MORE STOP THEN HOMEWARD BOUND

Marburg, Germany, was a pretty little university town located in the center of West Germany and the location of another U.S. Army Replacement Depot. However, the function of this Repo Depot was to process American soldiers arriving from the States to replace those who were homeward bound. It was under the command of the Second Army and I had to wear the Second Army patch, but we who had been in combat were permitted to wear the patch of the unit we fought with but on the right sleeve. So I wore two shoulder patches, the Second Army on the left sleeve and the Ninth Armored on the right sleeve.

I was housed in a small townhouse within walking distance of the office and the compound where the incoming troops would be assembled. A Lieutenant Mark Smith had already been there for some time before my arrival and was a big help showing me the ropes. We had a housekeeper who came several days a week and we would get our meals at the Officer's Mess at the compound. He had a toy Dachsund, which was cute but noisy. We walked down to the office, which was just outside the compound and I met several sergeants who were busy typing up lists of replacements.

My duties were not very clear and practically non-existent, which was fine with me. I was really amused when I was asked to be responsible for the coal supply since cold weather was setting in. They used these briquettes for the furnace and I wondered if I had come full cycle from my very first job in the Army at Camp Lee, Virginia, which was to keep the furnace going to warm the barracks there. Of course there was someone to shovel the coal and I only had to order more when the supply got low, a job I thought I could handle if I had a telephone. There were a couple of phones in the office so I was in business, and as it turned out I had to put in a call right then because they were just about out of the stuff.

An unfortunate incident happened when Smith and I were walking to the office one morning with his little dog running beside him. All of a sudden the dog darted into the street and was run over by a passing Peep. Luckily there was a Medical Officer riding in the Peep and he gave the poor little guy a shot of something to put him out of his misery. Smith picked him up and said he was going back to the house, so I went on to the office.

Just a week or ten days before Christmas I was offered a choice of three places to spend the holiday: Switzerland, the French Riviera or Paris. The trips to Switzerland and the Riviera were for two weeks and Paris was one week. I really wanted to go to Switzerland but they had just reduced the number of points needed to go home which made me eligible, and I did not want to be away if I should get my orders. So I took the trip to Paris even though I had been there a number of times before. Comparing this Christmas in Paris with the one the year before during the Battle of the Bulge was cause for reflection of all that had happened in the past twelve months. Each day in Paris seemed to remove me a little further away from the reality of that horrifying period which has made such an indelible impression on my life.

This visit also gave me the opportunity to photograph some places that I had missed on previous trips. After a few shots it was necessary to get more film so I bought a couple of rolls because I had not taken any pictures of Marburg and I wanted enough film to do that. If nothing else I seemed able to completely relax during that visit, something I was unable to do until then, an indication to me that I might not suffer from any post-combat trauma.

Upon my return to Marburg, since it was just a matter of time before I would be leaving, I made frequent tours of the compound in order to get a look at the men coming to Europe. Their facial expressions and unworried demeanor was so different from the serious and sometimes troubled look on the faces of my combat tankers. My guys had developed a strength of character that most of these men would take years to achieve. Every time I think of the men in my platoon, I can't help but feel a great sense of pride, which remains with me to the present time.

There was plenty of time for me to roam about town randomly taking pictures with my captured German camera. There was a picturesque stream running through the town and the ducks waddling along the icy edge of the stream could have been an artists' dream. Also the charming little foot-bridges over the trickling brook would make one wax poetic, but I was content to let the pictures do it for me. I had put one of the new rolls of film in the camera and by the time I had to leave Marburg I had used the entire roll.

The day that I had waited for all these many months finally arrived with my orders shipping me back to the States and home. A truck would transport several of us to a nearby train station where we were loaded into an old boxcar reminiscent of the "40 and 8" of World War I. There were only about twenty of us in it so we had plenty of room, but we had to sit on our bags, which could hardly be considered First Class accommodations. Although it was early January 1946 we had to keep the door open to let some light in since the car was unlighted. This did enable me to get some amazing pictures of all the devastation of the towns that our train passed through which included a severely-damaged Remagen. About every hour or so when there was a convenient siding out in the country, the train would make a ten minute rest stop. It was rather comical to see these guys jump out of the car, run across the field, do their business and run back to the train, which would always give a two minute warning by two blasts of its whistle.

After what seemed a long time but really wasn't, the train approached a rail yard and started to slow down and I was able to get a picture of a huge line of GI's waiting for chow. Our orders indicated that we would be fed after we boarded our ship, so we were eagerly watching for what might be our ship as we moved slowly on the edge of a very wide waterway where many ships were docked. Our train finally came to a halt at dockside just opposite what appeared to be a troop ship,

The railway station at Remagen. Photo taken from train en route to port.

and soon a sergeant came up to our car and said, "This is the end of the line gentlemen. Everybody out and follow me." He then walked us a short distance and said the Lieutenant would be there in a few minutes to give us our instructions for boarding and conduct aboard ship. While we waited I stepped away from the group so I could take some photos of the *Laconia Victory* that would carry us back to the land we left oh so long ago. When I walked back to the group the Sergeant returned and handed us a list containing the "dos" and "don'ts," one of which really got my attention. It stated that only one souvenir weapon per man would be permitted and here I was with five pistols that I had removed from surrendering German soldiers: a Luger, a P.38, a matching pair of Walthers, and an American Colt .45 which the German had obviously taken off of a surrendering or dead American officer. There was a warning at the bottom of the page stating that any violation of the above instructions could result in the removal from the ship and a delay of the man's return to the States.

I was then faced with the need for some immediate action disposing of the excess weapons. It so happened that in our group were some Air Force officers who reminded me that obviously they were never in the position to disarm any surrendering enemy and felt fortunate for this opportunity to obtain these valuable souvenirs. I sold the P.38, one of the Walthers and the American Colt .45 for twenty dollars each which today would bring at least a thousand apiece. I kept the Luger and one Walther because one of the officers offered to take one of them for me and give it back once we were on board, and I still have those guns. As it turned out, I could have kept all of my guns because there was never any weapons check either before, during, or after boarding the ship.

Amid a lot of 'booing and whistles, the P.A. system announced that the officers would move to the base of the gangplank and be prepared to board the *Laconia Victory*. There were less than fifty of us, and we all got a laugh as we stepped in front of the men and took our places ready to go aboard. While we were waiting my name was called, and I was handed an envelope informing me I was to be the Paymaster for the men and where and when I was to report for that duty. I believe I was the only officer who received an assignment but that was OK with me because it would help pass the time during the trip. Soon our names were called alphabetically and again the 'boo's started as we boarded the ship and were directed to our rooms which were on an upper deck. There were four of us in our room, one of whom was the officer who had my gun, making it simple to retrieve and on each bunk was a life jacket that we were required to wear whenever going out on deck.

I would estimate there were between five hundred and six hundred enlisted men but the harbor staff were so well organized that it did not take very long to move them onto the ship. This was an inland port somewhere in Belgium so it would be a while before we would reach the open sea, but soon we weighed anchor and were on our way. While navigating a canal we entered some locks which provided just inches of clearance on each side of our ship, requiring some masterful maneuvering to bring us through unscathed. All along the way we were able to observe some interesting sights that I had the good fortune to catch on film.

The ship that brought us home.

In due time the *Laconia* left the calm and placid inland waterways to break out into the open and frequently unfriendly seas off the northern shores of the European Continent. The next day the sun shone brightly but the increased motion of the ship was quite noticeable as we moved past the North Sea and through the well-known choppy waters of the English Channel. We passengers did not know at the time that we were experiencing the smoothest sailing of the entire crossing until the final day. It was common knowledge that the North Atlantic Ocean is consistently at its roughest during January than at any other time of the year, and we were to learn how true that was. Our first day on the ocean was reasonably smooth, but I couldn't help but feel the vast difference between the *Laconia* and the *Queen Mary* as we rode the waves toward some heavy weather. The next day started out well but by mid-morning the thickening clouds and increasing wind forecast a rather menacing future to our trip. Also this had been the day that the men were advised that they could obtain an advance of twenty dollars per man on their next pay. This would be done between 1900 and 2100 hours that evening, and a pay table would be set up in a designated room for me to disburse the money and have each man sign a receipt. I picked up the money at the Captain's stateroom, which had a safe, and counted the money before signing a receipt. The money was neatly stacked and each pack had the amount stamped on it so it was easy to count. Putting the money, the receipts and several pens in the moneybag, I headed for the room where the men were instructed to come. Although there were already some men there I locked the door until I could get set up, then I opened the door and told them to enter one man at a time.

I had decided to give each man a ten, a five and five ones so I set up three piles, one for each denomination, and counted out the money for the first man, who signed a receipt, took his money and left. Each man entered as the one before him left and things were going very smoothly but unfortunately the ship wasn't. The Captain had told me that the wind was approaching gale force and the sea was getting very rough. As I was counting out the money I was beginning to realize how that repetitive motion can affect one's stomach while sailing on some heavy seas. I had just finished counting out one man's money when it hit me, so I grabbed the money and jammed it with the receipts into the moneybag and dashed toward the head telling the men to wait there. I didn't think I was going to make it but luckily there was a large trash can along the way and I lost my entire meal in that trash can. Strangely I felt fine after that, and getting a drink of water I returned to the job at hand and finished without any further problem.

I counted the loose money and entered that on the disbursement memo and went back to the Captain's room, but he was up on the bridge checking on the storm, which had gotten worse. When he returned he told me that the winds were now officially at gale velocity and were slowing our progress.

I returned to our room and the three other guys were there sitting on their bunks discussing how rough it was getting, and when I told them what the Captain had said they told me "that wasn't something they wanted to hear." After a while we decided to turn in, but the creaking and groaning of the *Laconia*'s structural supports added to the roar of the wind and the ships motion made a peaceful night's sleep not too promising.

It pleased me that I was able to eat a light breakfast but I noticed that not very many chose to join me. The announcement over the PA system advised that the storm was still raging with winds remaining at gale force and it was recommended we not venture on deck. It is not often you get to sail into a gale and I wanted to get some pictures, so I bundled up, put on my life jacket and went out on deck. There is something awesome about sailing into gale winds over very high waves and I had to marvel at the power of nature that could create such conditions. I took some pictures but on the open sea there is nothing to compare them with so the waves did not look that high. There was a platform above our deck with some steps almost like a ladder leading to it and I thought I might see more from up there. I started to climb up there but as the wind picked up, I wasn't sure that was a good idea because I really had to hold on tight. Just as I reached the top one of the crewman called up to me "Sir, that is too dangerous, you really shouldn't be up there." I agreed with him and I hurried to get down, feeling that I had done something stupid. There wasn't a lot of rain but I was getting pretty wet from the spray of the waves hitting the ship, so I went on inside and told the guys what I had done and they all concluded that I wasn't very bright.

This kind of weather lasted throughout the day and night, then the next day it started to subside but still was very cold and raw. The *Sentimental Journal* printed by the staff stated that the ship had lost radio contact with the mainland during the height of the storm and had some officials on shore somewhat concerned.

During the remaining days on board the *Laconia* I made good use of my German Leica camera, catching the men on deck for some fresh air bundled up in their overcoats and the ever-present life jacket. Then there were the other ships going the opposite direction: a freighter, a tanker and a U.S. Battleship, each giving a greeting, which was returned by the *Laconia*. What a thrill when we first spotted land and everybody straining to see that beautiful Lady through the haze and finally coming into full view, bringing loud cheers from all of us. Soon the New York skyline, including the Empire State Building, provided a perfect setting for some of my final photographs, showing also the men watching almost in disbelief at what they were seeing.

At last the *Laconia Victory* docked and as we stepped off the ramp, there was this wonderful sensation of gratitude for making it safely home. It mattered not that there was no band or cheering crowds to greet us; it was enough that we were back knowing what we had accomplished. A lady standing nearby clapped her hands and said "Well done," and that was all we needed. We walked past a Red Cross stand where an attendant called out, "Have some hot coffee and donuts," but we were being led to our train and couldn't stop. We soon boarded a train that took us a short distance to Camp Kilmer, New Jersey, and after signing a few papers and getting some instructions we got on another train to be transported to Ft. Meade, Maryland. It was close to midnight when we reached Ft. Meade and we were getting a little weary, but I soon came to life when I saw none other than my Gracie. What a surprise. A long-time dear friend, Dick Garrett, had driven Gracie over to meet me and already had made arrangements allowing me to go home that night, but I had to return the next day for processing. Since they were not sure just when I would arrive, Dick's wife Virginia didn't come along. I quickly signed out and we jumped into Dick's car and were on our way home. What a way to end that rough, cold trip.

Some officers getting a breath of fresh air during the crossing.

These soldiers waited a long time for this view. They all stare as the skyline gets closer and closer.

When we saw the famous New York skyline we knew we made it home.

Chapter 20

THAT'S ALL FOLKS

The drive home took more than an hour and the whole time I kept saying that I could not believe I was back. It just would not sink in, and several times I told Gracie to pinch me so I would know that this was real and I was not dreaming. We would be staying at her parents place and everybody got up and came down stairs to welcome me home. Her mother fixed coffee and sandwiches that really hit the spot, and all the excitement made sleep impossible so we continued talking far into the night.

Gracie still worked for Doctor Hertzberg and since I did not know how long I would be at Ft. Meade, it was decided she might as well go to work. We managed a few hours sleep then I took the family car, drove Gracie to work and went back to Ft. Meade to be processed out of the service. My first stop was the examination room for a quick check-up where I was asked if I had any injuries to report. Once in a while my right knee bothered me, but I had heard that any complaints would have to be checked at the hospital causing a delay in my release, so I elected not to mention it. Next was the final interview by an officer who told me that the Army wanted to hold onto their combat officers, and advised me of the many benefits of signing over. I really liked Army life but I couldn't see being sent away, so I told him that I needed a break from the demands of the military. He suggested that I join the reserves but I wanted to think about it and needed some time to make up my mind. There were some papers for me to sign and I was handed my certificate of separation releasing me from the Army. Technically I would not be out until I had used up my terminal leave, which had over two months to run.

My next project was to get a car, but production was so far behind it would take months before a new car would be available. I was very fortunate that I was able to buy a used car because they were equally in demand, but I had a friend who worked for an auto dealer and he let me have a used Buick ahead of many others on a waiting list. I think wearing my uniform helped and it did not bother me to go before those who had not been in the military. Then we made plans to visit some of my relatives in Dayton and Cincinnati and Gracie's in Chicago, after which we would head to Florida to soak up some warm sunshine.

Our first stop was to see my Grandmother in Cincinnati who was living with her daughter's family of four in an apartment that left no room for overnight guests. Since I was home and alive I wasn't mad at anybody, and knowing Pete Zillick had lived in Cincinnati most of his life I thought he might know of a hotel nearby where Gracie and I could spend a few nights. So I called him and needless to say he was very surprised to hear from me. After exchanging pleasantries I told him why I called and he said he would check some things and call me back, which he did. He gave me directions to where he would meet us and lead us to whatever place he had located. It seems that the Zillick's had bought one of the double houses, living in one and renting the other and had called up the tenants who were visiting in California to ask if we could stay in their place. They obviously gave their permission, and Gracie and I stayed there for close to a week and Pete just couldn't do enough for us.

The house was heated by a coal-fired furnace and the first thing in the morning Pete was over shoveling coal and stoking the furnace. Then the phone rang and Pete said breakfast would be ready in fifteen minutes, and each morning Lois fixed these wonderful breakfasts for us. Most of the day we spent with my Grandmother and Aunt enjoying their company and some nice meals. We called the folks in Dayton and arranged to go up and spend a day with them. On the final day, I wanted to take Pete and his family to dinner to show my appreciation for all that they had done for us, but Pete knew the restaurant owner and had the check brought to him. It is hard to believe but that was the beginning of a lasting friendship, visiting each other right up until recently when poor health put limitations on their activities.

Soon we said our "goodbye's" with promises to come back often, then moved on up to Chicago for a couple of days with some of Gracie's relatives, which was pleasant but uneventful. Next was the long drive to Florida that was unhurried and relaxing, taking us to the little town of Lake Worth where we found a small cozy hotel, which was quiet and restful, exactly what I needed. Strangely, as I drove along I would often see a place that I thought would have been a strategic spot for an enemy emplacement but such thoughts never caused me any discomfort.

Back home it was now time to locate an apartment so I called Charlie Walker, a long time friend who was with one of the largest property management firms in the Washington area. He gave me an address in Arlington, Virginia, and Gracie and I immediately went to see it. It was fine and I told Charlie we would take it, thanking him profusely because housing, like cars was difficult to find. I called another friend who was in the moving and storage business and arranged to move in to the apartment. He did not charge me a thing for the move. Just another example of the value of real friends in the time of need.

Next on the agenda was to find a job and luckily I had friends in that area too. I got back into real estate, specializing in mortgage financing which I did right up until my retirement. I passed the exams required to become a licensed Real Estate Broker in three jurisdictions, Maryland, Virginia and the District of Columbia, giving me more credibility in my business dealings. I also became active in the Montgomery County, Maryland, Board of Realtors ascending through the chairs up to the Presidency of the Board.

In the meantime my Army terminal leave ended and so did my association with the military, although I did join the reserves, obtaining my captaincy before I had to resign after over five years due to the demands it placed on my time.

My return to civilian life presented many ups and downs, as did the military, which I presume is true of life in any capacity. Some of the "ups" were the early arrival of daughter Marilyn, the appointment as Manager of the Maryland Branch Office, the purchase of a home in Maryland, the successful rise to President of the local Kiwanis Club and many other activities of community service.

We have now reached the end of a long and hazardous journey that tore at every fiber of the human body and soul. A journey that took many of those who would travel with me and left them by the wayside. A journey that reeked of death every inch of the way and drove the mind to the very edge of insanity. A journey that presented opportunities for heroism without the realization of their being achieved. A journey that rips apart his sense of decency and releases his animal instinct that says kill or be killed. A journey that hardens the quality of compassion and grief so that he is unaffected by the death of those he had been close to. A journey that produced conditions that could cause a complete personality change, jeopardizing the return to a normal civilian life in the future. This is what that journey did to the average man, creating the gigantic challenge to dismiss the torment of combat so that he can unscramble the brain, soften the heart and return to the kind of human being he was before being struck by the soul wrenching violence of battle.

My life since the War has had its great moments and unbearable tragedy, but the strength and the will to move on that I acquired in combat helped me to overcome the low spots and reach the heights of my ambitions.

It is my hope and prayer that those who read this book will be filled with a sense of pride over what their country did during World War II in order to preserve the freedoms that they enjoy today. That they will recognize the abuses of these freedoms that are being committed today which actually threaten the future of this country. I would hope that an effort would be made to return to this country the high standards of decency and patriotism that made this country great but have hit new lows in post-war America. I would also ask the readers to share with others what they have learned from this book so that they too might benefit from knowing of one man's military experience in World War II.

For some time after the War, I would ask how I was able to survive when so many around me did not make it. Why our Supreme Authority saw fit to protect me during those many situations when death seemed almost certain. Then our daughter Marilyn was born and from that time I began to get the answers to those questions because of the many good things that began to unfold, some of which I have mentioned here. That list includes the production of this literary effort whose only purpose is to generate good feelings among the population toward this land in which we live. If that is the result, I can conclude that the time and energy devoted to this enterprise have not been in vain and can be considered my contribution to the betterment of our society. Now I will close with a little prayer that God will bless this piece of work and God bless America.

My military identification card.

"Bridging the gap."
I often give school talks. Here I am speaking to a class from St. Mary, Star of the Sea School. Note that I still fit in my combat jacket.

One of my talks at the Eisenhower Farm in Gettysburg, PA. I am holding up a print of me in my tank entitled "Taking the Remagen Bridge" created by artist Larry Selman (standing next to me). This same artwork is featured on the cover of this book.

A reunion of Company "A" men in 2001 on the farm of Frank Buck in Gettysburg, PA.
(L to R) Bob Janos, Ira Mullins, Clemon Knapp, Richard Lively, Jack Ward, Clarence Van Briesen, C. Windsor Miller, Bill Hess, and Howard Best.

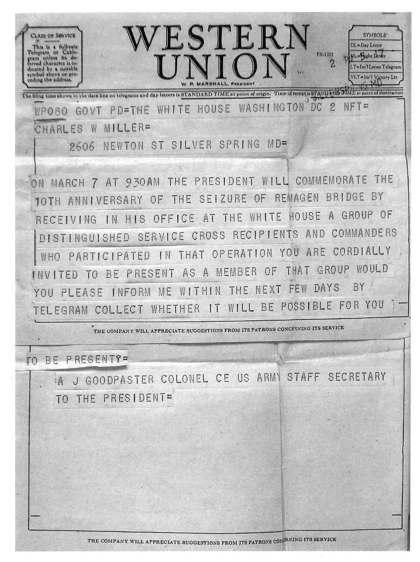

The telegram above was my invitation to the White House to meet with the President on the tenth anniversary of crossing of the Remagen Bridge. Below is a congratulatory telegram from Dwight D. Eisenhower.

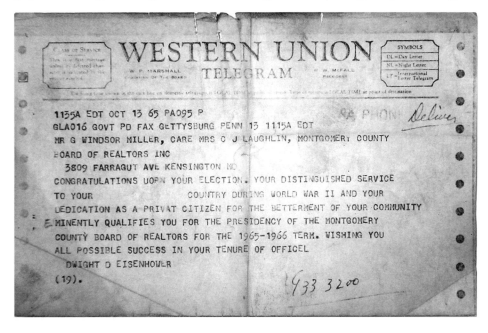

Appendix A

ROSTER OF COMPANY "A" 14TH TANK BATTALION

Compiled by George R. "Bob" Doering, Armorer

Akins, Tommy G.
Ashcraft, Robert L.
Auber, Charles L.
Baker, Melvin E.
Ballow, Eugene A.
Barszoz, Stanley
Best, Howard J.
Blincoe, Harold E.
Bowling, Smith W.
Brooks, Earl R.
Brown, Kenneth O.
Brownlee, Glen A.
Cagle, John T. Jr.
Cain, Walter E.
Captain, George F.
Caraway, Guy W.
Carter, Pat W.
Cerveny, Rudolph F.
Connell, Jack M.
Courier, Lawrence C.
Cow, Ivy R.
Culbertson, William N.
Curtis, Frederick B.
DeMarco, Walter P.
DiGrigorio, Thomas
Dickey, Charles L.
Doering, George R.
Dupree, Edmond J.
Ellis, Jonathan, R.
Engelman, Ralph
Estes, Lecil E.
Floyd, Randle J.
Flynn, Joseph
Fox, William A.
Frarklin, Hubert D.
Fried, Berthold
Garavaglia, Herman J.
Goodson, William J.

Grimball, John
Gustafson, Raymond C.
Gustwiller, Melvin H.
Hadley, Kenneth J.
Haines, Jarold F.
Halsell, Frank B.
Hannon, John M.
Herder, George S.
Hess, William H.
Humphery, Fred E.
Hunt, Andrew L.
Isaacs, Harry
Jackson, James R.
Jackson, John H. Jr.
Jacoby, George
James, Charles W.
Janos, Robert F.
Jarrell, Sam T
Jewels, Elwood C.
Johnson, Buren J.
Johnson, Clifford A.
Johnson, Glen A.
Jones, Robert A.
Knapp, Clemon
Knapp, Homer L.
Key, Chester
Kuchel, Joseph
Kuhlman, John J.
Lamphers, Frank V.
Large, Trig L.
Laws, Charles A.
LeMaster, Walter L.
Lester, Lark H.
Levine, Leonard
Littlejohn, George W.
Lively, Richard E.
Lovely, Fred
Mancini, Anthony

Marshall, John
Massingale, Calvin C.
Meredith, Robert W.
Miller, C. Windsor
Milligan, Hayden Jr.
Mills, Wallace J.
Mitchell, William B. Jr.
Moore, Carl J.
Moore, Charles M.
Moore, Richard S.
Morgan, Alfred E.
Moscowicz, Sidney
Moulton, William
Mounts, Henry C.
Mullins, Ira L.
Myhre, Lester L.
O'Daniel, Bernard P.
Owens, Raymond E.
Paterson, Walter D.
Patterson, Akie
Phillips, Joseph J.
Poeller, Fred E. Jr.
Raines, Fred C. Jr.
Reed, Paul W.
Reed, Roy
Richard, William E.
Rider, Zealand B.
Ritterband, Jerome
Roark, Darius S.
Roberson, Granger M.
Rose, Walter C.
Rounds, John I.
Rouse, Wilber V.
Russell, Melvin J.
Ruth, LeRoy T.
Ruzicka, Joe R.
Savage, Waldon
Schumacher, George F.

Scott, Ambrose A.
Shackleford, Hyatt
Shaffer, Howard B.
Shell, Carl L.
Smalley, Walter E. Jr.
Soumas, George P.
Stevens, James C.
Stiles, Waymond R.
Sucker, Donald R.
Sutton, John A.
Swayne, Lawrence H.
Taylor, Merschel J.
Terman, John
Thessen, Richard H.
Thomas, James E.
Thompson, Harold L.
Thompson, Lonnie

Trimble, Christopher C.
Trujillo, Joseph E.
Tucker, Burton G.
Tuma, George J.
Tunis, Charles E.
Utterback, Robert D.
Van Briesen, Clarence C.
Vario, George A.
Verducci, Vincent
Verkennes, Jacob H.
Vatale, Paul
Vlach, Joseph
Voepal, Warren M.
Volpe, John M.
Wahl, Elgart L.
Walsen, Harris C.
Walker, Joseph

Walker, Ray P.
Ward, Thomas E.
Warner, Everett
Weaver, Edwin M.
Weeks, Oakley M.
Wegman, Clement A.
Weis, Fred E.
Whitehead, John A.
Whitener, Clifford R.
Wills, Ernest E.
Wilson, William G.
Woodard, Howard J.
Workman, Daeeell
Yoho, Arnold, J.
Young, Adolph A.
Zills, James W. Sr.
Zinko, Anthony

Appendix B

FIRING TABLES

FOR

GUN, 76-MM, M1A1 AND M1A2

FIRING

SHELL, H.E., M42A1

W/FUZE, P.D., M48 AND M48A1

PROJECTILE, A.P.C., M62

W/FUZE, B.D., M66A1 AND TRACER

AND

SHOT, A.P., M79

Prepared by the
Ordnance Department, U. S. A.
January — 1944

Army Service Forces, Ordnance Office,
Washington, 22 January 1944.

The following firing tables (FT 76-A-4) for GUN, 76-mm, M1A1 and M1A2 are published for the information and guidance of all concerned.

These tables supersede FT 76-A-1 and FT 76-A-2 which should be destroyed. These tables were given limited distribution but were not printed.

FT 76-A-4 contains the same information as FT 76-A-3 as changed by FT 76-A-3, C-1 which may be continued in use, FT 76-A-3 and FT 76-A-3, C-1 were also given limited distribution but were not printed.

L. H. CAMPBELL, Jr.,
Major General, Chief of Ordnance.

(O.O. 063.2 / 2164)

FT 76-A-4 SHELL, H.E., M42A1 w/ FUZE, P.D., M48 and M48A1					MV — 2700 f/s
Range	Elevation	Change in elevation for 100 yd change in range	Range	Elevation	Change in elevation for 100 yd change in range
yd	mils	mils	yd	mils	mils
0	1.1	.7	3000	28.4	1.2
100	1.8	.7	3100	29.6	1.2
200	2.5	.7	3200	30.9	1.3
300	3.2	.7	3300	32.2	1.3
400	3.9	.7	3400	33.6	1.4
500	4.6	.7	3500	35.0	1.4
600	5.4	.7	3600	36.4	1.4
700	6.1	.7	3700	37.9	1.5
800	6.9	.8	3800	39.4	1.5
900	7.1	.8	3900	41.0	1.6
1000	8.5	.8	4000	42.6	1.6
1100	9.3	.8	4100	44.2	1.6
1200	10.1	.8	4200	45.9	1.7
1300	11.0	.8	4300	47.7	1.8
1400	11.8	.9	4400	49.5	1.8
1500	12.7	.9	4500	51.3	1.8
1600	13.6	.9	4600	53.2	1.9
1700	14.5	.9	4700	55.1	1.9
1800	15.5	.9	4800	57.1	2.0
1900	16.4	.9	4900	59.2	2.1
2000	17.4	1.0	5000	61.3	2.1
2100	18.4	1.0	5100	63.5	2.2
2200	19.4	1.0	5200	65.7	2.2
2300	20.4	1.0	5300	68.0	2.3
2400	21.5	1.1	5400	70.3	2.3
2500	22.6	1.1	5500	72.7	2.4
2600	23.7	1.1	5600	75.2	2.5
2700	24.8	1.2	5700	77.7	2.5
2800	26.0	1.2	5800	80.3	2.6
2900	27.2	1.2	5900	82.9	2.6
3000	28.4	1.2	6000	85.6	2.7

FT 76-A-4 SHELL, H.E., M42A1 w/ FUZE, P.D., M48 and M48A1					MV — 2700 f/s
Range	Elevation	Change in elevation for 100 yd change in range	Range	Elevation	Change in elevation for 100 yd change in range
yd	mils	mils	yd	mils	mils
6000	85.6	2.7	9000	193.9	4.5
6100	88.4	2.8	9100	198.4	4.5
6200	91.2	2.8	9200	203.0	4.6
6300	94.1	2.9	9300	207.7	4.7
6400	97.0	2.9	9400	212.5	4.8
6500	100.0	3.0	9500	217.3	4.8
6600	103.1	3.1	9600	222.2	4.9
6700	106.2	3.1	9700	227.2	5.0
6800	109.4	3.2	9800	232.3	5.1
6900	112.6	3.2	9900	237.4	5.1
7000	115.9	3.3	10000	242.6	5.2
7100	119.2	3.3	10100	247.9	5.3
7200	122.6	3.4	10200	253.3	5.4
7300	126.1	3.5	10300	258.7	5.5
7400	129.6	3.5	10400	264.3	5.6
7500	133.2	3.6	10500	270.0	5.7
7600	136.9	3.7	10600	275.8	5.8
7700	140.6	3.7	10700	281.6	5.9
7800	144.3	3.7	10800	287.6	6.0
7900	148.1	3.8	10900	293.7	6.1
8000	152.0	3.9	11000	299.9	6.2
8100	156.0	4.0	11100	306.2	6.4
8200	160.0	4.0	11200	312.7	6.5
8300	164.0	4.0	11300	319.2	6.6
8400	168.1	4.1	11400	325.8	6.7
8500	172.2	4.1	11500	332.6	6.8
8600	176.4	4.2	11600	339.5	6.9
8700	180.7	4.3	11700	346.5	7.1
8800	185.0	4.3	11800	353.7	7.2
8900	189.4	4.4	11900	361.0	7.4
9000	193.9	4.5	12000	368.5	7.6

FT 76-A-4

SHELL, H.E., M42A1
w/ FUZE, P.D., M48 and M48A1   MV — 2700 f/s

Range	Elevation	Change in elevation for 100 yd change in range
yd	mils	mils
12000	368.5	7.6
12100	376.2	7.8
12200	384.1	7.9
12300	392.1	8.0
12400	400.2	8.2
12500	408.5	8.4
12600	417.1	8.7
12700	425.9	8.9
12800	434.9	9.1
12900	444.1	9.3
13000	453.6	9.6
13100	463.4	9.9
13200	473.5	10.3
13300	484.0	10.7
13400	494.8	11.0
13500	506.0	11.5
13600	517.8	12.0
13700	530.1	12.6
13800	543.1	13.4
13900	557.0	14.4
14000	571.9	15.6
14100	588.2	17.1
14200	606.2	18.9
14300	626.3	21.7
14400	649.8	25.8
14500	680.0	
14600	731.2	
14610	758.5	

FT 76-A-4 PROJECTILE, A.P.C., M62 w/ FUZE, B.D., M66A1 and TRACER					MV — 2600 f/s
Range	Elevation	Change in elevation for 100 yd change in range	Range	Elevation	Change in elevation for 100 yd change in range
yd	mils	mils	yd	mils	mils
0	1.0	.7	3000	29.6	1.2
100	1.7	.7	3100	30.9	1.3
200	2.5	.7	3200	32.2	1.3
300	3.2	.7	3300	33.5	1.3
400	4.0	.8	3400	34.9	1.4
500	4.8	.8	3500	36.3	1.4
600	5.6	.8	3600	37.8	1.4
700	6.4	.8	3700	39.2	1.5
800	7.2	.8	3800	40.7	1.5
900	8.0	.8	3900	42.2	1.5
1000	8.9	.8	4000	43.8	1.6
1100	9.7	.9	4100	45.4	1.6
1200	10.6	.9	4200	47.0	1.6
1300	11.5	.9	4300	48.7	1.7
1400	12.4	.9	4400	50.4	1.7
1500	13.3	.9	4500	52.1	1.7
1600	14.3	1.0	4600	53.9	1.8
1700	15.3	1.0	4700	55.7	1.8
1800	16.3	1.0	4800	67.7	1.9
1900	17.3	1.0	4900	59.6	1.9
2000	18.3	1.0	5000	61.6	2.0
2100	19.3	1.0			
2200	20.4	1.1			
2300	21.5	1.1			
2400	22.6	1.1			
2500	23.7	1.1			
2600	24.8	1.1			
2700	26.0	1.2			
2800	27.2	1.2			
2900	28.4	1.2			
3000	29.6	1.2			

FT 76-A-4 SHELL, H.E., M42A1 w/ FUZE, P.D., M48 and M48A1				MV — 2700 f/s	
Range	Elevation	Change in elevation for 100 yd change in range	Range	Elevation	Change in elevation for 100 yd change in range
yd	mils	mils	yd	mils	mils
0	1.0	.7	3000	37.9	2.0
100	1.7	.7	3100	39.9	2.0
200	2.5	.8	3200	42.0	2.1
300	3.3	.8	3300	44.2	2.2
400	4.1	.8	3400	46.5	2.3
500	4.9	.8	3500	48.8	2.3
600	5.8	.9	3600	51.2	2.4
700	6.7	.9	3700	53.7	2.5
800	7.6	.9	3800	56.3	2.6
900	8.5	.9	3900	59.0	2.7
1000	9.5	1.0	4000	61.8	2.8
1100	10.5	1.0	4100	64.7	2.9
1200	11.5	1.0	4200	67.7	3.0
1300	12.6	1.1	4300	70.7	3.1
1400	13.7	1.1	4400	73.8	3.2
1500	14.8	1.1	4500	77.0	3.3
1600	16.0	1.2	4600	80.4	3.4
1700	17.2	1.2	4700	83.8	3.4
1800	18.4	1.2	4800	87.3	3.5
1900	19.7	1.3	4900	90.9	3.6
2000	21.1	1.4	5000	94.6	3.7
2100	22.5	1.4			
2200	24.0	1.5			
2300	25.5	1.5			
2400	27.1	1.6			
2500	28.7	1.6			
2600	30.4	1.7			
2700	32.2	1.8			
2800	34.0	1.8			
2900	35.9	1.9			
3000	37.9	2.0			

A.D.C.-76-A-1

GUN 76-MM M1A2 (ANTITANK) ON MOTOR CARRIAGE T 70
W/STRAIGHT TELESCOPES M70H, M72C, T93 OR T106
AND PERISCOPE TELESCOPE M77G, M47A1 OR M47A2

PROJECTILE, A.P.C. M62   SHOT, A.P. M79   SHELL, H.E. M42A1
                                          W/FUZE, P.D. M48

2600 F/S	2600 F/S	2700 F/S
0	0	0
400	400	400
800	800	800
1200	1100	1300
1600	1500	1700
2000	1800	2100
2400	2100	2500
2800	2400	2900
3200	2700	3300
3400	2800	3500
3600	3000	3700
3800	3100	3900
4000	3200	4100
4200	3400	4300

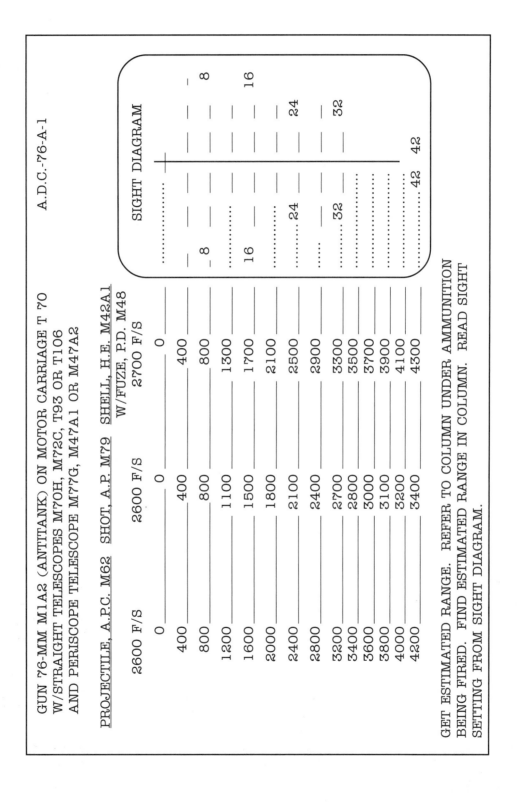

SIGHT DIAGRAM

GET ESTIMATED RANGE. REFER TO COLUMN UNDER AMMUNITION BEING FIRED. FIND ESTIMATED RANGE IN COLUMN. READ SIGHT SETTING FROM SIGHT DIAGRAM.

ABOUT THE AUTHOR

I was born in Dayton, Ohio on July 12, 1913 the younger of two boys who were taken to Washington D.C. after their mother died in 1918. There they moved in with an Aunt Florence Miller who broke off her engagement to marry in order to raise her two young nephews. When I was ten my father died leaving Aunt Florence to care for us by herself which was a difficult task for an unmarried lady who must be considered a Saint for the huge sacrifice she made to accomplish it. I went through elementary school, jumping one and a half grades and entered Central High at age twelve.

After my junior year, the summer I turned sixteen I took a job with the Capital Title and Guaranty Company, a subsidiary of the New York Title and Mortgage Company. I enjoyed the work with a Company that had a very impressive financial statement, which seemed to promise a great future for me so I decided not to return to school that fall. Also money was tight and my salary, small as it was, helped my Aunt with the household expenses.

This was 1929 and little did I suspect nor did anyone else, what was in store for our national economy. The stock market plummeted and our office suffered heavy losses making it necessary for the home office to take us over. In 1933 the New York Title and Mortgage Company closed its doors and I with millions of others was out of work. I managed a few odd jobs such as usher at the Earle Theater or delivering beer in my 1929 Ford roadster and the like until I was able to latch on to one of those temporary Government jobs where I rode out the Great Depression which qualifies me as a member of Tom Brokaw's "Greatest Generation." When the economy started to improve I located a position with the real estate firm of Boss and Phelps where I remained until the period in which this book has its beginning. I might add that I later finished high school by attending night school and receiving my diploma which is as far as I went except for the very thorough education received from a lifetime of on-the-job training.

The post-war era saw my return to real estate specializing in mortgage financing. Over the years I worked my way up to the position of President of the Montgomery County Board of Realtors which resulted in a congratulatory telegram from former President Eisenhower.

My Gracie passed away in 1971 and in 1978 I retired and moved to a cozy little home in the beautiful hills of Carroll Valley, Pennsylvania. I soon became involved in numerous local organizations thus completely shattering my dream of a totally inactive retirement. I now limit myself to giving talks and attending events relating to World War II plus spending time with my family which now contains three beautiful great-grandchildren.

The Author...

...Then

...and Now

...and in 1918 at age 4 in full World War I Army uniform.